BOOK II
HOW TO GET ANYTHING ON ANYBODY

The Encyclopedia Of Personal Surveillance

by

lee lapin

SPECIAL THANKS TO:

Bill Cheek
John Hancock
Laughing Lizards Athletic Club
Jonathan
Mike Russell
Steve Uhrig
and, as always, a number of folks who are shy about seeing their names in print...

Book II–How To Get Anything On Anybody
by lee lapin
©Copyright 1991 by lee lapin

Published by:
ISECO, Inc.
2228 S El Camino Real #349
San Mateo, CA 94403

ADDITIONAL COPIES OF THIS BOOK ARE AVAILABLE FROM:

ISECO, Inc.
2228 S. El Camino Real
San Mateo, CA 94402

How To Get Anything On Anybody (Book I) is available from:
CEP, INC. POB 865, Boulder, CO 80306

ISBN 1-880231-00-X

*S*ome of the techniques and devices shown in this book are illegal to possess or employ except by authorized law enforcement agencies. The laws governing electronic surveillance change from time to time and vary from state to state.

It is your responsibility to find out what is legal and what isn't before owning, operating, or employing any of these techniques and devices.

Talk to a good lawyer...

CORRECTIONS

A number of changes have occurred since the first printing of this book, and, I hesitate to add, I inadvertently left out a couple of items that should have been included so I would like to take this page to rectify the situation.

Full Disclosure, Box 903, Libertyville, Ill 60048 is a marvelous newspaper/newsletter that covers the fields of surveillance, intelligence and what the federal government is up to at any given moment. Subscriptions are more than reasonable and if you are reading this book you should probably be a subscriber...

SWS Security (whom I mistakenly refer to as SWS Technologies) 1300 Boyd Rd, Street, Maryland 21154, 301 879-4035 should be added to my list of "best countermeasures people". They have also added some really nice products since I wrote about them including a $450 repeater that works with ICOM two way radios (try and find this animal anywhere else) top quality wireless video transmitters (law enforcement only, the RPT-1 2050 is smaller than a 9 volt battery and will work as a video body wire!) a video switch that activates a relay upon presence of loss of a composite video signal for unattended CCTV's, and $10 9 volt lithium batteries for those really important transmitters or recorders.

SWS also sells the complete line of Universal night vision devices (the one on the cover is my personal Universal 'scope, I personally think they are about the best around), a pager intercept package and some hot new tracking toys.

Want a deal? Mention this book and save $100 on a repeater and an ICOM radio.

On page 200 I mention the Spy Shop in New York and hint they might have been involved in some shaky deals. This brought in nothing but heat; not from the Shop but from several people in the field who said, "they bounce checks to everybody, use phony names and don't pay bills etc. You should have been much harder on them, your defense is the truth." I hemmed and hawed about no personal experience.

Their check to us for a copy of this book bounced and no one seems to want to return our calls. Live and learn...

ADDRESS CHANGES OR ADDITIONS:

R.B. Clifton, now POB 888165, Atlanta, GA 30356.

Dailog Information Services 3460 Hillview Av, Palo Alto, CA 94304

Digital Security Concepts now 1230 North Simon Circle, Anaheim, CA 92806.

Marty Kaiser is at Box 1710, Cockeysville, MD 27130

Ross Engineering now 44880 Falcon Pl, #198, Sterling, VA 22170

Sheffield Electronics is 7223 Stony Island Ave, Chicago, Ill 60649

Sherwood Communications now Box 535L Southampton PA 18966 ph 215-357-9065

Tracer's Worldwide POB 48, Elmhurst Il 60126

Western Union Infomaster correct zip is 07458

Because of the large number of suppliers and sources that move or go out of business ISECO is in the process of assembling a master list (worldwide) that will be sold on computer disc and constantly updated.

CONTENTS

INTRODUCTION

The flat out aim of this book is to provide a look at the cutting edge of surveillance and investigative technology. If you are "in the business" it should qualify as a resource manual, perhaps even an encyclopedia of the whos and hows of personal, corporate and government surveillance.

This concept will please the vast majority of readers and piss the hell out of a few of them...Why?

Various reasons, some defendable, some not quite so—let's face it, people who have secrets like to keep them. People, even duly hired representatives of our very own government like to think they are the only creatures in the universe who *understand* what this technology is capable of accomplishing, and by guilt of knowledge association should be the only ones who are allowed to know *how* to do it.

Without waxing too philosophical, I would like to point out that, in a number of easily quotable instances over the history of this fragile world, this kind of thinking has generally screwed up whatever society was around at the time and has started uncountable wars.

To digress for a second, when I was a kid (so long ago lord) one of my favorite science fiction stories was set in the future, after a machine had been invented that could receive real time video and audio from any location on earth without a transmitter.

Access was first limited to the highest levels of government, then someone showed it to his friend and they told their friends...

Well, the upshot was that individual governments ceased to exist because *governments exist primarily to keep secrets.* See, if one could actually know what every scientist, warrior, politician et. al. was planning, where the resources actually were, what various forms of greed or foolishness were actually about to be implemented...

If everyone had access to the same weapons, personal insights—well you get the idea.

Now please, please don't take me for a socialist, or even a closet liberal, my personal belief, although God knows why it should concern you, is that if everybody had one acre of land to grow food on there would always be some son of a bitch that wanted two...

But, you see, if they didn't have any secrets...

And when you look at the laws that put the fear of God into the nice young lady at Nagra tape recorders when I inquired after the specs of their JBR recorder because "a man from the justice department came down and warned us that we could go to jail if we tell people..."

The Nagra JBR!!! This is a small, stereo tape recorder. Period. GOD FORBID the general public knew that our government had access to small stereo tape recorders! The great unwashed would rise in anger, structures would be pulled down thread by thread. Society as we know it today could crumble!—Silly?

Well, yes, and no. To me it seems like the initial step in oh-so-gently alleviating the first amendment is to deny existing information to the people who paid for it in the first place.

No, I don't think everyone should be given a set of instructions, some plutonium and a map to Iraq, but neither do I think unsuccessful laws should be used to eat away at the constitution in the name of law and order. It's just too reminiscent of other easily-shouted slogans.

In fact, personally, I could care less about enforcing the unenforceable laws—if some sleaze wants to nod out in a doorway, hey, don't stop him on my account; as far as I'm concerned it relaxes urban social pressure, opens up the job market for those who do want to work, and lets the cops concentrate on crime. Just make sure the fool doesn't have to steal my stereo or shoot my friends to afford his hobby.

But even if you don't agree with me that this is the "correct" pattern of thought, I still have trouble visualizing this scene on a dark New York street corner between a crack dealer and a customer.

"You got the stuff? I want 40 vials."

"Yeah, man you got the bread?"

"No, no, but I got Lapin's newest book, you

know the one where he explains the use of Tektronix spectrum analyzers to find frequency hopping transmitters."

"Far fuckin' out. It's a deal!"

A law enforcement person and I had the above discussion and he commented, "Yes. But he can hire someone to do a sweep for him."

I said, "From where?"

"The yellow pages, or from one of your books, where else?"

"And who are most of those guys?" I asked.

"Ah, former cops..." was the hesitant reply.

As this is written it is illegal, as in go-to-jail-don't-pass-go, in a number of third world countries to possess or use such innocent devices as phone scramblers.

Why? Because we love you, M-I-C, K-E-Y...

No, it's because the government doesn't want anyone to have the right to talk in private. No lie, it's that simple.

Sound like your dream retirement spot?

By far most surveillance jobs are not FBI or DEA-sanctioned probable busts but are, in fact, one spouse trying to get the goods on his/her partner, or a white collar businessman who has decided the best way to get ahead is to lie, cheat, and steal. It does go on every day, everywhere.

A number of other cases are unauthorized attempts by a person who actually is in law enforcement or employed by the government to spy on you and yours.

Okay, okay so much for Lee's political dissertation, I can see my secretary nodding off at the typewriter, believe whatever you want, but *know* this: Knowledge is power, knowledge is freedom.

Luckily, by law, set forth by the U.S. constitution, we are allowed (so far) to write about these things, so I ask you when you see a photo of an AID transmitter that is employed by the DEA and the CIA (not to mention the FBI and the IRS and the Justice Department) you don't scream for my head, or immediately feel I'm opening the door for the Medalin Cartel to ravage America ("Wow, look at this little plastic container with an antenna behind the wall Jose, I guess that's nothing, huh man?"—"No, no, I know that is an evil transmitter of the United States government designed to protect their hopelessly addicted population. I'm sure glad for that book.")

And the first time you find some low life is trying to steal what is rightfully yours by using something you wouldn't have recognized without this book, or the first time someone kicks you right in the privacy act, or, let's be fair here, the first time you use something I've detailed for reasons that may or may not be completely scrupulous...Try to think of me kindly. Lee.

AUDIO SURVEILLANCE—AN OVERVIEW

Audio surveillance equipment is normally the most effective method to monitor either telephone conversation, room conversation or in some cases, both. This section is designed to provide a look at the methodology involved in *effective* aural interception of intelligence.

The key to any operation is to remember this basic point: As an investigator it is your job to move information from one location to another without the participant's knowledge or consent.

There is always more than one way to accomplish this feat and, in most cases, the simplest avenue will also be the most successful. Read that sentence again. Any good intelligence agent or PI will tell you the best stuff is procured with equipment that is simple enough to do the job effectively but just complex enough so it will not be discovered by the target.

It does *not* require a degree in electronics to plant an effective bug, tap a phone or listen through a wall. Many of the units can still be purchased legally in the U.S. under the guise of "normal" electronic equipment or secured from overseas sources in ready-to-go formats.

Other units can be easily modified from available materials. In the following sections it shall be my distinct pleasure to walk you through a number of levels in the world of electronic surveillance from the simplest, off-the-shelf "wireless babysitters" to the most sophisticated units invoked by some of the top government intelligence agencies.

But first a word from our sponsors: Bugging and wiretapping is illegal, *in most cases*, the exceptions having to do with state and federal laws about recording conversations in an area that is owned by the person doing the recording or when a court approved warrant is in evidence. Some states are *one party* states and allow unannounced recording if one is participating in the conversation that is being recorded.

The hard truth of the matter is that only a few hundred court warrants are issued every year, usually on major narcotic or organized crime investigations but law enforcement agencies spend millions and millions of dollars each year on equipment to surreptitiously monitor conversations.

Where does it all go?

The practice of illegal bugging or wiretapping by law enforcement personnel is known as wildcatting. If usable information is turned up in such a manner, the personnel involved simply act upon it without ever mentioning the fact that it was obtained by employing an illegal monitoring device.

Law enforcement agencies are only the tip of the electronic eavesdropping iceberg. Far and away most bugs are planted by people to spy on their spouses or to gain an advantage in business.

The latter does not always mean spying on one's competitors—many bugs that have been found by countermeasures teams were obviously planted by someone in the same company, often to help secure a promotion or keep tabs on a personal competitor.

Most bugs, especially those planted by amateurs, can be found by amateurs armed with a rudimentary knowledge of the devices and techniques involved. With that in mind, let's look at bugs from the $29 Radio Shack specials to the latest FBI/CIA models and look at what they can do, how they are planted and how they can be found.

Remember, if the idea of surreptitious information collection appeals to your sense adventure it *is* a felony. In fact, under the laws now on the books it is a crime to possess equipment designed for eavesdropping. I strongly urge anyone who is considering the application of this information to consult an attorney and study the latest laws very closely.

BUGS

How many ways can you bug a room? A lot. There are lots of kinds of units available to accomplish the task of surreptitious information gathering. If we break these down by category of equipment the task of explanation narrows itself down to a manageable size.

What units are the most common in surveillance applications? RF bugs. Radio frequency transmitters. RF transmitters can have their own internal batteries or they can leech power from building wiring. Some can be remotely turned on and off from an outside source, but the initial planting usually requires one to get access to the facility to be brought under scrutiny.

A battery powered transmitter is the method of choice if one needs a quick implant for a short duration of time. If long term, continuous monitoring is required, go with something that has a multitude of batteries that would last for a year, or have something wired into the house, or even use a combination of the two.

BATTERY POWERED TRANSMITTERS

ADVANTAGE: Battery-driven transmitters provide a good, clean, and reliable signal. They may also be concealed almost anywhere since they contain their own power source.
DISADVANTAGE: Batteries need changing at regular intervals which exposes the investigator to detection. Range will be limited by power.

ROOM TRANSMITTERS 110 VOLT POWERED

ADVANTAGE: Once installed they operate indefinitely and require no further maintenance, providing they remain attached to the source of power, some use the lines of the building and outside power cables to transmit their signal making them very difficult to locate with normal countermeasures techniques.
DISADVANTAGE: Under certain circumstances, house power transmitters can transmit a low level background 'hum' if the power supply has been contaminated by the use of electrically noisy appliances such as faulty or old fluorescent lights, fan heaters, or other equipment.

The units, especially the carrier current models, are often a bit larger than their battery counterparts and may require a special receiver to demodulate the audio.

Both types of house powered transmitters can be easily concealed in such items as lamps, clocks, radios, video recorders and other items that will allow them to remain attached to the wiring without arousing suspicion.

In fact, many companies sell them prepackaged in just such paraphernalia but, following Lee's Laws To Live By #1: It's always cheaper to relive those halcyon days of your youth by mentally revisiting your high school shop class just long enough to do it yourself.

These units can be (and often are) mounted directly in the wall behind or under an electric socket.

Years ago when the concept of electronic eavesdropping really caught on, all the available units used discreet components (transistors) and averaged about the size of a pack of cigarettes.

State of the art today can be a unit the size of a fingernail or even a grain of rice. Many bugs are now made with surface mounted components and flat batteries so they take up no more room in an envelope than would a real letter.

Let's look at RF transmitters in general, their capabilities and limitations.

One of the most important specifications of a bug is its ability to remain on frequency within certain limits of operating temperatures. Frequency stability, as this is called, is critical if any form of unattended, automatic recording or repeating of the bugs signal is to occur. Two specifications are commonly used: a given number of plus or minus parts per million (ppm) and plus or minus a given percentage of the center frequency.

A common tolerance is + 10 ppm, if the center frequency were 100 MHz, then the frequency variation would be +/– 1000 Hz. A percentage tolerance might read +/– 0.0025% of center frequency. This corresponds to a maximum frequency variation of +/– 3750 Hz for a center, frequency of 150 MHz.

Two types of frequency control devices are used in most transmitters: resonant L-C (free-running) and crystal controlled oscillators.

Only those units with crystal control can maintain the above tolerances. Free-running oscillators, (tunable transmitters) should only be used with wide band, automatic frequency controlled, tunable receivers because they may drift outside the focus of a crystal controlled or synthesized version. Free-running transmitters may have a frequency stability specification for a given temperature range only. Battery voltage is also a determining factor in frequency stability, cheap units will experience wide frequency swings as the batteries wear down.

Most well-designed free-running or crystal controlled transmitters use tight voltage regulation for the oscillator circuits to control that problem. A typical free-running frequency stability specification is + 75 KHz from at an operating frequency of 50 MHz.

Frequency range specifications show the upper and lower frequency limits at which a transmitter may be operated and still be within its other specifications. A typical frequency range specification is one band such as low public service (30–50MHz), or commercial FM (88–108).

As long as the transmitter remains on one frequency any "locked" receiver, such as a scanner can continuously monitor it without adjustments. The best way to do this has traditionally been to utilize a crystal to maintain the frequency within tight limits.

The disadvantage to crystal controlled units is one cannot easily change the operating frequency if it turns out something else is using it in the target area.

One of the main questions people ask about any surveillance transmitter is how far will it transmit? Some of the variables involved are: How good a receiver is going to be used, power, the output of the transmitter itself, interference at the site, atmospheric conditions, metal in the target building, and even the weather.

Structural interference is the absorption of a radiated signal by buildings or other obstructions. The best signal is received when there are no solid objects between the transmitter and receiver. Obviously, this dream transmission path is not usually possible to achieve, so one should take into account the factors that affect signal propagation.

Transmitting from inside a building places at least one obstacle (the building's wall) in the path of the any signal. The loss from passing through a wall ranges from approximately 7 db for wood and plaster walls, to as much as 40 db for steel and reinforced concrete walls.

As a number of obstacles between the transmitter and receiver increase, the more the strength of the transmitted signal is absorbed in passing through them. Walls, outside obstructions and other buildings will attenuate any transmitter's signal. In complex structures, the number of floors and walls will greatly affect signal strength.

Translated: There is no accurate way to predict range without on site tests of the units involved. However the real problem with that particular question is that it's the wrong question.

Instead of range let's consider power. If one were going to buy a transmitting device to bug an office, what kind of power output would be ideal for the job?

And the survey says, the correct answer is minimum amount of power that will get the job done. Why would we want the minimum? Obviously the unit is not going to transmit as far as one with a lot of power would, but then consider conservation—batteries will last a lot longer and the unit will be much more difficult for other parties to find.

What kind of power are we talking about? The average walkie talkie puts out 1–4 watts and will reach out and grab someone at a range of somewhere between one and five miles. If necessary, the range of any small transmitter can be increased by the use of a repeater. One can actually use several repeaters if desired, to extend the signal as far as necessary.

What are the power output of most bugging transmitters? In the milliwatt range. There's only one or two companies that makes bugging transmitters (for law enforcement) in the 1 watt area. The biggest supplier would be AID in

Florida. In fact they have the biggest slice of the law enforcement business because of their line of body transmitters.

Physical specifications such as size, weight, shape, switch location, etc., are other factors that set a particular transmitter's usefulness for any application and should also be considered. Specifications such as spurious or harmonic attenuation, audio distortion, pre-emphasis response tolerance, are not easily verifiable and the manufacturer's specifications must be considered valid until proved otherwise.

Because of the exposure and concurrent risk involved in accessing an in-place transmitter to change a dead battery, it is important to estimate the length of time involved in the surveillance and the length of time the batteries involved will power the unit. How long would 2 9-volt batteries run and operate a 1 watt transmitter? Less than 2 hours...

How long would the batteries last in a 200 milliwatt transmitter? At least 5 times longer. In reality even longer because all that power creates heat and heat creates resistance and resistance requires more batteries, and, well, I'm sure you get the drift.

So a small, low power output is optimum for surveillance use. A lot of manufacturers of transmitters talk about power output, not as effective radiated power off the antenna, but as effective power as measured into a 50 ohm load or something like that, which has nothing to do with its efficiency at all. Don't be fooled by specifications of this nature.

One would not want to put a bug in place and have it transmit all over town anyway. People with scanners out there might pick up on it. Efficient, low power transmitters are the answer.

Some bugs actually put out only 5–8 milliwatts. How far will that power level transmit? Remember 5 milliwatts is only .005 watts.

Assume a 1 watt transmitter will transmit about one mile without outside assistance. A 5 milliwatt transmitter will transmit in most environments to a moderately sensitive

receiver for 500–1,000 feet. Would that be sufficient for most of bugging situations?

Hook the receiver up to a tape recorder and put the combination in a car and park it outside of the building. Is it sufficient now?

Damn right...

Now substitute a lithium battery. How long do you think our mic will transmit now? About 9 hours. 2 of those will provide 18 and 4 will last several days. The unit is still tiny but effective.

Another factor that affects battery life is the efficiency factor of the transmitter. Reasonable efficiency for a 100 mW xmitter is 35%. As we move up in power to 1 or 2 watts, 60% efficiency is not uncommon. The efficiency of a transmitter can be determined easily by measuring the initial current drain, multiplying by the measured input voltage, dividing into the rated power output, and multiplying by 100.

What kind of modulation techniques are used on these transmitters? Almost all of them are FM except for the real James Bond stuff that is both expensive and difficult to procure.

A few units are AM but most can still be detected with an FM receiver so it really doesn't make much difference in the end.

A number of brand new modulation techniques are making their appearance felt in the surveillance marketplace. Some of these ideas are more practical than others, some are not yet in use, but all are coming. All these ideas share one common advantage; they're very difficult to find with traditional counter measures gear.

When we get a little above the off-shelf items, things can be done to fool any observer and fool certain receivers.

I'm speaking of pulse modulation techniques, which is literally an off the shelf item, spread spectrums, subcarriers and, folks, I'm talking frequency hopping.

Subcarriers are secondary signals imposed on a particular frequency. The common version of this idea is the continuous elevator music available for a price in most cities. This music is actually broadcast by one or more major radio stations, buried in their signal. It takes 2 receivers to demodulate 1 of these complex signals, but it's still AM or FM. It's not anything special.

A subcarrier transmitter and matching receiver combo is marketed by Micro and Security Electronics in Germany, but this is one of the few places one can find a true sub carrier item on the surveillance marketplace.

Why aren't sub carriers used more often for bugging devices? This sub carrier by its very nature is only about 10% as powerful as the main carrier so a lot of the power as far as transmitting. It makes a very inefficient bugging device. If the main carrier is 100 milliwatts the sub carrier will only transfer 10 milliwatts.

One of the things on the market today that is a dramatic improvement on straight modulation is a frequency hopping system. The idea behind a hopper is that both the bug and the receiver change their frequencies a number of times a second. This skipping around makes it impossible to track the signal with any conventional receiver, and in fact hides the entire broadcast as the ubnits spend so little time on any one channel that the most a listener will pick up is a split second of static.

Hoppers are available commercially from law enforcement suppliers. In fact the FBI uses several different varieties of FH's. Most government agencies in Australia, including the local police, are equipped with a standard bug that runs off building power and hops.

If one looks at transmitted hopping signal on a spectrum analyzer it will show relative power in one area of the spectrum, but instead of transmitting on one exact frequency on a continuous basis, the signal will bounce around in a certain band.

Hoppers run a little larger than the normal transmitters but not to excess because the heart-the running chip, is only a bit larger than a postage stamp. It was first utilized as a secure means of 2-way radio communications for law enforcement. They have reduced them down in size now for continuous duty transmitters.

It's impossible to demodulate without the matching receiver. On a spec analyzer the operator may see it popping on and off but the signal is too fast for frequency counters.

Pulse modulation. Instead of creating a sine wave PM creates pulses and that can be either amplitude or frequency modulated. For FMing one would pulse shift, for AM one could shift the height of the signal.

This level of threat is only found in custom and/or government applications, but a counter countermeasure's operator should be aware of the existence of pulse modulation transmitters.

The next semi-exotic modulation technique that is rearing its ugly head in surveillance applications is known as spread spectrum, although to be technically correct I should point out that frequency hopping is actually a form of spread spectrum, but, in the venacular, spread spectrum is when the transmitted energy is dissipated over a wider portion of the band than normal. This form of modulation requires a broad banded receiver, or scanner with a wide band mode, in order to pick it up.

The good news is, from a reverse standpoint, most spread spectrum bugs will have at least one narrow power spike that can be demoded.

Remember according to the god fearing laws of physics one of the problems in hiding any small transmitter is the suppersion of harmonics. A harmonic is a multiple of the original frequency and it appears in spread spectrum transmitters as well as in the garden variety. A good operator will see them on a spectrum analyzer.

There may be little, or no evidence of harmonics in a 50,000 watt commercial transmitter, but they will be found to some degree on any bugging device, because they don't include suppression coils.

If the necessary coils were put in a unit to suppress most of the strays that little 5 milliwatt transmitter would grow to about 10 times its actual size.

However this handy rule of thumb is gradually being discounted because of a device known as a saw oscillator. These will produce spread spectrum output sans harmonics, and transmitters without harmonics means spread spectrums without spikes.

Saw oscillators are very very small in size and consume extremely little power and are very efficient. These small oscillators are actually grown, just like chips and transistors which means they're cheap and available to the masses.

Saw oscillators grown for the actual operating frequency, so they act as both the crystal as well as the oscillator. It is everything in one mini unit that can be as small as the tiniest transistor.

2 or 3 companies are manufacturing SO's as we speak, for use in inexpensive transmitter like garage door openers or key rings. They are taking over these markets because they're so cheap and work on a precise frequency. The other advantage to a code or data based spread spectrum transmitter is that one can get more data on the spread spectrum transmission because of its wider bandwidth. This means everybody in New York can have his own code for his very own garage door.

Right now SO's are pretty much limited to non-voice emissions but more than one company is experimenting with them for voice applications. This will bring the cost of spread spectrum bugs down into the low budget arena and will introduce them into surveillance roles.

Burst transmissions are another area of popular fiction with regard to surveillance transmissions. The concept in a burst transmission is that the audio is compressed at a certain ratio and then broadcast in a short burst that is difficult to find because of the short time it's on the air and difficult to decipher because of the burst algorithm.

Burst transmissions have been in use since WW II, pioneered by our old friends the Germans to limit the value of U-boats when they had to surface and report. Some have conjected one could use a hidden tape recorder to tape a conversation and then have the transmitter broadcast it in a burst upon a remote activation signal.

It's not a bad idea. At least one company, APPLIED SYSTEMS CORPORATION is marketing a burst system for voice and data transmission but, as far as I know, no one has actually combined the necessary modules to record and then burst on a remote signal.

It is, however, possible...

IR transmitters convert audio into infrared and transmit the information on a fairly narrow beam of light. Good IR units use a laser diode to provide the beam. An IR receiver is needed to demode the audio back out. The main advantage of an IR system is the fact that no rf is generated and normal counter measures will not turn up an IR bug.

Disadvantages include a strict line-of-sight operation that will not go thru walls or draperies and is attenuated by closed windows. They have been used in the field, often by placing a microphone in the target room, and running the microphone out to where the IR transmitter is hidden in the eaves of the building or on the roof. This placement also allows for convenient tapping of the building's power supply. IR attacks are high level attacks.

PK and MICRO AND SECURITY ELECTRONICS sell prepackaged, miniature, IR systems. It is also possible to use commercial systems that are designed to transmit television room audio to a tiny receiver to let the user enjoy private television. This systems require the user to boost the incoming audio to line level (A $15 RADIO SHACK amplifier will do it) before transmission and are limited in their range, (say to 150 feet) although this can be increased by using a better light receiver or mounting a good photographic lens in front of the receiver.

The simplest way to bug any room is to hardwire it. Hardwired microphone systems are nothing more than a mike in a room with a pair of wires going to it. That pair of wires could lead right to a recorder hidden in another room. This system does work and is in use, but has a couple of disadvantages including the fact that it doesn't take a Rhodes Scholar to follow the wires (if discovered) to their termination point.

And possibly terminate the operator.

Hardwires are limited by the type of mic, amplifier and wire involved. A standard mic will have a range limitation of a couple of hundred feet or so unless a powerful preamplifier is employed to boost the sound.

An alternative to installing an amplifier at the collection point is to "phantom power" the microphone element boosting the signal at the point of origin. A good PP mic will transmit a couple of thousand feet down a standard twisted pair.

Hard wires can be led out to transmitters, combining the advantages of both systems into one package.

CARRIER CURRENT

A high level/low cost attack is to use a system known as carrier current. On one level these units emulate RF transmitters. They turn room audio into modulated signals and, like their RF cousins, require a receiver to demodulate but rather than going through the air, CC's radiate very low frequency waves that hang on their "antennas" so their output stays with the house wiring.

Radio Shack sells 3 or 4 different models that work on several different, very low frequencies. They are very difficult to ferret out in a countermeasures search and the chance of accidental listeners is about zero.

The main problem with CC bugs has been that the signal travels down the wiring only until it reaches the local utility company transformer. The transformer blocks the signal from going any further unless one has the guts and ability to climb a pole and "strap over" the transformer creating an path for the RF-based audio.

A few years ago that statement would have been absolutely correct. Today it's not necessarily true because the power companies are bypassing their own transformers to allow carrier current RF to pass through them automatically because they want to send their own signals around town. This set up can be used for internal power company communication or, more likely remote meter reading.

In one system a small RF transmitter is placed on the meter and the meter reader just drives down the street and hits a button to read any meter out onto his car.

The important thing to us is that these modifications allow carrier current bugs to transmit considerable distances courtesy of the power company.

The Radio Shack units are easy to use—many folks simply plug them in. A bit more creative approach is to incorporate the small circuit board in a RS unit into an electrical appliance in the target room. This will provide an unbroken stream of intelligence as long as the unit is plugged into a wall socket.

There is one other pertinent fact to remember when using carrier current transmitters. How many power cables go into most houses? Three.

Why three? Because U.S. homes use two phase wiring. The power cable comes into the house and goes into a box of some sort, either a fuse assembly or circuit breakers. Between the ground and any one wire the potential is 110 volts. Across the 2 hot wires gives 220 to operate major appliances.

If one is going to put a carrier current system in a house and monitor it in another building it will be on only one phase. In order to monitor the unit one has to attach the receiver to the *same phase as the transmitter.* It's simple , if it doesn't appear on the first try, check the other phase.

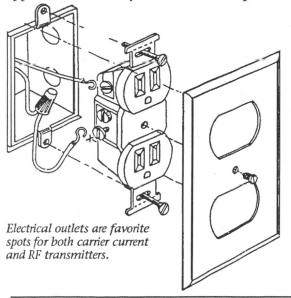

Electrical outlets are favorite spots for both carrier current and RF transmitters.

Room TRANSMITTER
TELEPHONE LINE POWERED

Usually called an infinity transmitter because it will operate over an infinite distance—even internationally—this device transmits room conversation via the telephone line to which it is attached and from which it draws its power. The subject remains unaware of the trans-mitter's presence since his telephone instrument is 'on-hook' and apparently not in use. The normal telephone functions remain unaltered.

The infinity transmitter pretty much disappeared from the scene a few years back when the telephone operating system (in the U.S.) was changed to electronic switching, but, as we will see in a few moments, clever new developments have brought it back to life.

There is also a telephone *carrier current* room monitor on the market that is very efficient and very, very hard to find...

Next likely method of attack? Take a crystal, squeeze it and it produces electrical energy in proportion to the squeezing. Put the crystal against a solid surface, amplify the resulting energy and you have a contact microphone that turns vibrations into sound. Place it one side of a wall and you can hear what is going on on other side of the wall.

Refinements on this technique include the use of "spikes" that actually penetrate thru the wall until the touch the far side, or the application of small, hollow tubes to guide sound waves from one area to another.

These latter types are known as keyhole mics for reasons that should be obvious.

Briefcase RECORDING

An old, but effective trick for spot surveillance is to stash a small recorder in a briefcase (preferably a locking briefcase on the off chance that the target is a nosy as you are) which is suitably "forgotten" after a conference meeting or job interview.

The operator then returns after a critical time period to retrieve his lost case and walks away with a full recording of the crucial period after he made his pitch...

BR's can also be used in one party states to legally record any conversation you are a participant in, regardless of whether the other party(ies) have given their consent to the process.

Many of our suppliers will be more than happy to sell you a briefcase system, or one can apply Lee's first and enjoy the thrill of construction. Everyone needs a hobby.

These methods constitute the majority of all bugging attacks.

Telephone MONITORING

There are essentially two effective methods of monitoring a telephone, hardwiring or drop out recorders which are generally known as 'wire tapping' and telephone line transmitters which are commonly, albeit incorrectly, known as 'telephone bugs.'

TELEPHONE TRANSMITTERS
LINE POWERED (SERIES TAPS)

Series telephone transmitters use the line power of the telephone system for their operating power. This feature limits the operator's exposure to a one time installation. They are by far the most common type of telephone tap and can be attached in the phone itself or on the line within a reasonable distance from the unit. Favorite placement spots are junction boxes and phone rooms.

ADVANTAGE: Once installed they operate indefinitely and require no further maintenance. Chance of random discovery is limited because they are only operational when the telephone is in use.

DISADVANTAGE: In order not to cause an off hook line condition, series transmitters are designed to be low powered and as such have a limited range. One can expect to receive an audible signal for a 100 feet or so on an inexpensive unit and more with better receivers and environmental conditions. Line conditions vary considerably and it is therefore possible that a particular transmitter will operate very well on one line and badly on another, even when the lines are located in the same building.

Professional series transmitters can be found prepackaged in modular wall jacks, or in replacement parts for the interior of the phone itself. LORRAINE ELECTRONICS sells a "parallel" series transmitter that is attached across the lines (rather than in series with one side) that will transmit from an extension phone if the target phone is unavailable.

TELEPHONE TRANSMITTERS/PARALLEL TAPS
ADVANTAGE: Parallel transmitters employ their own batteries which gives them a more powerful signal and makes them harder to detect with line measurement type counter-measure sweeps.
DISADVANTAGE: They can be placed some distance from the telephone unit itself but do require periodic battery replacements. Best suited for short term surveillance.

DROP OUT RELAYS/AUTOMATIC TELEPHONE SWITCHES
Automatic telephone recording is undoubtedly the most reliable and cost effective method of telephone monitoring. A drop out relay connects discreetly to the telephone line acting as an interface to a tape recorder. Each time the telephone line is used, the interface and cassette will switch on and record both sides of the conversation, terminating when the handset is replaced. The system is efficient, cheap and can be left unattended for long periods of time collecting information without human participation.

Radio Shack sells a couple of efficient drop outs, including a parallel model which is quite difficult to uncover in a standard search.

Some cassette recorders can be wired directly to the telephone line by simply using a .01 mfd cap and 10 or 20 meg resistor as the audio path allowing them use their built-in VOX components to control the recording process. Long play recorders can be substituted to allow several hours of conversations to be recorded before the tape must be changed.

Simple, cheap and easy to install, drop outs are the most common type of, ah, "significant other" surveillance.

Microphones, Acoustic Analysis, and Hardwiring

A microphone is a transducer, a device that turns sound waves into equivalent electric waves. All microphones convert sound energy into electrical energy that can be amplified, recorded or transmitted. In order for a microphone to accomplish the conversion of sound energy to energy useful for our purposes, electrical conductors and other circuitry must be provided.

Certain microphone characteristics dictate which type of microphone is best suited for a particular application. These characteristics are: frequency response, sensitivity, impedance and threshold sensitivity.

Frequency Response: Is the actual range between the highest and the lowest frequency to which the microphone "hears."

Sensitivity: Is defined as the rating of electrical power output that a microphone will produce when subjected to a certain sound level. How well it "hears."

Impedance: Is the AC resistance measurement of the microphone. This is important because the output impedance of the microphone and the input impedance of the device to which it is connected must be more or less of a match for the system to function properly.

Threshold Sensitivity: The lowest sound level that will produce an output. It most cases the smaller the mass of the microphone's diaphragm, the lower the threshold sensitivity.

Microphone Types

The microphone most often employed for intelligence gathering and investigative operations is the "electret" version of the condenser microphone. Advantages of the electret include an excellent threshold sensitivity, low response to mechanical vibration and low output impedance coupled with small size.

The electret is a marked improvement over earlier dynamic microphones for intelligence gathering purposes. The diaphragm of an electret microphone is a thin film of plastic material which makes it very sensitive to weak sounds. The light diaphragm also makes it quite impervious to mechanical vibrations.

Electret mics come in all shapes and sizes, some with a built-in amplifier located close to the mic element. It is possible to walk into your friendly Radio Shack and purchase a number of suitable versions for most surveillance work (avoid clip on "tie clasp" types because they are designed to be less sensitive) for a minimal cash outlay, *BUT*, it is well advised that anyone who is collecting important information, or being paid to collect information utilize mics designed specifically for surveillance applications.

A top quality sub miniature surveillance mic will run $100+, but remember *no system can out perform its microphone.*

Most of our suppliers offer one or more models, my personal pick is a tiny gem custom made in Japan and sold to Saul Mineroff, who in turn, installs it in several items and resells it to law enforcement types. It is also sold by one other U.S. supplier, SHERWOOD COMMUNICATIONS.

I took one of these mics wrapped in tightly in my fist, put my hand in my pocket and recorded room conversation...Quite sensitive, tiny and ready to operate or be wired into a system...

Any room in which an audio surveillance operation is to be conducted requires an application of acoustical knowledge (acoustical survey) that can spell the difference between success and failure. The first step is to determine the likely point of conversation. Every inch the investigator can move the microphone closer to the targets increases the chances of a successful operation.

Rooms finished with solid walls and furnished with such items as desks and filing cabinets that reflect sound waves are called "hard rooms." Hard rooms are highly reflective of sound waves and tend to give a sense of loudness even when no loud sounds are present.

Rooms with sound absorbing tile on the ceilings or walls, and furnished with carpets, drapes and stuffed furniture are known, as one might suspect, as "soft rooms." They are sound absorbent and tend to give a sense of quiet even though substantial audio may be available.

Oddly enough, the problems associated with soft rooms are few in number compared to those associated with hard rooms. Multiple sound reflections in a hard room can produce serious distortion and all interference tends to be intensified in a hard room.

Acoustic tile, normally found in soft rooms, is often referred to as "sound proofing," even though the tile does not sound proof at all, but merely reduces sound wave reflections within the room by appearing transparent to local sound.

Microphones or transmitters can, and often are, placed behind acoustic tile to pick up sounds within the target room.

STASHING THE MICROPHONE

There are several points to consider when selecting a location for a concealed microphone or xmitter. It should be placed as near as possible to the area where conversations are most likely to take place while any placement that would subject the microphone to reflected sounds must be avoided. A microphone situated in a file cabinet for example, might pick up so much reverb and standing waves as to render speech unintelligible. Electrical interference is another problem and if the sources can not be eliminated, careful placement of the microphone and cable routing is mandatory.

Transformers, motors, heavy appliances and light dimmer switches are all sources of AC hum. Whenever possible, microphone cables should be routed away from those units. If the microphone cable must cross electrical wires, it should cross them orthogonally.

Look it up...

Remember that most people tend to view only those areas which they can see easily. Areas above eye level as well as those below eye level are not normally seen by the average person. All these areas should be considered to be prime bug locations.

Another trick is to visualize the fact that people tend to view things that appear solid as if they were really solid. This concept applies to

doors, hung ceilings, curtain rods, books and so on. This idea makes them unlikely to be considered capable of concealing anything. Therefore these items can be considered as potential microphone locations.

Placing a microphone/transmitter in or near the ceiling offers several advantages: Concealment of the cable is much easier when an attic or fake ceiling provides some working room. And, because sound passes right through acoustic tile, a microphone can be placed on the far side of the tile without having to drill a telltale access hole.

HIDING THE WIRE

Long cable runs present special problems both electrically and visually, therefore an investigator should always try for the shortest possible cable run that includes the maximum amount of concealment.

Carpeting provides an excellent camouflage for microphone cable. By separating the pile down to the carpet backing, wires can be tacked onto the backing with staples. The pile can then be brushed back to cover the application.

Most wall-to-wall carpeting is installed with a tackless strip which is fastened to the floor along the baseboard. These are thin strips, usually made from some sort of wood, with short points protruding through the upper surface. The carpet is stretched to and pressed down over these points to secure it against the wall molding.

It is a simple matter to unstick the carpet, separate the layers and lay a wire far from prying eyes...

The wire itself can be simple twisted pair or super fine varnished wire that is just slightly thicker than human hair for some distance between the microphone and the recorder. As the runs increase in distance simple wire will start to cause an unacceptable signal loss and be subject to electrical interference.

It is possible to place an amplifier at the recorder end (and possibly a filter) to somewhat compensate for this problem but the amplifier will boost *all* the signal including audio and electrical noise so this becomes only a medium term solution to the problem of long runs.

Another stop-gap measure is to run the thin wire while in the target room and then splice it into shielded microphone cable (which is much more obvious) as soon as possible to help preserve the signal for the rest of the run.

The real solution is to employ a device known as a line driver amplifier at the front end of the system placed as close to the microphone as possible. Line drivers are "phantom powered" meaning the electrical power for the amplifier is fed down the same wire (but in the opposite direction) as is the incoming signal. This further means there are no batteries to change in the target room.

Line drivers boost the audio at the microphone end of the cable feeding a much stronger signal down the wire and minimizing line loss and induction effects and will greatly improve the signal to noise ratio on any cabling run of over fifty feet.

AID offers a variety of electret condenser microphones and subminiature line drivers to the feds and claims a working distance of 500 feet without any problem.

"Civilian" models are available from a number of sources including SHERWOOD, VIKING, MICRO SECURITY, and so on. A wise investment for any surveillance kit the only practical alternative being a compressor-amplifier like VIKING's which increases the "range" of any microphone and makes any conversation easier to understand.

Hardwiring offers many advantages: it's simple, inexpensive, provides the optimum audio from any location, needs no attention after installation, and will literally last for years. It can be combined with a transmitter to eliminate the possibility of doing a Hansel and Gretel routine back to the LP. In most cases the transmitter can be located in an area that is convenient for maintenance purposes.

Wanna see something really special children? Can you say CIA? I thought you could.

Here's how the big guys take the art of hardwiring to an exact science.

FINE WIRE KIT

A few years back some genius with the above named agency reportedly contracted with a here-unnamed civilian art supply manufacturer to design a very secret something known as a fine wire kit. The idea was to be able to lay a totally concealed hardwire any place, anytime.

Even though you might not be able to get your greedy hands on an official kit, the techniques are valid. Hell, there are more than valid, they're *outstanding*.

The kit itself consists of several items that are used to lay a concealed wire. The "cable" can be forced into cracks or actually embedded in soft building materials without damage to the fine wires of which the cable is composed. The wire used in this kit does not have to stripped mechanically before soldering. The heat from the soldering iron will dissolve the varnish used as installation. To make the connection, one merely twist the ends of the wire together or about terminals on the associated equipment and applies solder.

Two types of spools are included with each kit. Five spools each contain a minimum of a 100' of two-wire cable No. 30 gauge. This pair of wires has been twisted together to prevent magnetic pickup. The kit also contains 10 spools, each containing a minimum of 250' of a three-wire cable No. 38 gauge. To visualize 38 gauge wire reach up and pluck a strand of your hair out and examine it.

The 38 is a little thicker but not much. Now take this wire and split it into three sections by running it against a super sharp razor blade. Now it's a bit thinner than your hair…

Now visualize running this super fine wire into a minute crack in a floorboard and sealing it with tacky beeswax that can be blended into almost any surface.

Add a built-in continuity tester to verify the circuit as it's being laid. Pretty slick, huh?

Two of the wires in this cable are of one color while the third has a distinguishing shade. This third wire is fastened to the center strip on the printed circuit on the spool and is common or ground wire. It can be distinguished at either end of the circuit.

The knife/laying tool is the main piece in the kit. To use it the blade is forced into a crack in the floor, wall or ceiling and the wire, as a result, will also be introduced to the crack. The use of the walking lever prevents the tool from jumping forward as it would if it were merely being pulled along the crack. It also allows the operator to exert more control over the sometimes large forces required to open the crack and thereby reducing the danger of breaking the thin wires being laid.

It's important to note that the blade of the tool is not pushed so deeply into the crack that the entering end of the wire falls below the surface.

The other major tool in the kit is a bee's wax caulking syringe. The wax gun has two important functions. The bead of wax extruded from this gun can be used to cement a wire to the wall or into a crack, holding it in place and preventing it from popping out. It can also be used to fill in and conceal the crack in question. The tackiness of the wax makes it suitable for coloring with dust and powders after it has been laid down to further hide one's handy work.

It is important to use the wax sparingly to push it as far into the crack as possible to make full use of existing cracks or to cover or paint it, particularly if the concealed wires stay concealed for weeks or months. In use, the wax gun resembles a regular caulking gun. A bead of wax is extruded over the wire after the latter has been laid. Two tools are used alternately with the operator laying a little wire and then tacking it down with wax.

It is not necessary, in fact it is undesirable to lay a continuous bead of wax over wire. A little experience will show that it is necessary only to tack the wire in place once every foot or so in most instances. The wire-laying tool contains a circuit to monitor the wire laying operation and will warn the operator should a break occur in the wires being laid. As it is difficult in some locations to lay the wire without covering the bulb window with the hand, it is wise for the operator to pause occasionally and check the bulb. If the bulb is lit, a break has occurred and the wire must be dug out of the wall and repaired or a fresh circuit must be started.

The kit also contains a screwdriver for changing blades in the wire laying tool, wedges for holding cracks open, extra batteries, extra blades for the wire-laying tool, sharpening stone, tubes of wax, wax gun, blade cleanout wire, needles for threading wire through the wire-laying tool, wax gun, and eraser for wire-laying tool.

Really, really a nicely executed concept that can be duplicated in part by anyone with clever hands, thin wire and a few bees. Or some glue and an exacto knife…

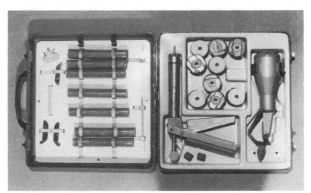

CIA fine wire kit with wire, cutting/laying tool, caulk gun, and tubes of bee's wax caulk.

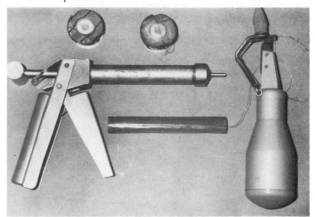

Close-up of fine wire laying tool and caulk gun.

A TRICK:

> *Electronic supply houses stock a type of "pencil" that is used to repair printed circuit boards. The nearly invisible conductive track produced when the device is run over any hard material effectively substitutes for thin wire in many instances.*

Other, hi-tech, hard-to-find, options include using existing wires (telephone, alarm, cable TV, or electrical) to serve as a path for surreptitious routing or even the recent concept of *"fortunious conductors."*

The latter is a rather unique routing system that enjoys the idea that *any metal object can serve as a conductor of signals!* Great agents have employed chair legs, drain pipes, metal moulding, file cabinets, stereo housings, computer cases, doorbell wiring, furnace control cables, sliding glass door frames, and coax *shielding,* and even studs in the wall as one or, on occasion, both legs of a hardwired system.

Let the countermeasures person that will check these routes for extraneous signals step forward...

This is a high level attack that has been used in a number of government applications. Say no more, say no more...

FIBER OPTIC MICROPHONES

Picture a hardwire microphone system with the following qualities:

—Sub miniature in size

—Doesn't look like a microphone

—Uses NO metal in its construction

—Uses NO wire to carry the signal

—Better audio quality than conventional mics

—Long distance capabilities

—Phantom powered

—Simply will NOT show up in most counter measures searches

The fiber optic microphone fulfills all of these requirements. Although not on the surveillance marketplace at this very moment they are available or can be constructed, and I predict they will soon be found in a wall near you.

Fiber optic microphones, which are currently used for medical applications, employ low priced laser diodes to send coherent light down a single strand of fiber optic cable (sized somewhere between a single strand of hair and the finest linguine) that culminates in a tiny diaphragm or movable housing.

When outside sound strikes the membrane at the proximal end it moves, modulating and reflecting some of the light energy from the transmission diode. This reflected light is demodulated by a simple photodetector circuit and amplified.

This system is in use in interferometers and vibration detectors as well as in specialized microphones.

The fiber optic system gives no tell tale hints of its existence. A single plastic strand passes the information so there are no wires to trace, no microphones to squeal, nothing to tip off a metal detector or alert a non-linear junction detector and it can be pushed into a tiny hole, down a floorboard and then through a wall...

The signal characteristics and physical attributes of fiber optics means no interference, no spurious radiations, little signal loss and outstanding stability.

Fiber optic experimentation and construction kits can be ordered from our friends at EDMUND SCIENTIFIC.

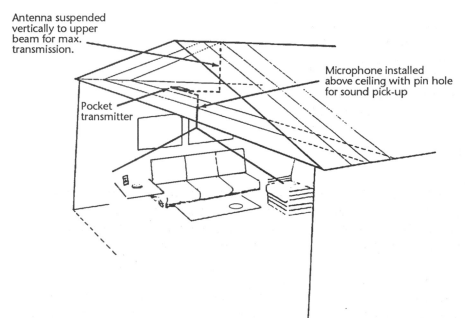

Antenna suspended vertically to upper beam for max. transmission.

Microphone installed above ceiling with pin hole for sound pick-up

Pocket transmitter

Room bugs can be installed above a dropped ceiling by using a pin hole for sound pick-up. This arrangement (above) allows the antenna to be suspended vertically for maximum transmission range.

Other typical locations include: behind venetian blinds, under a chair or couch, in the box springs of a bed (spring noise may override room sounds), under a table lip, behind a painting, under the bottom lip of a chest of drawers, or under chairs. Extend the antenna as far as possible and try for a vertical placement (below).

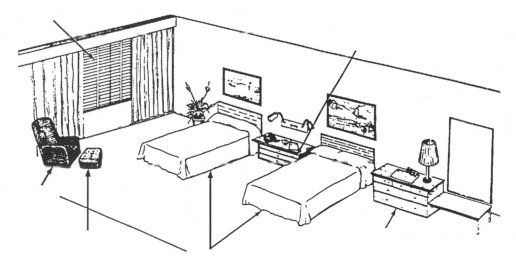

ACCESSIBLE HIGH LEVEL BUGS AND TAPS

The surveillance marketplace operates much as does the military: First the big guys get the new technology and then it gradually filters down into other hands.

Here's a close up look at several units, that are available in the correct situations, for export say—when you need to take that little something special back to your maiden aunt still in Czechoslovakia.

The rather mundane shrink tube packaging does not do justice to these units the exceptional electronics inside were designed by a gentleman who we'll call Mr. Partridge. (Sorry, that's a private joke, they can't all be gems.)

Anyway the first unit is an infinity *carrier current* transmitter. It hooks anywhere on the phone line, picks up local audio, mixes it with very low frequency RF that clings to the phone wire. A thousand or so feet later a modified Radio Shack CC receiver picks the signal off the wire.

Try and find this with any sort of usual sweep gear—the RF is too low to be received on anything but a carrier current receiver or a spec analyzer and it's right where it has no business being—on the phone lines.

This constitutes an attack that 99 and 44/100th's of the countermeasure's people won't find. At least up until this writing.

A wonderful little development for those among us who love to mind other people's business or just appreciate fine craftsmanship. Not available from the Franklin Mint, not sold in any stores, it can be purchased for about $800 from a company known as S7.

No they're not in the suppliers section. You're all smart or you wouldn't be reading this enlightening publication, you figure it out.

Second shrink wrap bundle is a parallel tap that has a built in nicad battery. The latter is trickle charged from the phone wire when the phone is not in use. This gives the advantages of a parallel tap (very hard to find, no current draw during transmission, high impedance) with the advantage(s) of a series unit, i.e., no

batteries to change, and like an indoor jogger it runs in place for a very long time.

Great range, over 1,000 feet when I tested it, the only disadvantage is that it does need some time to recharge and constant phone calls may wear the battery down and cause a temporary transmission failure.

Partridge telco carrier current bug and rechargeable phone tap (above). Surface mounted wafer transmitter (below).

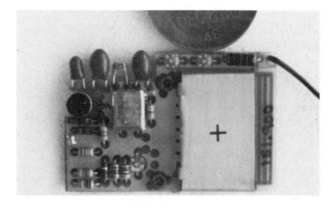

HOW THE GOVERNMENT DOES IT

Not all bugs necessarily have to be state-of-the-cutting-art-fancy. Do you really need a frequency hopping, pulse modulated, wide band FM, remote start unit, to take down the local sleaze or can you live with a plodding and proven workhorse?

Did Anhauser Busch need Sea Biscuit to pull the beer wagon?

Following is a picture of an AID (Audio Intelligence Devices) TX703. It is a wide band FM unit with an internal electret microphone and a flexible antenna. It could be the most popular law enforcement bug on the market today.

This is pure speculation on my part, of course, because AID will not talk to folks like me. Not that I can blame them, half of my friends feel the same way...

The TX-703 has the unusual attribute of varying its radiating power congruent with the power source—in this case add one, two, or three button cells and the power will automatically adjust from 0.5mW to 1.5mW and then up to 2.5 respectively.

Of course the operating time varies inversely to the output power, i.e., 270 hours with one silver oxide button, 60 when three are stacked together.

The TX-703 operates in the 36–39 MHz band, (exact frequency on demand) and will set the legitimate law enforcement supplier back a cool $695.00.

The unit pictured was found during a countermeasures sweep by one of the companies listed in our sweep section.

Six hundred and ninety five dollars... Maybe I'm in the wrong business...

Audio Intelligence Devices TX-703

BEST BUGS ON A BUDGET

For that matter, some of the best bugs anywhere, budget be damned. The first (pictured) is a model AE3 from DIJIRO ELECTRONICS. It sports several features not found in other units that sell for 10–15 times the price.

The unit is crystal controlled for stability that's good enough to allow automatic monitoring and recording from an unmanned listening post, or use with a repeater for increased distance. The crystal supplied transmits in the 49 MHz citizens band and the output power is limited to under 100 milliwatts by using 6 volts (four 1.5 batteries in series) with a legal antenna of one meter.

If the power is upped to 9 volts the output is increased proportionally and the crystal can then be switched to achieve 50–54 MHz (6 meter amateur band) operation.

A sensitive microphone picks up ambient sounds (although it would be a simple matter to substitute a jack for remote mic placement or telephone interception) and then connects to an internal VOX that can be adjusted to compensate for the local audio level. The VOX can also be set to turn off immediately after loss of signal (when someone stops speaking) or automatically remain on for 30 seconds before cut off.

This means that the unit will transmit ONLY when there is audio present—no noise, no go. In a quiet area a single nine volt battery will power the unit for about 3 weeks in a standby mode making this unit ideal for placement in little used/important traffic areas like conference rooms or, say, bedrooms.

Harmonic suppression is excellent, the audio is clear and I was able to command a range of about 900 feet using a AOR 1000 scanner with a no-gain antenna.

The unit is sold only as a kit (due to the FCC regulation Part 15.119 governing home built, low powered devices) and does require some grasp of electronic theory to construct and tune.

If you are functionally electronic illiterate (a mind is a terrible thing to waste) have it put together by an electronics technician. I did just that for an outlay of $25 plus another $25 to align and tune the finished product. The basic kit is about $75, so all-in-all it's a bargain in any light.

Next on my private hit parade of budget bugs would be the kits sold by Sheffield Electronics, a company owned and operated by one Winston Arrington. For a number of years (since 1966 to be exact) Sheffield has manufactured all types of electronic surveillance gear for cops and feds including such things as zero subcarrier transmitters.

Their gear was regarded as on a par or better than the German firms. Then Mr. Arrington had a, well, sort of a run in, I guess would be the correct word, with the authorities concerning his method of livelihood.

He retired many of his products and published a book of circuits (Now Hear This) from his products. He also sells several kits which are unique because they operate on out of the way frequencies, specifically 65–119, 145–180, 160–240 and 235–305 MHz, are efficient, fairly stable and don't produce too many harmonics.

I built and tested four of his units, the TEL-6, TEL 11, R-8 and R-9 and found them to work as advertised, the small telephone tap reached out to my scanner at 800 feet the powered units grabbed ranges of between 2,000–3,000 feet.

These kits only cost $30–$60!

Next would be the Deco bug and tap, both sold for about $30. These too, are kits and operate normally on the 88–110 commercial FM band but can easily be tuned to go above or below the band, hiding them from the curious or clumsy.

Cony transmitters are pre-made, tiny and cheap. They are not overly stable but for the price are quite reasonable.

Upward in price and stability would be the crystal controlled units from Japan (see suppliers) and the Ruby units from England.

And don't overlook our old friend the Radio Shack carrier current wireless intercom.

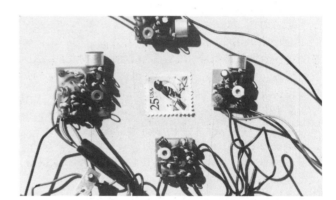

Sheffield Electronics high level units.

Inexpensive Deco bug and tap.

Best Bugs

This is a purely subjective list of what I consider to be the best electronic surveillance devices available today. In order to make my list each item must be available to civilians, practical, efficient and inexpensive or unique and not *too* expensive. The order is rough; beginning with the cheapest and easiest to obtain, moving into the quite cheap but a little harder to get and/or assemble and ends up with some great, moderately expensive units.

1. Radio Shack wireless mic. Take off the false cover behind the battery and adjust the frequency above or below the commercial FM band. Under $35.00.
2. Radio Shack wireless mic (Canada). 50 meg unit is hard to find, same price.
3. Japanese. Cony and or Micro Electronics. Cheap, tiny, assembled, buy them from the factory for $30–$100 and instead of the $300 demanded by most U.S. resellers.
4. Deco Electronics. Very simple kits that operate in the commercial FM band but can be adjusted up or down. About $35.00.
5. Dijiro and Bond unit. A bit harder to assemble but should sell for $800.
   A great device, see photo and spec sheet. About $80.00.
6. Sheffield Electronics. Any one of their wonderful tiny transmitters that are stable, operate in odd bands like 170 MhZ and do a great job. Kits average about $45.00. See photo.
7. Radio Shack "wireless intercom." Carrier current transmitter works on power lines. Receiver must be on same side of power transformer (unless strapped). Really hard to find, mount behind wall socket or in electric appliance. Under $100.
8. S-7 Coded room transmitter. Needs decoder to hear audio. Hard to find.
9. S-7 Turd unit, or wafer transmitter. Latter has surface mounted technology, package it with a flat Poloroid battery and mail it to someone you love, or hide it somewhere flat. Both around $700.
10. Super fancy units from Micro and Security (Germany) or PK (Germany). Crystal controlled, IR or coded units in a variety of sizes and shapes. $500 up. Way up.
11. S-7 "Partridge" unit that uses telephone wires as a carrier current transmitter. About $800.
12. Modify any commercial unit with remote start transmitter. Under $50.00, numerous sources.

Telephone Taps

1. Use a split hard wire. Almost free.
2. Make an induction tap (like the Kel model pictured elsewhere) put a powerful amp on it. Cheap, hard to find.
3. Direct start recorder that is designed to attach to telephone line. Radio Shack (Canada), or modified Sony or Marantz. $100–$150.00.
4. VOX start recorder with a capacitor/resistor that allows direct wiring to phone line.
5. Drop out recorder. Starts remote start tape recorders when phone is lifted from cradle. Radio Shack series model only works on one phone, works from quite a distance. Radio Shack parallel model starts on all phones on line, harder to find, needs to be close in. About $30.00.
6. Commercial models of dropouts from many suppliers/spy shops. $50–$100.00.
7. Japanese imports. Cony and Micro. Same rules apply as above. Under $50.
8. Deco Electronics. Easy kit, tune above or below FM band. About $30.
9. Order off premise extension. Attach recorder or run through manual call forwarding (cheesebox). Audit phone bill.
10. Listen Electronics dialer tap. Dials you when target gets a call. About $150.00
11. Slave units. If access to line can be coupled with spare pair. Listen Electronics, Sherwood Communications. Starts under $100.

12. S-7 super nice parallel transmitter with auto recharge feature. Needs no attention, powerful, hard to find. Several hundred dollars.
13. German fancy transmitters from the usual suppliers.
14. IR unit out window and then via hardwire. Modify Sharper Image type TV audio transmitter or buy Micro Electronics ready made. $75–$500.

HARDWIRE AND INFINITY

1. Duplicate fine wire kit. Use good mic. Cheap. Or just hide a VOX recorder in room. Very cheap. Radio Shack, various recorder sources.
2. Phantom powered mic. Sherwood Communications or Viking. $100.00 up.
3. Defeat the hookswitch on the phone. Hook up audio amp to wire at first appearance or from phone room.
4. Pinhole one wall and use a tube mic. Under $100.
5. Use piezo electric paper to make through wall mic. Easy construction, maybe $100.00 including amp.
6. Good thru wall pick up with built in FET amp. Sherwood Communications.
7. PK or Micro vibration mics. $300 up.
8. Add spike to any of above. Construction cost a couple of dollars.
9. Infinity transmitter. Shomer Tec or Listen Electronics. Under $200.
10. 2500 phone with built in infinity transmitter. Listen Electronics, $250.00.
11. Modified infinity. Sherwood Communications. Under $300.00.
12. Make a fiber optics mic. Right next to impossible to find. Cost of components
13. Constant line monitor. Acts as both infinity transmitter and telephone tap. Automatically transfers functions when call is made. S-7. Several hundred bucks...

14. Use a fortuitous conductor with good mic. Little cost, much smartness required.
15. Pennwalt piezo foil as a hidden mic or in a thru wall application. Buy the kit.

VIDEO

1. Mini camera and mini coax hardwire. About $300–$400. Sherwood, VMI, etc.
2. Same with fiber optic transmitter and receiver. Add a couple hundred bucks.
3. Use wireless distribution amp (DAK, Sharper Image, ads in magazines. Short range but cheap. About $50–$75 without camera.
4. New, unlicensed wireless transmitters. $175–$600 (with camera).
5. Complete "security camera" set up. Under $300 various suppliers.
6. Stash long play recorder or modified 8 mm camcorder in area. Say $800.
7. Pinhole through dropped ceiling or wall, use pin hole lens or fiber optic viewing bundle. Several hundred dollars. VMI, Sherwood, Olympus Corp.
8. Hide camera and or recorder in TV, appliance or cute stuffed animal. Spy Shop, NYC. Several hundred bucks.
9. Commercial law enforcement type transmitter. $2,000–$6,000 Tron Tek, PK, STG, etc. ALSO SEE VIDEO SECTION FOR ADDITIONAL IDEAS.

Passive, not aggressive

It's still the dream of every eavesdropper to find the ultimate passive bug—one that requires no access to the target premises in order to operate and is virtually undetectable. A number of units that meet these demands do in fact exist, but by in large they are expensive and never, but never, work as well as simply hiding a microphone in the room.

The common thread that binds these attacks is that they all focus some sort of energy at the target and then receive back a percentage of that same energy that has been reflected from the target. The return energy has been modulated by the sounds in the room and can be demoded at the receiver.

The energy source can be one of several varieties but the two types that actually seem to work and can be purchased or assembled are Lasers and microwaves.

For reasons that can only be explained by cultural anthropologists, the Russians (you remember them? They used to be the bad guys) seem to prefer to employ microwaves and US, we like Lasers...

The first documented instance of successful passive electronic eavesdropping occurred some thirty odd years ago when the Russians presented our Ambassador with a beautiful, carved Seal of State to put in his office (following one of my rules to live by I might add— if you need to plant a bug, give it away). Our folks went over the unit and found no evidence of electronic devices or RF fields and gave the seal the seal of approval.

It hung in the embassy for some time before a countermeasures search found powerful microwaves being beamed at the building from a nearby residence.

The embassy was researched and a small, apparently inert cavity covered by a flexible fabric diaphragm was found in the seal.

The design was so damn clever we couldn't even get it to work and had to loan it to MI5 in Great Briton where some smart chap got it to function by hitting it with a beam of the correct frequency of microwaves that were then modulated by the diaphragm (which was reacting in turn to the room noise) and bounced back to the receiver.

In 1990 the U.S. made a decision to tear down their new embassy building in Moscow, then under construction because of the plethora of devices, many of which were microwave sensitive, that were already in place courtesy of the Russian contractor.

The key fact in this last incident is not that those dirty sons of XXX's tried to bug our embassy, of course they tried to bug our embassy, that is, after all, their job, nor is it that we were afraid we couldn't find the devices, but that we didn't want to reveal our search methods.

Hence we simply tore the building down and started again with more control over the materials and personnel involved in the building process. There are rumors to the effect that the Ruskies tossed handfuls of diodes in the cement mixture to set off our non-linear junction detectors and mask any real devices but this is "neither confirmed or denied" by official sources.

What is known is that they did make extensive use of fiber optic microphones and cabling in order to beat traditional countermeasures sweep equipment.

The CIA started experimenting with lasers at about the same time as the Russkies were designing Great Seals. The concept is to take an infrared laser bounce it off of a reflective surface, such as a window, pick the returning energy up at a wide angle of reflection and feed it through a simple photo transistor demodulator.

This does work and has been demonstrated a number of times, the major problems are that outside noise also modulates the window and that some thick window panes simply do not move enough to affect the light.

Solutions to these problems have come by aiming the laser at something in the target room itself that will reflect the beam. Interior mirrors have been utilized along with stereo speaker cones to name but two.

The government has pioneered a reflector boost system that employs tetraethyl shaped reflectors constructed from simple Mylar and stuck on windows, lamps, or walls. The operators try to orientate them so they get a clear shot of the reflectors when the drapes are opened or half-pulled. This is a very high level attack and would only be used in situations where competent countermeasures were expected to be encountered.

A "reliable source" tells me they can pull off about 500 feet with a good installation.

You want to play with a laser reader? Your choices are few:

Buy PK ELECTRONICS' off-the-shelf version. The laser is hidden in one 35 mm camera housing and the receiver in another. This is an ideal mount as it is innocuous, has lenses already mounted for beam focusing and collection and can be tripod mounted.

In their demonstrations PK has shown varying results at a distance of 200 feet. The unit requires a fair bit of set up and tweaking to work correctly. The audio is not hardwire quality.

Oh yes, figure on $25K for this little gem.

An English firm has built a couple of lasers that use multiple beams, four apiece I believe, one beam for the source and the others for a noise cancelling effect that reportedly work well. Again in the 25 thousand neighborhood.

The government in at least one country is looking for the recipient of one of these English devices and I doubt it's just to have a "are you satisfied with your new laser?" chat with him…

Option number two is to build your own unit. Plans (that really work) are available from DIJIRO and were also printed in *Radio-Electronics* magazine.

The DIRIJO plans were originally published with the specific purpose of eavesdropping but after, I believe, a short but serious conversation with a dully appointed agent of our federal government about the legality of eavesdropping devices, it was modified into a laser communicator.

The receiver still works well for the original purpose and the total unit price will be measured in hundreds, not thousands of dollars.

An additional source for a laser receiver is GENERAL SCIENCE AND ENGINEERING, POB 447, Rochester, NY 14603. A simple check for $198 gets an assembled receiver with a number of sophisticated features including a pivoting mirror for beam focus. This unit would have to be modified with some sort of front end collection lens since it is designed to collect a direct beam, not miniscule reflected energy, but this should be a fairly simply modification.

Option number next: modify a commercial laser communicator. Again the primary difference is the necessity to collect low amounts of light, something which can be rectified by lens additions.

Microwave reading equipment is a trifle harder to come by, certain non U.S. (okay, they're British) non linear junction detectors, devices which beam microwaves into walls and look for return bounces from diodes and transistors, operate at frequency ranges (400 MHz, U.S. units are above 800) and power levels which allow them inadvertently, to bounce off objects in the next room and reproduce the room's audio.

The CIA has custom manufacturers of microwave flooding gear.

A friend of mine is also experimenting with the concept of bouncing very low level microwaves from a window with a directional horn antenna and demodulating them. If the initial tests bear fruit it would mean a handheld unit that could be aimed at any window, up to a distance of 200' and audibly recreate the room's audio.

He plans on a price of about $500.

High level attacks like RF, high voltage, lasers and so on do work in specific situations but it is easier and generally better to stick a transmitter in the room.

Recorders

Recorders, usually tape recorders, are still the basic currency of the surveillance trade. A recorder can function in a stand-alone mode by simply secreting it on one's person or in one's belongings to record conversations (legal in one-party states), left in an "on position" in a room where a target conversation is expected to take place or be added onto or manufactured in any one of a number of household and automobile at-home items.

Even low-end recorders have made significant gains in their performance as well as their range of abilities during the last few years. One might point out their prices have also come down substantially, in fact, if you stop and think about it, technology is probably the only field where prices actually decrease as the product gets better. But I digress, enough of Lapin's theory of economic development, let's get back to recorders—the first surveillance recorders used flexible rubber belts to acoustically etch sounds on, for later reproduction.

Sort of.

The next step up was wire recorders which recorded the magnetic impulses on a fine spool of wire and offered longer recording times, better fidelity, and improved search capabilities. One interesting fact of life with wire recorders is that the wires were always stretched to the nth degree before their breaking point, which normally occurred at least once every couple hours of use. If you think trying to splice an errant audio tape is a pain in the ass, let me tell you that trying to splice mangled, chewed, and coiled fine wire is the surveillance equivalent of sysiphsus and his big rock.

Even in just the last few years, significant technological advances have been acquired or at least moved down from higher-priced recorders to run-of-the-mill recorders; i.e., VOX (Voice Operated Relay) starting capability is pretty much stock on $50 up mini cassette recorders, my little four-year old Panasonic offers two levels of voice activation for automatic unattended recording while my nifty new little $150 Radio Shack actually has a variable threshold setting that uses the volume control to adjust the click-on level of the recorder. The sensitivity has increased dramatically in these units while the size has decreased dramatically and motor noise has been brought under control.

Most of these capabilities were available at accessory prices on early recorders or could at least be duplicated with the use of outside black boxes which, although they work well in most cases, double or triple the size of the original recorder. Not the optimum arrangement for undercover recording.

Always record everything. Any intelligence that's worth gathering, is worth recording. Tape is cheap. Use it. In many cases, today's recorders will actually record more than the human ear is capable of discerning, thereby going "up" half a generation in sound quality right off the bat. Audio tape enhancement techniques have also increased dramatically and many times allow for the reproduction of sound that otherwise would have been lost due to poor signal strength or outside interference.

The Unit Itself

Before purchasing a fancy high-priced surveillance recorder, make a list of the probable applications and priorities that will actually be needed to accomplish the jobs one expects to be involved in. Is clarity the most important specification? Is conviction level audio a necessary requirement for jobs you may be working on or will intelligible audio be sufficient for your purposes? How much recording time is needed? Will the unit be secreted as a body wire or inside custom equipment or even an attache case? Will the recorder likely come under electronic scrutiny by a recorder detector? Do you expect direct telephone line recording capabilities without modifying the unit?

These are some of the types of questions that should be answered before a budget is earmarked. As one would expect, several of the specifications are direct tradeoffs; as recording speed decreases providing more recording time on any particular tape, audio intelligibility suffers at an inverse ratio unless special equalization and compensation circuits have been added to the recorder. Even in the latter case, there will be audio degradation as recording time increases because that's simply the nature of the beast.

A low-end recorder (under $200) may fulfill every application necessary. My own little Radio Shack is practical, quiet, offers two speeds (allowing 90 minutes on each side of a microcassette at the lowest setting with fair intelligibility), a built-in VOX that can be accessed directly to a telephone line by simply using capacitors for the audio path, and adding the correct loading resistor to make extremely clean telephone recordings.

It's reasonably quiet, small enough to fit in a shirt pocket, and offers enough sensitivity to fill the role of "hidden reporter," or it can be stashed in a very small package for the old "leave it behind at the meeting while you go out and take a phone call or leave it behind you after a job interview/meeting so you can see what kind of impression you actually made after you 'remember' the missing recorder and come back for it." It seems reasonably rugged and has a fair battery life.

One step up the ladder are recorders which have been modified for surveillance use. The typical modification is slowing down of the recording motor by one technique or another to provide longer recording and playback time on a single cassette. The larger modified machines, those that use standard size cassettes, can actually record anywhere from 8–12 hours on a standard TDK D-120 cassette. Please note when perusing advertising data for extended play cassette recorders that the total time quoted normally includes both sides of the cassette and some of the recorders require manual intervention to turn the cassette over before they will record the full time.

Extended play recorders allow more recording versatility by limiting the amount of access necessary by the investigator to change his tape and pick up his messages. Their primary use is probably for in-place hardwire monitoring of telephone taps, although they can certainly be used to record radio bugs just as easily by simply running a line to a scanner and using a small (available) interface to turn them on when audio is received from the scanner. Their third obvious use is to be stashed in attache cases where they can record entire meetings (or entire evenings, one must suppose) of audio activity.

If you should just happen to be planning to use a surveillance recorder in the latter application, something else you might want to remember is that many recorders make an audible "pop" when they run out of tape and kick the record key back into the off position. There are some situations in which this noise can prove to be embarrassing, or even worse, if it's not physically muffled.

Extended play recorders are never better than their original machines so the higher quality unit one begins with, the better chance of ending up with a useable final product. If one buys a $120 recorder, expect to receive $120 worth of service from the recorder. As the prices go up, so should the quality. Check with the modifier to see what changes have actually been incorporated into the design of the recorder. Some extremely low-level "designers" simply pop the rubber doughnut off the capstan to reduce the speed of the tape. As one might imagine, this modification produces rather simple results. That is to say, it doesn't work very well. Speed varies, tape gets worn, and all-in-all, it's just sort of an easy way out of a situation that should be handled with a bit more aplomb.

Are there new circuits to be designed and inserted to compensate for higher bias (since this same bias is now saturating more tape) or for the difference in audio frequency produced by a slow speed recorder? Good modified units will answer a hearty "yes" to these questions.

Also bear in mind that most VOX-started recorders do drain the battery power even when not recording as the VOX circuitry needs to be powered up. This drain is significantly less than if the recorder was actually running, but on some recorders it is definitely a consideration and may empty the power pack in as little as one day, thus defeating the concept of extended play recorders that can be left in place to capture and condense long conversations.

In the standard sub-mini recorders, it has been my experience that there is not a lot of difference between Panasonic, Pearl Corder, Olympus, and even Radio Shack within each price strata. Most of the recorders are made from similar, if not identical chips and Japanese motors, and seem to work about the same. If at all possible, try the recorder before purchasing to become familiar with its ease of operation and little details like how loud the motor runs.

Next step up is to use miniature, but not sub-miniature units, that use a standard cassette and are designed for high fidelity recording. A good example of this is the Marantz PMD-201 or Marantz PMD-430. These recorders have become the work horses of audio electronic news gathering operations as they are durable, rugged, and offer very high-quality recording.

One important aspect is they offer stereo recording. Stereo may seem simply like a useless add-on in most surveillance applications, but this is not true! Stereo recording is almost required in evidence-level audio and should be employed whenever more than one person is speaking or there are noises which may interfere with the conversation.

Stereo expands the human ability to discriminate between individual audio sources and will increase the comprehension of any conversation. This is known as the "cocktail party effect" and can be the single most important factor in picking out a single conversation from among a mass of conversations, or recognizing a speaker.

Stereo also offers the option for "losing" one track if the other track is cleaner. Virtually all good law enforcement units are now stereo.

Top End

What do you do for a recorder if you're the DEA, CIA, FBI, or almost any other outfit with three letters and enough money to indulge in your wildest surveillance fantasies? You go to our old friends at Nagra, of course.

For years a small Swiss company, Nagra Magnetics, Inc., has designed and produced quite simply the best recorders on the market— anywhere. Nagra's were traditionally the only recorders used for film sound in feature-type films and, in fact, are still widely used for that application. Most Nagra's are crystal controlled, besides laying down audio on the tape, a precise reference frequency is recorded separately on the tape. During playback the recorder uses this reference frequency to "look ahead" and precisely modify the speed of the playback to compensate for any variables in tape stress, wear, operating voltage, etc. This feature alone makes Nagra a very high profile applicant for surveillance recording.

Most Nagras up to this time have been open reel rather than cassette and offer a variety of recording speeds as well as superb electronics and mechanicals. For the last few years, two ultra small Nagra recorders have been produced, again primarily for the film and audio industries, but have found wide spread use in well-heeled surveillance operations. These recorders are based on the Nagra SNS, a miniature open reel recorder that used a special small tape to provide the necessary fidelity. In order to bypass anything that would increase the size of the unit, one of the models had no facility for rewinding and requires a hand crank or external rewind unit to bring the tape back to its original position.

Nagra's are for recording...

Recently an FBI agent by the name of Jim B. Reames decided that the Feds needed something a step up from the mundane ($2,000 plus) SSN's. The result was that Mr. Reames worked directly with Nagra designers to come up with a sub-miniature recorder designed for law enforcement recording only. I mean, this unit is so secret that Nagra refuses to admit it exists and, at the moment at least, has no advertising data available on the unit. In a more or less confidential conversation, a Nagra employee told me that they had been contacted by the Justice Department and threatened to have all their government contracts yanked if they advertised the unit in law enforcement publications or, God forbid, anything farther down the tree of legality.

Apparently marketing is accomplished by word-of-mouth between agents and narcs and at closed trade shows.

Mr. Reames apparently did such a good job, they named the recorder after him. This secret Nagra is called a JBR and it's a gem. It's sub-miniature stereophonic with two totally inde-pendent channels and a third central track which records a reference signal of 461 Hz for adjustments during playback. The unit uses a special Kudelski cassette, provides two hours non-stop recording, and requires three "N" size batteries which allow 10 hours of operation.

The machine is designed to be unobtrusive and completely concealable. No erase head is provided and no playback facility is included with the recorder. This has the triple effect of reducing the unit in size, requiring one to pay for a separate playback unit from Nagra, and making sure that the agent or informant the unit is taped to/carried by, cannot modify the recording in any way. The bias oscillator has been moved from the typical 19+ Khz to 32 Khz which offers the same radiation frequency as a quartz watch, making it extremely hard to detect by handheld recorder bias detectors which ferret out hidden tape recorders.

The JBR checks in at a tiny 110 x 62 x 20 mm, weighs 143 grams, offers remote control capa-bility, extremely good microphone sensitivity (10 mV/PA), better than 51 dB signal to noise ratio, and 170 Hz to 4.5 khz at less than 3% harmonic distortion. It has a built-in compres-sor with a 2-to-1 compression ratio and an operating range of 80 dB.

To say this unit provides fantastic recording is an understatement. In fact, this unit provides sound so good you want to go to court and listen to your voice.

Well, maybe not, but you get the idea.

So you're all set to run out and order a JBR? Can't say I blame you. It's a dynamite little machine, without a doubt far better than my $150 Radio Shack special, besides the rather strict advertising policy, are there any other differences?

Well, a minor one. The JBR costs $4,337 without playback. However, you'll be happy to know that a complete stereo playback machine with a time base corrector goes in a package deal for just an additional $6,195. The tape grinder will only set you back $290, each mic-rophone $170, and the degausser a mere $477. (*$477 for a degausser?* Sure, that must be the solid gold model with the emerald pilot light.)

On the other hand, the two hour tapes are a reasonable $14 a piece, somewhat making up for the unit's price tag.

Coming down from the Nagra, we find various privateers who have taken good recorders and added a few modifications to make them surveillance bound. DANIEL TECH-NOLOGY, INC., a Connecticut-based firm that sells primarily to law enforcement, takes the Marantz PMD-201 and performs several modifi-cations, moving the recorder from the Acura Integra of surveillance recorders in to the Mercedes range (well, a low end Mercedes at least). Their modifications include:

— Adding an efficient remote control that will start the recorder from about any type of switch and uses about the same power as normal shelf battery drain.

— A "Silent Stop" at the end of the tape that is effected by replacing Marantz's mechanical solenoid with an electronic shut off.

— A built-in a source of power for phantom powered electret microphones as normally employed by law enforcement agencies.

— Stopping the unit down to half speed from 1-⁷/₈ to ¹⁵/₁₆" per second while maintaining high recording capability (same speed as the JBR), for two hours of continuous recording.

— Changing the internal telephone input of the unit as to record in the offhook condition and not inadvertently replay any of the recorded signal onto the target's phone line, something these units have been known to do.

Very tiny recorders are also made by Panasonic (model RN3) by placing only the record electronics in the credit card sized unit which must be inserted into a larger case housing the playback amplifier and speaker.

Saul Mineroff also offers a tiny, slowed recorder (modified RN-36) but he sells to law enforcement folks only and demands a brisk price.

VIKING INTERNATIONAL supplies virtually the same recorders as DANIEL and MINEROFF at bargain prices...

THROUGH WALLS

For some obscure reason, probably a marked lack of discipline in my upbringing, the concept of listening through a wall has always appealed to me. While other children were out fishing or playing baseball, I was secreted in the basement with my Cub Scout super amplifier and a modified guitar pick-up, listening to the teenage girl next door entertain her latest date.

The woman knew the meaning of the word entertainment...

The esoteric joy of (ah, in a metaphorical sense only, as, of course, this would be illegal without the correct court ordered paperwork) aurally piercing a solid barrier and bringing home the sound has remained with me to this very day.

Morally I would be remiss not to point out that, besides the obvious legal technicalities involved, it can be rather embarrassing to explain this type of equipment—point of fact when I was testing out several of the units pictured here, my next door neighbor (again a rather nice looking lady) stopped by to see if she could help out by holding something while I took my pictures.

And, by the way, what exactly was I doing with that little rubber thing taped against the wall of her house?

Among a variety of other things that spring to mind I was also a much faster liar when I was a child.

Through wall sound can be garned in two basic fashions: The first is by using a tiny microphone that is sealed from acoustic pressure by the addition of deadening material relieved only by a plastic tube. The tube can be either flexible or stiff depending on the application. The second method is to use a transducer that picks up the actual vibrations on the target wall caused by sound on the far side.

The former (tube mic) can be used in a variety of amusing ways; in this configuration the microphone diaphragm is exposed to air pressure only through the tube attached over the microphone aperture. A plastic tube will carry sound pressure waves over considerable distances, depending upon the material, the microphone, and diameter of the tube. The actual microphone must be sealed with an airtight seal that connects it to one end of thetube.

The open end of the tube is then inserted into any opening that gives access to the target area. Adjoining hotel and motel rooms as well as condo style houses frequently have back-to-back electrical wall outlets which fulfill this requirement quite nicely.

Simply removing the cover plate on the listening post side opens a path for the tube into the target room side of the outlet. Television antennas, cable television carriers as well as telephone inlets/outlets may also provide a ready-made hole in the wall.

The plastic tube also reduces the risk of detection by a conventional countermeasures person since it keeps the microphone and associated wiring away from the wall of the target room. The tube may be flexible or rigid but should be insulated along its entire length to protect against building vibration.

A TRICK

The best modification one can make to a ready-made tube mic is to wrap the tube itself with a thick blanket of foam rubber and duct tape to improve the quality and quantity of the sound.

Tube mics are easy to make: Surround the best miniature electret mic element that's within your budget with some sort of sound-deading material from the local hobby store. Cast it in plastic, glue it in styrofoam, whatever.

The entire element must be enclosed except for the plastic sound tube which is glued directly onto the front of the mic, extending out to the necessary length.

NO HOLE

What if the target has the gall to locate himself in a place that does not have prefabricated listening tunnels? I say find another target...

Just kidding. Here's a look at the exact

science of wall holing as taught to some of our best federal agents. You didn't read it here.

Drilling Through Walls

If a hole between the target and the LP rooms is not available, one must drill or cut a hole through the adjoining walls. The trick to this is to go slow and use the old "Extreme Care" so the hole is not outwardly noticeable from the target room.

One method is to place the hole behind drapes, furniture, or pictures for ready-made concealment. The downside to this is that a loss of sound may result from the material blocking the hole in the target room.

The other, more widely-used approach is to create only the tiniest of pinholes in the wall as this is all that is necessary to allow sound to pass through the wall, and is much less noticeable than a large hole.

If one has access, the start point of the hole should always be made from the target room going toward the listening post. This avoids flaking or chipping of the surface surrounding the hole, although it defeats one of the reasons for using a tube mic—lack of access. The pinhole location on the listening post side of the wall should be cratered to a depth of about 1/4 of an inch and should be aligned so the twain will meet once the crater is prepared and the tunnel is drilled.

A rule of thumb, or in this case, eye, is that if the pinhole is to be above the target's eye level, the hole should be made at an upward angle; if it lies below eye level, at a downward angle. This reduces the possibility of anyone seeing the hole itself.

The actual pinhole should be made with an angle-pointed instrument such as a 16–18 gauge hypodermic needle. A needle will punch right though wallboard, if one needs to puncture wood surfaces which tend to splinter, a small dental burr should be used to start the hole. Or, of course one could hire a moonlighting dentist to do it up right.

All drilling, even from the "safe" side, should be done with hand tools as opposed to their power counterparts to avoid damaging the wall surface with a slip of an electric drill. If the hole is started from the operator's side of the wall, compressed air should be blown into the finished hole to scatter any chips or drill dust.

Even though sound waves that manage to crawl through a pinhole will be much weaker than those on the hot side of the wall, an interesting effect transpires: When sound passes through a pinhole in a wall it will cause the sound on the other side of the wall to act as though the pinhole was the originating sound source.

In effect it no longer matters what the relative angle of the sound source to the pinhole really is, as the sound will pass through the pinhole in such a way as to make the microphone think the hole itself is the source of the audio.

Since the sound waves on the LP side of the wall behave as if they were coming from the pinhole rather than the direction of the original source, a microphone can be directed at the pinhole without regard to the direction of the original source.

Because the relative strength of the holed sound waves will be considerably lower than that on the source side of the wall, one must affect an airtight seal with regard to the wall in order to preserve as much of the remaining sound as possible.

The easiest way to do this is to use caulk or water tight bathtub sealing compound that can be molded around the tube itself, protecting it from ambient sound and misc. vibrations.

CONTACT PLEASE

An alternative to the tube/pinhole setup is the contact microphone. This is a device which "reads" the mechanical vibrations of the wall itself, translates them into electrical differences, amplifies them some 5–20,000 times, and turns them back into sound.

The first, and still most popular form of contact mics were a variation of electric guitar pick-ups. They took advantage of the fact that when a quartz crystal is compressed it produces electrical impulses in response to the original signal. When brought into tight contact with a wall the crystal picks up minute vibes caused by sound striking the wall.

If this signal is amplified enough the audio can be reproduced with some degree of accuracy. Many contact mics still sold use this very same technology to "listen to mechanical noises" or "tell if your office is subject to this kind of attack."

Yeah, sure...

The audio quality of most contact microphones is barely okay at best. Mechanical vibrations of the target wall caused by normal ambient sounds can cause severe interference problems.

Still, this represents a viable attack profile, especially if combined with modern technology which incorporates field amplified contact elements and piezo-electric transducers coupled with updated mounting techniques. Whew...

The rules for successful contact mic attacks include:

1. Use the best mic element and amplifier one can afford. See the tests...

2. Test various locations before selecting an installation site. Walls work in mysterious ways.

3. Secure the contact element as tightly as possible to the surface of the target wall. How? If it is a smooth, slick wall, tape it down tightly with gaffers tape; if the surface presents a less than perfect surface, use a strip of elastic cord that is tacked down at either end to make a tight contact.

4. If at all feasible, drill into the target wall and affix a spike (a solid, usually light metal "nail") directly onto the contact element in order to increase the amplitude of the signal.

TWO TRICKS

> A. 3-M makes a thin double sided adhesive tape that transfers the vibrations with little loss. Place a strip of the tape on the wall and press the contact element onto it.
>
> B. Use electro sonic gel from medical supply houses designed for gluing electrodes onto various portions of the human anatomy to provide a constant contact surface.

Contact mics provide a viable alternative to the old break and enter concept if the ambient noise is not too intense and the gods cooperate. Every agent should have a couple of good CM's and low noise amplifiers on hand for that job that one just doesn't want to go to jail for...

The contact element can also be hooked directly to a transmitter by modifying almost any mini transmitter, placing a jack between the mic element and the xmitter. This alleviates the all too prevalent problem of the target following the wires to the source and terminating the connection.

For those of you too lazy to make, modify, or create, several suppliers (PK, MICRO) sell contact mic/transmitter units that are designed to be placed on an outer wall and received with the appropriate receiver.

CONTACT TESTS

Contact Mic's consist of two parts: the pick up and the amplifier. The pick up can be a flat metal surface in contact with a quartz crystal, a plastic stud pressing against same, or a piezo board that produces electrical signals as it contracts and expands.

The crystal arrangement has traditionally been the most sensitive, but the other methods are breathing down its neck. A unique example of a very good pick-up element is one from CSI that uses both a plastic/crystal element and a piezo board, combining the best of both worlds.

The second consideration is the amplifier. A good thru wall amp will have an amplification factor of at least 10,000 times—some double or triple that—and do it with little added noise.

I hired several unsuspecting civilians in order to conduct a consumer survey of contact mics. We tested a variety of models, both thru a hollow door and a solid wall, and came up with the following best-of list:

1. The 4020 Mini stetho (with dual contact head) outstanding performance, good clarity, some feedback protection, from CSI.

2. Micro Security contact mic. Almost as sensitive. Very good performance.

3. Research Electronics Ear-200. This unit uses a plastic stud and the entire amplifier must remain in contact with the wall. Okay.

4. Ruby suction cup mic. Sold from the factory, thru Edmund Scientific and numerous retail outets. Last on the list, but still acceptable. Suction cup will not stick to rough surfaces and leaves a rubber scar on smooth walls.

A TRICK

A brand spanking new product can be used for both thru wall applications as well as for no-find hardwire microphones. This product is a paper thin piezo film made by PENNWALT, POB 799, Valley Forge, PA 19482.

This poly vinylidene flouride acts as an active capacitior that varies its charge with any difference in pressure upon its surface. The Pennwalt product is used in medical and industrial applications to sense minute changes in solid surface vibrations as well as changes in air pressure, and convert the signal into an analog electrical current.

This means, best beloved, that a tiny portion of this film can be stuck to any surface where it will act as a very sensitive contact mic, turning any good amplifier or transmitter into a dyamite thru wall device.

The same foil can be used as an unlikely looking microphone by simply backing it with a piece of plastic or styrafoam and stashing it anywhere in the target room. The innocuous looking foil will act as a great microphone.

A couple of foreign suppliers are packing the foil in coax cables, replacing the usual foil shielding. Hook it up to a television and it functions as a cable television supply cable while it sends room audio back down the line.

Find that.

Pennwalt sells a great sample kit for $150 that includes four different foil samples (one with a built in FET amplifier) and instructions to let any curious person play Mr. Wizard.

This stuff is going to appear in many surveillance applications.

VISUAL ACCESS

Seeing through walls is a trifle harder than listening thorough them, but by no means is it an impossible task. If a tiny hole, say one millimeter in diameter is punched/drilled through the wall, (slightly larger than the period at the end of this sentence), a number of companies will be only too glad to supply fiber optic viewers that will provide a wide angle view of the room on the opposite side of the wall.

These viewers can also be used for the covert examination of suspicious packages and other legitimate purposes and can be set with an eye piece or hooked to a video recorder.

Due to the flexibility of the fiber optics utilized in these viewers, they can also be poked under doors, through keyholes, shared electrical outlets, and so on.

Rigid pinhole lenses can be used with only a slightly larger opening, see the video section.

A TRICK

A simple, instant way to see through some doors without any drilling or poking? Sort of. The INTELLIGENCE GROUP makes a reverse viewer that uses six lenses housed in a small tube that fits over in-door peephole viewers and provides a crisp picture of the room beyond the door.

Olympus Corporation thru wall fiber scope.

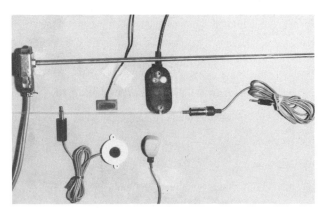

Examples of tube, spike, and contact microphones.

K I T S

Walkie
RECORDALL
*REG. U.S. PAT. OFF.

BRIEFCASE CONFERENCE RECORDER

SELF-POWERED

LIGHT • COMPACT

Model CCB

**IT'S ALL
IN THE BAG
NO HARNESSING
TO YOUR BODY**
No Wires,
No Plugs,
No Reels,
No Bulk,
No Heavy Load

**Authorized Catalogue
and/or Price List**
1960 – 1961

Authorized Federal Supply Schedule Price List
FSC GROUP 74 PARTS III AND II
Contractor Miles Reproducer Co., Inc.
Contract No. GS-00S-31614
Period July 1, 1960, through June 30, 1961
General Services Administration
Federal Supply Service
GSA Distribution Code 87

TRANSISTORIZED

★ AUTOMATICALLY RECORDS VOICE AS FAR DISTANT AS 60 FEET ... NO WIRES

★ PLAYS BACK EVERY WORD ... FILTERS NOISE INTERFERENCE

★ RECORDS IN OR OUT OF CLOSED BRIEFCASE

★ STARTS-STOPS AUTOMATICALLY BY TELEPHONE OR VOICE-ACTUATION (optional)

★ 8 HOURS OF UNALTERABLE INDEXED RECORDINGS ON SINGLE BELT (3¢ PER HOUR)

Manufactured in U.S.A. by

MILES REPRODUCER CO., INC.
812 BROADWAY • NEW YORK 3, N. Y.

Everyone
should have one closet in their house that is
stacked from floor to ceiling with black, non-
descript, briefcases. Each case contains everything necessary for a particular surveillance job
whether it's just your basic hardwire audio job
or a super sophisticated video production
starring somebody's wife and...

Or maybe it's your wife and...

Forget that, let's get professional here, I know
none of you people would ever, ever, consider
something that is not totally above board and
completely legal.

So let's say you're an FBI agent who wants to
be prepared for any unexpected surprises.

And you have a beautiful wife...

One-stop-shopping intelligence and surveillance kits are a useful methodology for storing
and integrating all the equipment that is
necessary to accomplish a particular type of
job. Besides, they're sexy.

Some kits can be purchased from non-title III
suppliers in a plug-it-in and you're ready to spy
mode, but it is usually less expensive and more
exacting to construct a custom kit based on
one's own requirements, but before we get into
homebrewing, let's look at what used to be:

The first intelligence kits were probably made
by MILES REPRODUCER CO., see the ad... These
kits did not use audio tape, instead they employed a plastic belt that groves were cut into
like an Edison phonograph.

The real genesis of IK's was manufactured by
Bell and Howell and was known as the Kel Kit,
a "self-contained recording system packaged
into 3 businessman's briefcases. The system
serves to record voice messages received from
any room. Remote transmitter through a
receiver on a recorder."

Intelligence kits? Ask any big city cop who
has worked intell or narcotics, well, ask any *old*
big city cop and he will tell you about the Kel.

Kel systems employed a number of concepts
that are still valid and in some cases unbeatable
even with today's technology. Let's let Mr. Kel
tell it in his own words:

*"...A plug-in receiver with companion transmitter
to record sound to originate at a distance from the
location of the briefcase. The receiver may also be
removed from the briefcase and used separately.
The system is available with a built-in receiver
offering up to four channel capability. These
systems provide a built-in microphone exposed by
an unobtrusive small hole in the briefcase connected to the AGC2 amplifier to record conversation
in the vicinity of the briefcase. The unit is turned
on and off by a concealed switch in the carrying
handle.*

*"The AGC2 audio amplifier's detachable and
when used for hard wire inputs directly through the
recorder. The incorporation of VOX control relay
circuits allows the unit to record only when conversation is present to conserve tape time. It may be
switched to continuous recording operation. The
recording system is powered by replaceable alkaline
standard DC cells, regular D cells, 115 volt AC,
230 AC, 12-volt vehicular power supply. Battery
test meters are provided to check battery condition
and two separate cables are provided for AC and
vehicular operation.*

*"An accessory ni-cad rechargeable battery pack
and battery charger are available."*

Kel's first appeared on the scene in the early
60's and were still in production well into the
80's. The basic kit has a two-track tape recorder
offering 1-7/8 and 15/16 IPS speeds, a record-
playback frequency range of 300–3,000 hertz
plus or minus 3 dB at both speeds, sharp noise
rejection at frequencies over 3500 cycles per
second. A rechargeable nicad battery pack
provided approximately 18 hours recording
time or 100 hours standby. A battery charger
for the nicad battery pack (24 hours full charge)
allowing charging for 110-volt AC to 220-volt
AC power. A non-rechargeable battery pack
utilizing replaceable mercury alkaline D-cells,
providing approximately 40 hours recording
time or 200 hours standby was also available.

Monitoring and other electronics necessary to operate the AGC2 amplifier or the R2 receiver are also included. A non-directional VHF antenna for the R2 receiver is built in the briefcase cover plus there are provisions for an external antenna to boost the effective range.

Plus, a microphone built into the briefcase with a concealed opening to the outside for use with the cover closed. A concealed external on or off switch for unobtrusive manual operation with the cover closed. Automatic recorder activation facilities offering voice only triggering of the recorder. Detachable equipment included: AGEC2 audio amplifiers, suitable for operation with *2 miles of line,* remote powered at 100 dB gain, 40 dB compression range, R2 receiver available in 30–54 MHz for low and 148–154 in high band. Double conversion with crystal filters plus or minus 6 kilohertz full deviation acceptance. Sensitivity is 0.5 microvolt for top flight dB signal and noise, 2 milliwatt into 2,000 ohms, output power consumption less than 100 miliwatts at 6 volts DC. R51 headphone antenna for R2 receiver, briefcase and playback amplifier R50, auto antenna and external recorder adapter, T2 transmitter, VHF FM low, VHF high. 200 miliwatts RF power, 100% modulation at 5 kHz deviation, 40 dB compressed audio gain, power consumption under 900 mil at 13-1/2 DC.

T50A microphone antenna for use with the T2 transmitter, *automobile antenna adapter* allowing simultaneous use of the automobile broadcast receiver and T2 transmitter, sets batteries, earphone for silent monitoring, one T57 clamp-on pickup for telephone monitoring *via induction link,* one A4 gutter mount antenna.

The kit was modular in the sense that items were designed to do double or triple duty to extend their usefulness. For instance, the transmitter's input was a jack so a microphone could be hooked up to it or a small female-to-male jack that accepted the lead from a normal automobile radio antenna and then passed the incoming signal onto the radio.

This meant the unit could be snapped into place underneath an auto dashboard, plugged into the vehicle's own antenna, and still let the car radio function as normal. This installation took only a matter of seconds at worst. Have you ever tried to bug a car? It's hard to get the signal out in a coherent fashion. This unit did.

Kel kits can take a two mile line of mike cable. Any kind. Twisted pair, coax, antenna cable, anything laying on the ground, and bring the audio home where it can be notched and filtered to pass only voice bandwidths.

The telephone tap input is an induction coil built into what appears to be a plastic spring operated clothes pin. It could/can be clamped around a phone pair instantly and works well enough to bring the conversation back to the recorder and is just about impossible to find with any line measuring counter measures gear.

A modern version of this could be easily constructed by adding a small FET preamp right at the clip to boost the low level signal at the source before any extraneous noise is acquired.

The first Kel's were reel-to-reel, the later one's cassette based. The kit comes with a complete manual which shows one how to wire up a room, wire up a car, wire up your friends, wire up your enemies, truly an all-around intelligence kit. The price was reasonable, cops bought the bulk of the Kels, but then, during the days of Vietnam and protesting, the army bought thousands of them at $600 at a crack from X's[1] dad.

After one of the unit's primary designers left Kel he went directly to work for AID and they subsequently began to sell copies of the Kel, although the new units do not contain as many accessories as the originals and the price is considerably higher.

Manufacturers have discovered there is more income involved in selling a basic kit and then allowing the customer to purchase "options."

---

[1] *Name deleted at the insistance of publisher's lawyer.*

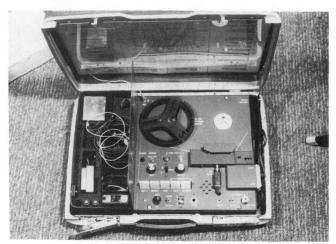

Early Kel Kit still offers unique features not found in later, more expensive copies.

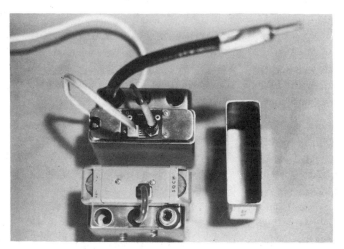

Kel transmitter works in room or automobile. Crystal-controlled with antenna connector.

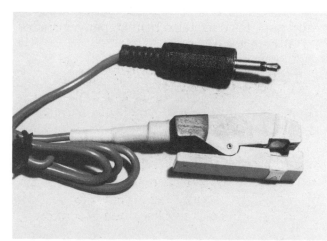

Kel induction tap is virtually impossible to locate electronically.

The following
is a series of suggestions: a kit for every kid, as it were, make them, modify them, or ignore them as you see fit, or just consider the permutations possible with the components.

Each kit (except where noted) should fit into a Haliburton Zero sized briefcase.

HARDWIRE KIT

One or more sub miniature, super sensitive mics, stiff and flexible plastic tubing, line driver mic and power source, piezo paper mic, one contact element and amplifier (with spike?), elastic band and thumb tacks, double-sided 3M tape, contact paste, mini shielded cable, superfine varnish coated copper wire, electronic conductor pencil, liquid conductor paint, long play recorder, VOX activation unit, small active filter unit, headphones, bee's wax, superglue, exacto knife, filament tape, small drill with a variety of bits, VOM, wirestrippers, screwdrivers, black light paint, and a bottle of New Skin.

BUGGING KIT

Long play recorder, sensitive mic, shielded cable, VOX, scanner, gain antenna, earphones, carrier recorder starter, at least one crystal controlled transmitter modified to take external mic, one Sheffield type xmitter, one Deco broadcast FM unit, "adjusted" or Canadian Radio Shack unit, Carrier current transmitter/receiver, mains transmitter or AC power supply for crystal transmitter, preamp, small bandpass filter unit, adapter to hook onto car antenna, selection of battery packs and wire. Drill hole in case for mic placement and remote recorder start switch.

Sources include, Sheffield, Dijiro, Deco, Micro, Capri, Grove, Sherwood, AMC, AOR, Radio Shack etc.

VIDEO INSTALLATION KIT

Mini chip camera, mini coax cable, twisted pair, fiber optic transmitter/receiver and 500 feet of fiber optic cable, pinhole lens, fiber optic 1 mm viewscope, drop ceiling mount, IR light source, square of "trick" black plexiglass,

Watchman® type mini monitor, BNC connectors, gaffer's tape, lens chart, speciality mounts (sprinkler, clock, planter, radio, as needed).

Sources: VMI, Sherwood, etc.

VIDEO WIRELESS KIT

Above plus transmitter (good, TRON TEK, VIKING, or other title III units, medium WIRELESS VIDEO, VMI) and/or cheap home video distribution transmitter, mini receiver/monitor, gain antenna, VCR or camcorder.

VIDEO IN PLACE

Camcorder with C-mount removable lens, pinhole lens, remote on and off switch, motion detector, date/time coder if to be used as evidence, or "time bomb" motion sensitive time lapse VCR with mini camera, pinhole in briefcase, foam padding, mounts to hold equipment in place, light source or intensifier if needed for application.

TELEPHONE MONITORING KIT
(and room via telephone line)

Punch down tool, can wrench, telco wire and cable, handset, line finder or Fox and Hound type injector unit, VOX recorder (preferably long play), direct capacitor-resistor direct wire tap, inductive tap, Tele-Monitor or Listen infinity transmitter, slave, several transmitters, some modified to take a plug in tap element, color code chart, parallel and serial recorder drop outs, telco ID, telco helmet, pen register or DTMF detector.

EXECUTIVE UPGRADE OPTION: Trickle parallel transmitter ($700), carrier current telephone line monitor unit ($800).

LISTENING POST KIT

Continuous scanner, gain antennas for various frequencies, long play recorder, carrier sensing recorder start device, external battery packs, car power adaptor, active filter, notch filter, Radio Shack amplifier and speaker, good headphones,

REPEATER KIT

Good scanner or crystal controlled receiver, pre-amp and gain antenna, external batteries and car/AC adaptors, VOX operated or carrier current start commercial FM walkie talkies repeater module from VIKING (Viking number 2).

PHOTO KIT

Motor drive, bulk loaded camera with point and shoot features, remote shutter release, pinhole lens, IR and fast speed film, red 1 filter, mini camera with fake cases, (cigarette pack etc), fiber optic view lens, IR light source, IR strobe, trip wires, timer, motion detector shutter release, small drill. Make hole in case, securely mount camera and pinhole lens.

COUNTERMEASURES KIT(S)

Cheap: OPTO frequency counter, CPM 700, OPTOELECTRONICS APS104 pre-selector amplifier, sensitive audio amplifier, Fox and Hound type induction amplifier and injector, VOM, resistors, wire, tools, adapters, clips, walkie talkies.
Better: Above plus TDR, Scanlock reciver, combination wire matcher/tester for phone cables, spec analyzer, scanner, Range lock unit.
Best: Above plus frequency computer memory for Scanlock, Non-linear junction detector, ICOM receiver, wide-band carrier current amplifier.

CELLULAR INTERCEPT KIT

Handheld scanner, 800 ground plane antenna (CELLULAR SECURITY), Yagi gain antenna or Nearfield type gain antenna, frequency bank guide, recorder, CAPRI recorder starter.

Receivers and Scanners

You wanna listen to transmitters—big transmitters, little transmitters, your transmitters, someone else's transmitters—you gotta have a receiver...

There are many different receivers being marketed at this time. The most popular selection of general receivers is probably that marketed by ICOM.

Their receivers can tune from 25 to 2000 MHz and allow the addition of a spectrum display unit effectively turning them into spectrum analyzers.

Other brands (Grove for instance) offer electro-luminescent displays that are compatible with receivers allowing them to duplicate, at least in general terms, the $5,000 receiver/analyzers for far less money.

What should a buyer look for in a receiver? One of the first necessary qualities is selectivity. Also referred to as resolution, this property is the ability to discriminate between two signals. In a visual display we will call it resolution, if audible thy name be selectivity.

Selectivity is an important factor because the radio spectrum is a hotly contested and fought for war, with many factions trying to get frequencies, licenses, allocations, operations and assignments, crowding the band beyond the limits of human tolerance.

If the operator is going to try and pick out one signal from this killing field he needs all the help he can get. A surveillance transmitter will probably be unlicensed and operating on only a few milliwatts. Nearby, enormous transmitters will be pumping out thousands of watts. It makes little difference if these monsters are physically nearby or close; in terms of frequency, they're nearby.

Selectivity then is the ability of the receiver to discriminate the desired frequency from adjacent signals. Normal selectivity varies depending upon the mode you want to hear. Surveillance lovers are interested mostly in narrow band FM so we want a selectivity factor in the neighborhood of 10 or 15 KHz.

Another characteristic that goes with selectivity is the shape factor of the filter employed in this process. How quickly does that filter which allows only one very narrow slot to come through, suddenly cut down and say no more signals, regardless of how strong they are, we have what we are looking for; the job is taken.

Some filters taper off poorly, even though they begin to roll off at 15 KHz they do it so gently that strong signals can still over power them and come thundering in. Try to get a filter with good sharp, steep numbers to allow for correct adjacent channel rejection.

Most filters are rated when they begin to roll off 6dB. They roll off at 6dB but the next specification listed is usually 60 decibels. At 60 decibels, exactly how wide is the filter?

Use the 6 and 60dB points for reference points along with a ratio of roughly 2 to 1. If a filter in question offers a bandwidth of 15 KHz at 6dB down and then approaches 30 KHz at 60dB down, it's doing its job.

Dynamic range refers to the ability of a receiver to respond to the very weakest signals offered, and to be effective it should do this even in the presence of stronger signals. Many inexpensive receivers, especially low-end scanners armed with a whip antenna, can garner about 40 frequencies at one time.

Inter-modulation, images, and a Noah's Ark of horrendous RF creatures can rush into the front end of the unit, overwhelming it if it lacks selectivity and dynamic range.

Even with good dynamic range one can be listening leisurely and suddenly hear something of interest that doesn't jibe with the area of the spectrum being searched. This is often due to a spurious product generated by the receiver itself. The signal may actually exist, but it lives somewhere else in the spectrum.

In this case the unit has revealed the presence of a suspicious signal, and that may be enough to start the search, but it's just an indication and doesn't give one the real story as to what frequency it's truly on. This is a manifestation of poor dynamic range.

Any receiver will come apart (electronically speaking) if too much signal is present, offering all sorts of unusual indications that don't really exist in what we have come to know as real life.

Scanners are absolutely atrocious in this respect.

An indication of good dynamic range is the presence of what is listed as third order intercept capability. If this phrase appears on a spec sheet the receiver is strong in the DR department. To further qualify it—plus 20 is very good—plus 30 dBm is excellent.

Dynamic range becomes the most important feature of a receiver when it is operated in any area where very strong signals are present.

On the other end of the scale is sensitivity. This is the ability of the receiver to respond to an extremely weak signal. Can it do it in the presence of very strong signals? If so, the unit has good dynamic range as well as sensitivity.

Sensitivity figures on the order of less than one microvolt are best for surveillance purposes.

Most scanners and short wave receivers can now easily check in at under one microvolt at least in certain frequency ranges. The lower that number, the better the sensitivity.

Communications receivers that operate on just a single channel, such as two-way radios, offer figures on the order of a quarter of a microvolt, maybe even one tenth, because they don't have to tune wide frequency ranges. All of their selective circuitry can be concentrated on that one frequency, making the receiver really sensitive as it is able to reject everything else from causing interference problems.

Next the buyer should look at the frequency range covered: DC to daylight, is what we're hoping to find in our perspective receiver; 25K–1 Gig is what we will settle for, although 30 to 400 is where the most of surveillance transmitters operate and is the area where most counter measure gear is designed to operate.

Economics operate in electronics just like they do in the field of used car sales. The more

one is willing to pay, the more one can expect in terms of performance.

LISTENING POSTS

An LP is the place where the signals from the surveillance transmitter are received and often recorded. An LP can be as simple as a pocket receiver carried by an agent or it can be as complicated as a fully equipped command post staffed twenty four hours a day with monitoring and transcribing personnel. An LP can take one of several forms depending on the type of site under surveillance, the type of equipment in use and, of course, the budget of the operator.

A stationary LP is the type favored by law enforcement types but has several limitations: the first being that it must be located within the range of any surveillance transmitter. This could range from a couple hundred feet for the low power, micro-transmitters to one-to-three miles for powerful body wires.

This type of LP usually takes the form of a rented room near the surveillance site, unless, of course, one has some interesting neighbors.

The stationary LP often starts out life as a simple operation with only a receiver and recorder (plus a backup receiver and recorder in the event of equipment failure). However, as things progress, new information that comes to light due to the intercept could point to the necessity of phone taps at the location under question, auto's to be tailed, or new sites to be bugged in order to continue the investigation.

For this reason some buggers keep additional receivers, recorders, and telephone equipment in the LP, along with additional monitors and vehicles stationed nearby. This arrangement alleviates some of the problem of having the correct equipment on hand for a large job.

PERSONAL

When the LP consists of an agent wired with a pocket receiver, the purpose is usually to provide backup for another agent rather than for use as a permanent facility. This type of operation is used extensively for any situation that involves contact with a possible hostile.

This not only provides backup for the investigator who may become involved in a life threatening situation, but also provides a witness for any subsequent developments.

MOBILE

The mobile LP can be as simple as a pocket receiver installed in a vehicle, or as sophisticated as a surveillance van equipped and staffed much like a stationary LP.

Normally, the mobile LP will have at least a receiver and recorder with automatic carrier or voice activation on the recorder (CAPRI ELECTRONICS, SHERWOOD). In those operations where anticipated countermeasures necessitate the use of micro-miniature low RF power transmitters, a mobile LP may be the only way a receiver can be established within the transmitters range.

MP's can also be equipped with repeaters to re-transmit the received signal to a more permanent LP to minimize contact with the vehicle during the surveillance.

Note that a couple of suppliers (in the section so named) sell, or in at least one case, rent, complete surveillance vans that can be used as mobile listening posts.

TAKING A WALK THRU THE RF SPECTRUM
Where the bugs are, someone waits for me...
Before attempting to locate surveillance transmitters and especially before laying out next month's mortgage payment for a transmitter or surveillance receiver one must have some idea of where (electromagnetically speaking) these units operate successfully.

The Federal Communications Commission defines the radio spectrum as that swath of electro-magnetic activity in which an antenna or radiating device oscillates forth a signal from an antenna at the rate of 9 kHz up to 300 GHz.

This is an enormous range of frequencies. At the top end it borders on light, the lower end is well within the audio range.

An electronic bug can be constructed or tuned to operate almost anywhere in this spectrum. However a couple of common factors cause many of the units to cluster in certain frequency ranges.

The AM (long wave) broadcast band takes up an area from 1.5 to 1.5 MHz. Below this range there are very few communications signals emitted. If one goes below the broadcast band about the only thing that exists down there is a small band of frequencies ranging between 160–190 kHz. Here live the carrier current based wireless intercoms, units that do not require anything other than being plugged into a wall in order to broadcast audio over the electrical wiring of the building and for some distance beyond.

1.6 and above, up to about 30 MHz, is known as the HF (high frequency) or shortwave spectrum. In this band one can listen to everything from hams, ship-to-shore, air-to-ground and even the most socially-deprived portion of humanity—CB'ers...

What's the lowest frequency bugging transmitter (besides the above mentioned carrier current units) one is likely to find? 27 MHz. Most of the units here are homemade from plans or kits on the market today and are based on CB transmitter technology, using CB crystals.

Radio Shack in Canada sells a 50 MHz cordless microphone and another unit that's just under the U.S. FM band. They also sell several carrier current devices.

Several factors work against bugs into this part of the radio spectrum. First of all, in order to get an efficient radiating antenna, it must be monumental in length, even if it is coiled, it requires lots of noticeable wire in order to get a good output.

The second reason small transmitters are rarely inserted here, is that the average signal level available to a receiver's antenna in this portion of the spectrum is substantial. Everybody from the Voice of America, the BBC, and Radio Moscow, runs all sorts of multi-kilowatt transmitters in here. We're talking hundreds of thousands of watts of transmitting power. A few even boast effective radiating power in the millions of Watts. With the factor of propogation, (the paths that signals from around the world take) you can fry a receiver trying to find a little tiny bug transmitting a few hundred feet away.

Thirdly we have noise. There's a great deal of noise in the AM band because both man-made and natural sources of interference tend to be amplitude modulated in their makeup. This is ignition noise territory plus the area where lightening crackles and computer noise lives. Incidental radiation lurks in this section of the band in preposterously high levels.

The last factor stacked against surveillance transmitters in this region is simply the crowding factor. One can hear things from all over the world, the bands are as crowded as the Santa Monica freeway during rush hour, virtually bumper to bumper, there's very little room to put in a device that has a controlled frequency and hope no one turns a 1 kW transmitter loose on the same frequency.

CBer's utilize 27 MHz. 30 to 50 is commonly called low band, or low public service. There's a ham band stuck in at 50–54 Mgs and 54 up to 72 is designated as TV channels 2–4.

72 to 76 is generally a low powered band in which some devices can be found. There are some wireless mikes made to operate in here and it's an area that few people realize exists.

From 76 up to 88 is television channels 5 & 6.

The most common approach among amateur eavesdroppers who need certain information on a subject, is go to the friendly neighborhood bugging supplier, sorry I meant Radio Shack, and buy a wireless microphone. In order for these units to be operated legally and sold in the United States, they have to be FCC type approved. The FCC limits these low powered transmitters to certain frequencies. Any manufacturer that wants to produce these products in volume, to hit the retail consumer market, is going to construct them to these guidelines.

88 to 108 is the standard FM broadcast band and where the typical inexpensive wireless mic or amateur eavesdropper's bugs (Radio Shack, Cony, DECO, etc.) operate.

The disadvantage to transmitters in commercial bands is, of course, they can be easily found by anyone who is looking for them and often times by people who are not. Case in point was a small unit planted in a women's apartment, actually her bedroom to be specific, in a large apart. complex where I once lived.

The bug was placed by her jealous boyfriend and left to free run for several days, during which time one of the neighbors discovered the rather graphically entertaining programming and spread the word around the complex.

Finally another resident took pity on the hapless victim and told her of the impromptu audience she had garnered. End results included a boyfriend told to get lost, and a resident who shunned all contact with her neighbors until she finally moved out.

The program was so popular during certain hours that I always felt she could have sold a little advertising and at least made some money from the experience.

The advantage to commercial bands are the easily available receivers and the fact that a good amateur (a professional amateur?) can "smuggle" a bug right next to a high-powered radio station so that only someone with a hot receiver in the right place is going to be able to find it.

Just up above and below the commercial FM band is a good area because many wireless mics can be tuned to slip outside of their original operating frequencies. In fact, the FM band in most receivers and many transmitters will go up to 112 megs. The FCC has never assigned anything to this area so it is a frequency that one could use and nobody's going to be scanning it.

If a particular transmitter can't reach this band, one can make minor modifications in the coil and it will damn sure go up. Most of these units are extremely low in power and their operating frequency will tend to shift and change a little bit, but a good wide band receiver with a wide window will pull them in.

108.1 all the way up to 117.9 is the aeronautical navigation band. There's little voice communications here but whirs, clicks and beeps produced by VOR and other aid to navigation type radio stations.

118–136 includes civilian and military aircraft communications.

Japanese firms offer body transmitters in the 120, 130, 140 MHz range. These units are openly obtainable and KANT (in Japan) offers low priced, crystal controlled transmitter/receivers configured in both a room and telephone bugging unit.

From 137 to about 138 a careful searcher can find down link data transmissions from satellites and not much else. It's a nice cozy little electronic neighborhood in which to stash something. This is a place that people just don't look. Most observers of the spectrum do not think to look for communications in the 137 to the 138 range and even if a weak carrier is located, most listeners will figure it's just a satellite and ignore it.

The military has air-to-ground and some base communications all the way from 138 to 144. Then hams check in from 144 to 148, to utilize the 2 meter band. This band is the most congested part of the amateur radio spectrum (hams). This means nice ready made repeater gear is available over the counter for this area of the spectrum.

There are some other frequency ranges now which are also becoming popular in the field of electronic surveillance. Just below 50 MHz a wide variety of ready made equipment will transmit including cordless telephones, which are sometimes hot on hook or rigged to serve as emergency bugs by both law enforcement and private eavesdroppers. This can be done legally because the cordless phone, unlike it's brother the cellular, fell outside the 1986 Electronic Communication Privacy Act, which forbids anyone surreptitiously monitoring communications that are intended to be private.

Wireless babysitters that operate on RF are another available type of transmitter intended for consumers that is often adapted to surveillance purposes. The actual frequency of these units falls between 46.6 and 46.99. Occasionally these operate as in place bugs without any effort on the part of the eavesdropper.

Drive around a residential neighborhood with a scanner some day and see if you don't pick up "private" conversations in a house or two where someone has a free running "babysitter" switched on.

Note if one were to sweep through those frequencies where the base repeaters for cordless phones operate, you'll hear both sides of the conversation because the base repeats the handset. The actual telephone handset is radiating at a frequency 3 MHz higher than the base, in the area of 49.6 to 49.99.

Then we jump up all the way into the 150's. Fast food restaurants use 150–154 to talk to there little clown or other plastic order taking robot. There are also provisions by the FCC for devices to be placed in this band and they do exist on the commercial market.

151 goes back to the federal government, mostly military bases. Next comes the most densely populated portion of the two way commercial radio spectrum, 151 to 174. This is called high band or high public service.

This particular band is divided roughly in half. 151 to 162 is a civilian portion while 162 to 174 is federal. The agencies that utilize this particular frequency range are for the most part base-station fixed and mobile operations of federal agencies.

If one had a bugging device that was going to be thrown on the air in that area, one might best check the frequency out on a spectrum analyzer or a frequency counter or something before placing the crystal in the circuit and locking it to a particular frequency. One might find oneself setting right on top of a paging system or a taxi cab or business band or law enforcement. It is an area where a lot of things have been appearing.

A bunch of signals and a bunch of surveillance signals live in the 167 area. Professional surveillance transmitters used by the FBI and other law enforcement agencies (made by AID, HDS, etc.) are often placed here. The FBI tends to use 167.4 through 167.985 for most of their communications.

174–400 megs contains several types of surveillance transmitters. Sheffield Electronics made several good units that fell right in there and some are still around.

Sheffield is selling kits and schematics now for the units they used to sell in a complete version. See the review of their products in another spot in this sterling publication...

170–174 MHz, is pretty thin listening as there aren't too many people up at this end of the band. Some industrial stuff, but it's not as crowded as the 150's and there are some good places to put a little transmitter there.

174 to 216 is TV channels 7 to 13. The amateur 6 meter band is also located in this area. TV bands are again both good and bad from the standpoint of placing a surveillance

transmitter. Here's a place where one can essentially hide a transmitter—not physically but electro-magnetically in the spectrum— and it takes a good counter surveillance man, employing a good receiver or preferably a spectrum analyzer, to spot a tiny little carrier and break it out from the enormous strength of a nearby TV signal.

Professional wireless mics designed for television and film applications, but often employed as body wires or stationary bugging transmitters, are typically here between television channels in the 170's and 180's. Some wireless mikes are also available in the 457's and 467's, from commercial video suppliers.

216 to 220 is for inland water navigation communications and it is a very thinly populated part of the spectrum. This is another example of an area waiting to happen. Scanners cover it, transmitters can be made for it.

220 to 225 is a ham band although the top 2 MHz are gradually being taken away being handed off to UPS for truck communication.

An interesting spot is 400 to 406. This area is reserved primarily for space-to-earth devices. This also would be a good area to put something one doesn't want casual listeners to stumble upon.

Next consider the UHF area: Equipment is available for law enforcement and taxicab communication in the 400 meg area. Law enforcements uses it. Private security uses it.

406 to 512 is the UHF land mobile band, 406 to 420 is for the exclusive use of federal government agencies. 420 to 450 is shared in some areas of the country but exists primarily as a ham band, 450 to 512 is a civilian section.

500–800 megs. Not much. Sheffield and a couple of other manufacturers have reportedly made devices that transmit here at one time or another. It's feasible and the technology is evolving.

If one is going to build an RF bug there must be a receiver available to pick it up. Up until

ICOM and ACE developed their new continuous line of receivers and scanners, there just wasn't much available. One had to either take a receiver and modify it so it would pick up the listening device or make a receiver from scratch, although a few Japanese companies do make matching xmitters/receivers in this band.

There has been very little manufactured in the 500, 600, 700 MHz range or even in the 800, 900 MHz range because no one was sure it could be successfully done until cellular phones came along.

Now there's a tremendous amount of R & D going on in this band. The FCC has now opened the low 900's for wireless video and a number of inexpensive transmitter/receivers are already available with more to come.

A company in Italy sells two sub miniature units (one phone tap-one bug) that operate right at or around 900 MHz. These units are sold to law enforcement in the U.S. by KNOX SECURITY.

One gigahertz? The FCC has just opened up something at 1.2 and 2.6 for law enforcement video transmitters. These are covert video transmitters like the ones sold by HOUSEHOLD DATA SERVICES, TRON TEK and SWS. These are good video transmitters and they are omnidirectionial without requiring big disk antennas. They offer high gain with small, phased arrays or cavity dipole antennas.

3 or 4 gigs? We aren't there yet, stayed tuned to this channel for more information.

THE PHONE COMPANY

This book is not designed to be a basic text on either electronics or telephony, there are a number of good texts available on either subject for the uninitiated, however a solid grasp of how a telco (a commonly used contraction of the words telephone and company) operates is crucial for anyone concerned with wiretapping or data interception.

Regardless of which particular side of the fence one finds one's self on...

Besides a general overview of the system's functions it is important to understand a little bit about signal flow and distribution points as these are the main areas targeted by wiretappers.

The natural starting point for our little discussion is the central office (CO) or telephone exchange. The CO houses the equipment that directs calls, processes the audio, furnishes dial tone and the electrical power required to power individual telephones.

The CO in turn consists of one or more exchanges each processing up to 10,000 lines. The exchange a subscriber "belongs" to is identified by the first three digits of the phone number in question.

Thus, all numbers that begin 495–XXXX live on the same exchange.

From inception until a few years ago an an exchange consisted of crossbar circuitry, that being electro-mechanical relays which opened and closed to connect and direct phone calls. These relays were powered by 48 volts DC which was drawn from the local power company and then backed up by banks of automobile batteries that stored enough energy to power the exchange for about 24 hours if the normal power supply was interrupted.

When a customer lifted the phone from the hook it began to draw power, pulling in a relay and providing dial tone.

The 48 volt operating power was referred to as "battery" or "battery power."

Modern exchanges consist of computers and sophisticated software known as ESS for electronic switching or DSS for digital switching. Gone too are the batteries, most systems are now backed by diesel generators producing somewhere between 48 and 52 volts, but the term "battery" is still used to refer to telco current.

In the electronic versions no audio path is completed to the actual telephone instrument until the called telephone is signaled with a 90–105 AC voltage that produces the ring and the phone is lifted from it's cradle.

This lack of audio path is a small but important point, the "ring" the caller hears when dialing on an electronic system is not the other phone ringing but actually a synthesized signal produced by the exchange computer.

Exchanges and CO's are connected by truck lines or "trunks." Until the proverbial few years ago trunks were just that—large cables that contained many individual wires each capable of carrying one conversation. Some time ago Bell Systems began multiplexing trunks allowing each separate wire to carry many conversations simultaneously to increase their capacity without laying new trunks.

Today most trunks are either fiber optic lines that transmit light rather than electricity (also multiplexed) or microwave links. Because of the number of conversations taking place on each wire (or fiber) trunks are not normally associated with eavesdropping.

With one major exception: While researching this book I asked a number of professional, read employed-by-the-government, surveillance personnel if, indeed, every phone in the US is tapped.

A simple question, right?

Now let me preclude my favorite answer by reminding you that for years and years, probably since the first transatlantic cable was laid, the agencies in the U.S., in particular the NSA have monitored ALL overseas calls, cables and telegrams.

First manned by humans the task is now delegated to computers that "listen" for key words before recording the ensuing conversation.

Several of the people hedged their statements but one gentleman said, "Microwaves may travel in a straight line but the signal spreads out quite a bit before the receiving antenna and it is a simple matter to pick up this scatter. Most calls made in this country travel at least part of their journey via microwave links or satellites. It should not be assumed that these calls couldn't be monitored."

Now carefully take a razor blade and cut out a few of the stock government phrases in that answer and see what's left behind…

Interesting isn't it?

Also in those halcyonic times of yore, telco's were known as a walk in the park for anyone with a law enforcement contact. General policy was for company personnel to install taps or bridges right at the exchange on the say-so of cops and government agents—pro bono.

Even such sleazy creatures like private detectives had no great problem obtaining these unofficial listening posts.

Besides this semi-authorized interception a number of CO's were fond of simply listening in on interesting subscribers. Sort of as a replacement for daytime television.

A number of lawsuits have passed under the bridge since these days, like the one in MIll Valley California where a number of the office personnel and lineman seemed to dedicate an inordinate amount of their working hours listening to the explicit adventures of a couple of local women, and the pendulum has swung back in the other direction.

Most telco's now require a court order before they will supply records or place a tap for any agency. This does not, however, mean that all CO traffic is safe from the prying ears of curious telephone employees.

Along with the computer hardware CO's contains giant walls of electrical connecting posts known as frames or main distribution frames. This is where the connection is made from the CO's equipment to the actual telephone line leading to the customer is affected.

Lines are run from the CO to various distribution points in the system. Older lines are mounted on telephone poles, new ones are usually underground. Once a line leaves a CO it becomes open to attack by eavesdroppers. The lines start out in a large cable and gradually filter out to smaller cables until the termination point is reached.

The first stage of this journey occurs in a large duct (or main feeder) cable that contains up to 3,600 individual wire pairs. Junction points in the duct cable are usually under ground with manhole access. These splices are usually pressurized and sealed to protect their environmental integrity. and are difficult to sucessfully compromise.

Branch cables or branch feeders break off from the main cable at these splice points. These smaller cables have up to 900 separate pairs contained within them. When the main is spliced to a branch, the outer cable bundles (higher pair numbers) are the first to be connected. These junctions may be sealed or filled with a weather resistant petroleum jelly.

The branch branches off into even more compact cables called distribution cables. DC's are the last grouped link between the CO and the subscriber's own telephone line and normally contain somewhere between 25 and 300 pairs.

DC's may be mounted on poles or buried depending on the local regulations and ground conditions. A single DC can feed a medium sized office building or apartment complex. In a residential neighborhood the DC will cover a set group of houses or neighborhoods.

On older line runs (usually pole mounted) the DC will enter a rectangular metal splice box (sealed) and is permanently joined to a set pair in both the branch and main feed cables. This set up will have two large (branch cables) and one smaller line (DC) entering/leaving the splice box.

The wires from the DC are usually paralleled to the branch feeder's wires so any individual pair can be used in several locations depending upon demand. The fact that one pair can appear at several different locations is an important factor to anyone concerned with aural interception.

If the splice box has one-side-one large cable (branch from CO) and other side two smaller (branch and distribution torwards subscribers) is a series connection without the parallel multiples appearances.

If the area to be served has underground cables the branches and DC's are spliced in an above ground pedestal box or a buried pedestal box that can be opened and then allows the interior terminal board to be removed for access to the splices. Cable TV also utilizes pedestal boxes but they are usually unmarked. Telco equipment is always marked.

Once a box is opened the splice connections themselves will tell the observer the type of connection—two wires (one in one out) at each

connection is a series splice—two is the parallel version.

The latter is the favorite of compromising persons because it means there will be more than one appearance of the target pair and more than one opportunity to place a bug, often blocks away from the actual location of the telephone itself. Multiples can be traced with the proper equipment or their location gotten from friendly phone folk.

In fact any phone wire can be traced by hooking an rf generator to it and "followed" with a radio receiver. JENSEN TOOLS sells a low cost unit that will allow the operator to trace the wire even it is buried four feet underground.

Newer systems often use a cabling run system called serving area concept or connect through plan. A SAC can be readily identified by the appearance of cross connect cabinets rather than splice cases.

Cross connect cabinets can be a God send or a trouble spot, again depending if one happens to be in the business of snooping or discouraging snoops. A CC cabinet consists of three panels that are prewired on the back with leads (pigtails) and nut-on-bolt wiring terminals on their surface.

As the system is installed a telco employee joins each pigtail with a wire from a branch feeder or a DC. By design the center panel handles the branch feeder and the side panels serve as home for DC's.

The feeder panel is connected by wires (straps) to the DC panels. This strapping allows the telco to connect pairs to DC's as directed by demand. To facilitate this these connections the binding post are numbered to match the cabling numbers.

WIRETAP METHODS

The areas of risk of a telephone system include the phone itself, the inside wiring, drop wire, protector block, splice boot, pedestal, cross connect boxes and multiple appearances of the line. The probability of a tap drops off after the first loading coil or central office.

PARALLEL

Parallel taps go across the two active (tip and ring, usually red and green) wires in a telephone cord, across binding posts in a cross connect cabinet, on the splice block in an office building's telephone room, on the screws of a house's splice block on a multiple (B box) appearance of the phone cable, in the house wiring or in the phone itself.

The simplest, and probably the most effective, type of parallel tap is a bridging tap. This simply involves connecting a separate wire pair, in parallel, with the target wiring. The bridge wiring, in effect, becomes an extension of the subject's phone and leads to some sort of listening device, usually a tape recorder.

The main advantages of a parallel tap include the fact that it will work when any extension phone on the wiring is activated, draws less current (and thus is harder to find) than a series tap and can be installed almost anywhere on the line, even miles from the target phone.

Parallel taps are the type usually found in cross connect boxes, splice boots and other appearances of the line.

Parallel taps are an oft-used form of domestic surveillance, usually concealed in a garage or attic of the target house. A parallel recorder starter such as the Radio Shack 43-236B is often used to control the operation of the recorder.

Amateur tappers tend to stash the tap on or near the premises; pro's will use a multiple appearance or do something clever like dig up the drop wire as it leaves the telco pedestal or distribution box, attach his bridging wire, run it to a weatherproof box and rebury everything.

Cross connect cabinets are a big favorite of good surveillance folk. Most CC cabinets will allow their panels to be pulled forward and a pro will install wiretap gear behind the panel, backstrapping the correct terminals. This area is rarely checked by telco personnel.

Office building bridging is often done in the splice cabinet at what is known as a 66 block. This block uses V-shaped terminals to connect the drop wires to the phone lines. A pro will use a telco seating wrench (about $15) to seat his bridge wiring so it will go unnoticed by anyone except the most dedicated searcher, or pull the block forward and attach his wire to the back of the 66 post, running it out of the block, allowing a remote installation of the listening equipment.

Parallel transmitters can be attached in any of the above locations (except buried, unless the telco wiring is used as an antenna) as easily as a hardwire.

The advantage of a parallel unit picking up all extensions will turn to a disadvantage if not planned so persons other than the target will not be intercepted, burning up valuable tape.

SERIES TAPS

A series tap breaks one side of the tip ring combination and is installed so the it is in series with the wire. Simple drop out relays, such as the Radio Shack single line recorder starter and single line "tele secretaries" sold by mail order houses fall into this category.

Series drop outs will only record the extension they are installed upon unless one places them between all the phones and the CO, such as on an outside drop wire.

The exception to this rule is that a VOX operated tape recorder that is wired in series with a capacitor and resistor to pass the audio will start on any *noise* on the line rather than a drop in voltage and as such will grab all conversations that come down the line.

Series transmitters use the phone line for power, requiring no batteries but are typically low in output power and require a close in LP.

Series drop outs usually have to be physically close to the phone in question in order to sense the necessary voltage changes.

With these limitations in mind it is possible to install a series tap in most of the same places as a parallel: Favorites include the protector block on the outside wall of a house, in the phone itself, on the drop wire or at the first telephone pole or pedestal.

Pro's place them on the line, amateurs choose areas such as inside a splice boot where the chances of discovery are high because they are accessed by linemen installing other phones in the area.

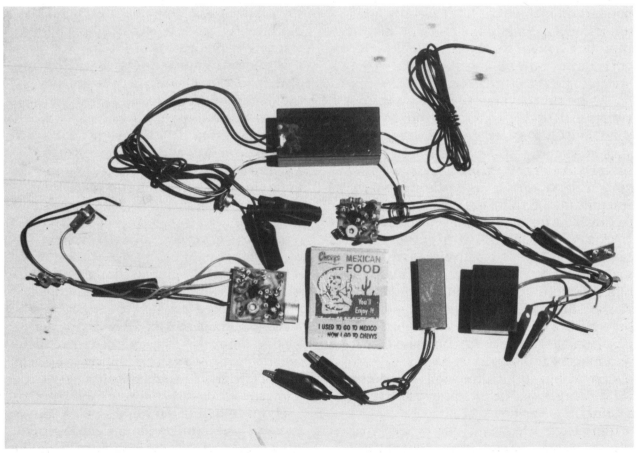

Examples of series and parallel taps.

A Phantom

Phone tap or two...

Under certain ideal circumstances, it's possible to literally produce a phone tap out of thin air. Bear in mind this doesn't work in all situations, but if the ingredients are there a clever eavesdropper can produce his own phone tap between two particular targets.

This is a situational condition that involves a little bit of social engineering but no actual hardware. The first necessary factor is the quick availability of persons who have something in common to talk about that our hero desperately needs to overhear. It is also necessary to have a telephone or telephone service that offers a hold function, a conferencing function, and preferably a speed dialing or at least an automatic re-dial function.

When these requirements are met, the eavesdropper dials one of the targets and as soon as the phone is answered, the agent puts him on hold. Then he hits the speed dial or re-dial function to which the other target's number will have been already programmed into so it will dial his number immediately. When the second party answers his phone, the eavesdropper simply hits the conferencing feature and the two targets will be on a phone line talking together.

It may seem strange that two people can engage in a meaningful conversation when neither one has actually called the other without finding something suspicious in the event, but in reality, it works out pretty well because the two parties have something in common that they're going to naturally talk about. One generally assumes the other one called him. If the calls are timed correctly, the first caller will be going "Hello, Hello" just as the second caller picks up the phone and the conversation, most times, proceeds from this point in a normal rhythm.

A couple of points to consider: Call the person who picks up his phone slowest first and call the fastest respondent second in order to slim down the awkward pause before conferencing. The same thing applies if one target has a secretary and the other doesn't, in fact it's also possible to become his secretary by asking the first target to "please hold for Mr. Jones." This embellishment not only covers any pause between the two connects but makes the first target think that the second target has indeed called him.

Likely candidates for this social tapping include lawyers and their clients, people about to close a business deal, a customer who is about to order from a usual supplier, or even a husband and a wife.

This particular technique works best for people who have a nice sense of the absurd and a polite manner...

Another true-to-life story was engineered by a friend of mine (but, then again, I think of everybody as a friend) and did actually take place.

Bear in mind my friend is an upper level programmer and part time hacker.

The head of an engineering group for a major Silicon Valley software company put a microphone on his computer to digitize voices, not an uncommon practice. He left the mic in place while he worked on other projects.

Inert.

My friend had seen the mic on a visit to the company's office, went home and thought things over. After a suitable pause he decided to call the other person's computer via both their modems.

It took him three tries to get the microphone to turn on and broadcast the resulting audio out on the phone lines to my friend's computer. He heard every sound in the other office until he logged off.

INFINITY TRANSMITTERS

In the mid-1960's an engineer working for the George Cake company developed an unique method for using the telephone line, and in some cases, the telephone instrument itself, as a room bug. Note this is not (at least in a pure form) a telephone tap but rather a device that reproduces room audio just as an RF transmitter does except instead of broadcasting over radio waves, the infinity transmitter utilizes telephone company wires to transmit the room audio to the listening post.

The first infinity transmitters were small black boxes designed to be placed inside any telephone instrument in a room that was to be placed under surveillance. A Cake model utilized its own tiny condenser microphone for good audio transmission quality. Later models tended to use the microphone in the telephone instrument itself as these microphones became higher in quality as opposed to the original carbon mic buttons.

Once the unit was placed inside the telephone instrument, the two lead wires were simply clipped across the red and green wires from the telephone cable. The infinity transmitter lay dormant until the user dialed the phone number of the telephone the device was installed in. While dialing the last number he simultaneously blew a small harmonica that had been taped to allow only one, or in some cases, two tones to function. The infinity transmitter unit sensed these tones coming down the incoming audio path even before the AC ring voltage was applied.

As soon as the unit sensed its audio signal, it detoured the ring voltage so the phone would not ring and simultaneously activated its own microphone to pick up any nearby sound and transmit it down the phone wires just as if the call had been completed.

In most cases the phone would never ring but the audio path would remain open processed by telephone company equipment to provide a nice clear path from any direct dial telephone in the world to the room under surveillance. If other parties attempted to reach the target phone during the active surveillance they received a busy signal. If the target in the room picked up the phone to initiate a phone call, the unit would disconnect automatically and allow normal outgoing dialing procedures to continue.

The infinity transmitter was a wonderous device. Although first sold only through authorized law enforcement suppliers, it soon found its way into civilian market places and thousands or maybe tens of thousands of the units were employed in various situations.

Although the theory of infinity transmitter is still valid, upgrading of telephone company equipment from mechanical crossbar type switching at the central office to ESS or electronic switching, which has now been accomplished in virtually every market in the United States, has made the original infinity transmitter obsolete. In ESS systems there is no audio path to the telephone being dialed until the phone is picked up, therefore with the original infinity transmitter it becomes impossible to prevent the phone from ringing or exercise the necessary control over the transmitter.

Infinity transmitters all but disappeared from the marketplace for a number of years because of the infusion of the ESS switching system; however, technology marches on and now there are a number of infinity systems that work quite well on ESS lines.

The simplest system is an infinity transmitter designed to work on a dedicated line. These units have been available for a number of years from various suppliers and average about $200 per unit. They are ostensibly sold as audio burglar alarms, allowing the owner of the premises to dial up his own unit and check for suspicious sounds in his building while he's away from the premises.

Due to the present interpretation of privacy and wire taping laws, it is also legal, in some cases, for this type of unit to be installed in a business so the employer can legally dial up the transmitter and listen to all audio that his employees may be producing. In some states it would also be legal to install such a unit in your own residence and employ the unit for off-premise surveillance of anyone else who lives in your domicile (read your spouse here).

Although this law may be subject to change, as this book is written there is no legal expectation of privacy in your own house when you share it with someone else: spouse, roommate, or relative.

These more modern infinity transmitters don't rely upon a mechanical tone signaling device, but rather employ a handheld two-tone oscillator that activates them when held to the mouthpiece of the telephone. Some units have been marketed that simply use a touch tone dialing code, much as most answering machines do for retrieving messages, to activate the transmitter.

The drawback to these infinity transmitters is that there's no provision for normal operation of a telephone. The units automatically answer the line in order to have an audio path. Then they wait for a prescribed period, usually about 30 seconds, for their signalling tone in order to activate their microphone and broadcast room audio. This means these units must have their own dedicated line in order to function. One can simply not put a telephone on this line.

These units were originally used by having the telco install a separate line in the building or on the premises to be monitored and then the infinity transmitter was plugged in and simply left in place. Most of these infinity transmitters came equipped with the modular telephone jack designed to be plugged directly into the female jack the telephone company installed on the end of the line.

However, exact placement was up to the installer and if the device was to be used on a surreptitious basis the new, dedicated phone line normally terminated in an area where the unit could be secured from prying eyes such as behind equipment, inside a locked cabinet, or in the ceiling or even inside the wall in an area which was to be covered by the microphone.

The modern way to employ this infinity transmitter is for the user to have the telephone company install a new line in the same drop wire as the target's normal phone lines are run. The eavesdropper then takes this active, dedicated pair and connects across an unused pair in the room to be monitored. In a typical residence phone, this would be the yellow and black wires as the red and green wires would be utilized for the working telephone instrument.

The infinity transmitter is then connected to this new spare pair (the yellow and the black) and secreted in the area to be monitored. An even hipper version is to make a simple modification inside the infinity transmitter itself. To do this one either connects one's own microphone or simply disconnects the built-in microphone from the infinity transmitter and then plants this tiny microphone in the area to be monitored, running a pair of wires back to the infinity transmitter which can then be physically removed from the premises and attached to the dedicated line at any convenient point including appearances outside the room or even outside the building itself.

A slight modification on this concept is to hook the infinity transmitter somewhere along the drop line and then use the spare pair to hardwire a tiny microphone inside the target room or even in a telephone in the target room. It's much harder to find a tiny microphone than it is to uncover a fairly bulky infinity transmitter.

In an office building that has hundreds of line pairs, it's extremely easy and efficient for an eavesdropper to place a single telephone line to function as a dedicated line as an infinity transmitter. The unit itself may then be secreted inside a telephone instrument in the ceiling or anywhere in the target area.

Once the unit is concealed, it is a simple matter to employ the building's own cable distribution system to connect their new dedicated telephone line to the area which is to be placed under surveillance.

In summary, this type of infinity transmitter works extremely well as long as you have a single phone line that is never expected to ring, but is just in service to allow this surveillance operation to function.

The other option would be to attach this type of unit onto a normal phone line when you are indeed away from the premises and simply wish to use the line for room monitoring purposes rather than as a conventional telephone circuit.

NEW AGE INFINITY

In the last year there's been a new entry into the infinity transmitter market. This concept has been marketed in a couple of different systems. One of the better examples I've tested is manufactured by LISTEN ELECTRONICS. This outfit sells a number of unique surveillance devices including an infinity transmitter, or to use their terminology, a time-sequence coded room monitor, for under $100 that actually provides nearly the same level of service as did the earlier infinity transmitters on non-ESS circuitry.

How is this accomplished? LISTEN's unit is modular and designed to be plugged into any phone jack in the area to be monitored, although it's possible to also remove the jack and simply attach it across a drop cable or pair or active ring-and-tip pair. Once installed, the unit hibernates in its own little corner, remaining dormant until a certain sequence of events transpires.

In order to trigger the unit, the eavesdropper dials the phone number of the line the unit is attached to, waits until it hears one ring tone, hangs his phone up, and then counts off 12 seconds. The unit senses the ring signal and activates an electronic timer which counts off the seconds until it reaches 12 (actually it goes off slightly before that to allow for human error).

At this point, an electronic window is opened up and for a couple of seconds the unit places itself on alert waiting for another ring signal. If the unit receives the second ring signal within the time window, it takes that as an instruction to connect itself across the wires and activate its microphone, sending any sounds in the immediate vicinity over the telephone lines.

In actual practice the unit works much as advertised; the time window takes only a bit of practice (one Mississippi, two Mississippi, kind of practice) to establish the rhythm of the window opening. There is a disadvantage involved in that the phone will ring once in normal circumstances. It's possible that a ring will not actually emanate from the telephone instrument on the same line because in some telcos the electronic ring audio is not actually timed to the AC signal sent down the wire. In other words, just because you hear a ring on the telephone when you're dialing the number doesn't necessarily mean that the phone on the other end of the line has actually rung. Most of us have experienced this at one time or another when the person you're calling picks up the telephone before you actually hear it ring.

When installed in the telephone unit, LISTEN's device doesn't use a separate microphone but rather employs the sensitive microphone in the telephone handset.

Once LISTEN's unit is activated, it acts as an ordinary infinity transmitter and if anyone tries to call the phone while the unit is in use, he/she will receive a typical busy signal. One has to be slightly careful with the unit because of the possibility of the one ring signal. If the party on the other end is extremely suspicious, over-use of the device could cause some measure of concern in the owner of the target telephone as it appears to ring once every so often and then no call follows this solitary ring. However, this is hardly noticeable and extremely difficult to identify unless one is cognizant with state-of-the art infinity transmitters.

The other minor problem is that in theory at least, it is possible for an innocent party to dial a phone, hear it ring once, hang up because they're distracted for some reason and dial the number back just in time to turn on the unit and begin receiving room audio. In real life this scenario rarely comes to pass.

The modular version of this unit is an innocuous box approximately 4' 1/2" by 1' 1/2" and is quite sensitive, allowing the normal room level audio to be picked up and clearly transmitted from a distance of 30' to 45'.

For an extra $50 LISTEN will furnish their infinity transmitter already built inside a standard 2500 series (choice of beige or black I believe) phone. By direct wiring the circuitry of the infinity transmitter into the telephone itself, it becomes extremely difficult to find the modification without knowing exactly what one is looking for.

LISTEN's circuitry is professionally laid-out on a circuit board that closely resembles the circuit boards already installed in the telephone unit. It's a very clean job and unless you are familiar with the inner layout of this telephone unit or have another unit on hand with which to physically compare it, it is likely to slip by even close scrutiny unlike "added" black box transmitters or modifications. A correctly installed circuit board appears to be simply that—a correctly installed circuit board.

See the photo of the LISTEN-equipped phone in the countermeasure's session.

Because infinity transmitters require no outside power, emit no RF energy, do not inhibit the normal workings of the telephone instrument or line they're installed on, and remain inactive until instructed otherwise by the user, these units are justifiably popular. One simply needs to have access to the phone lines once or install the modified telephone itself one time and the bug is in place and ready to go until it is physically removed.

Infinity transmitters have the added advantage that even if found it is nearly impossible to find out who has been accessing the unit since the only record kept is on the user's phone bill. It would be difficult to prove that calls made to a particular number were performed to take advantage of an infinity transmitter's capabilities.

LISTEN ELECTRONICS seems to appear under the same general guidelines as most car manufacturers; i.e., you buy the basic stripped down model which gets you where you're going just fine or you listen to the salesman and before you know it, you're adding leather seats and defrostable outside mirrors. Lay out another $50 and not only do you get the infinity transmitter, either in module or telephone form, but you gain the capability of monitoring both sides of any telephone calls on the line or in the telephone instrument as well as monitoring the room audio. This option operates in the same fashion as the infinity transmitter. You dial it up, do the time code routine, and if there's a telephone conversation going on, you will be able to monitor both sides of the conversation rather than the room audio.

Both of these units are outstanding from an operational as well as an economical viewpoint and I recommend them.

SHOMER-TEC sells a very pleasant infinity transmitter (made for them by a good "private" designer in New York) that has at least one additional step of security included. The SHOMER-TEC unit requires a touch tone code to activate the microphone. The operator simply sends the correct code during the "window of vulnerability" and the device switches on automatically. The unit (Tele-Monitor 2000) also features remote switching that will allow up to three separate units to be hung on the same line (placed in different rooms) that can be activated by different touch tones, or all three can be brought on line at the same time to provide blanket coverage.

The unit works well and is priced under $200. It is also sold by SHERWOOD COMMUNICATIONS which modifies the unit by adding a very sensitive external mic element that allows the user to stash the infinity transmitter some distance from the telephone pair for remote monitoring. Place the unit on a wire, or in a phone and run a pair of fine wires to the tiny mic and presto, any room is wired.

Add $100 for this modification.

What about all those old style infinity transmitters lying about unwanted and forgotten? There's still some application...

For instance, VIKING (the one in San Francisco) sells a very tiny "black box" that can be dropped on a dedicated line, or if one is really clever, the unit can made to work on FAX lines if the operator waits for the FAX to time out and turns the transmitter on.

This cute idea also applies to lines equipped with an answering machine, wait for them to time out, let the machine disconnect and quickly punch the activation tone.

And you're on line.

SLAVES, LOOP ENTENDERS AND DIALERS

One of the most popular telephone taps employed by all levels of the law enforcement community was developed in the last few years. This device is known as a slave unit and consists of a capacitively isolated demand-bridging tap. Physically the slave unit is a combination of an infinity transmitter and a parallel or bridging wiretap. It is usually housed in a small, modular plastic box but can take on other configurations.

Slaves are installed across two telephone lines that are located (physically) near each other. One line is owned (or borrowed) by the operator, the other is the target's phone line. When the operator dials the number of the first line the slave will silently bridge itself across the target's line allowing the operator to hear and/or record both sides of any conversation taking place.

Slaves are used by law enforcement folks because they can easily order up a new phone line and have it appear in the same vicinity as the target's line BUT slaves can also be used by nefarious civilians who have an apartment or office in the same building as the target (because the lines will appear in the same junction box or splice board), by those clever enough to employ spare lines or place an order for a buried phone or off premise extension close to the line to be monitored or by folks who, for one reason or another, want to spy on some-

one who lives or works in the place that hosts the target line.

This latter application requires them to simply order up a new phone line that terminates in the same junction box or even runs down the spare pair of the target line.

Of course, in many applications this method would be illegal. Please remember that...

If the two lines (the target line and the access line), don't appear in close proximity in a multiple box or in a cable, it is possible to access a spare pair by hooking an audio tone generator up to the unused wires and then following the tone to see if the new pair appears at a terminal box or multiple box that is near the line that is to be used as the access line. Another trick for civilians employing slave devices is to bury a telephone in an friendly apartment or office in the same complex as the target line, thus assuring at least one common point between the two lines respectively.

LISTEN ELECTRONICS manufactures a slave unit that is installed inside a normal telephone wall jack. The unit has modular connectors that allow one to plug the target phone line into one jack and then install the lease line in the other input jack. This is usually accomplished by running the new line down the spare pair (normally the yellow and black) of the telephone line itself.

Titled the modular telephone tap, this slave unit is innocuous enough to be passed over in anything but a dedicated physical search or a good electronic countermeasure's survey. By removing the cover of LISTEN's unit, it is possible to bypass the modular jack installation that's provided and simply wire the unit on an existing cable or cross terminals on a accessible multiple block.

When the law enforcement units were first introduced, they listed for approximately $700 from a couple of different suppliers. The LISTEN ELECTRONICS modular telephone tap, at the time of this writing, goes for $88.

Law enforcement slaves often offer enhanced latch on and grab techniques; BARTEC's DLP-11 unit uses three lines to operate: #1 is the line being monitored, #2 is the line connected to the dial in side of the slave, and #3 is the remote LP or telephone decoder.

The friendly side (always a good place to be in my opinion) has to be equipped with a cancel on disconnect (C.O.D.) feature from the local telco and the call-waiting feature should NOT be present on the good guy's side.

This unit allows a 2100Hz decoding tone to accuate the slave and allows complete electrical freedom from the bad guys' line as the user must actually dial up the friendly line from a good phone.

Whew...

JSI TELECOM offers a handshake connection to prevent unauthorized access of the slave and automatic redial if the unit drops off line as well as a programmable pause for "behind" PBX operation.

Their unit is housed in a tiny cylindrical tube and can be connected on most systems.

COI takes the slave concept a step further by offering a room audio, or infinity slave if you will. This unit works like a normal slave except it transmits room audio down the friendly line instead of phone audio whenever the line is accessed and will release the subject line when the operator's phone is returned to a on hook condition.

Reminder that COI is law enforcement only.

Automatic Tap

Another brand new edition to the line of interesting phone taps is the automatic or lazy man's tapping device. Like the slave this unit bridges two phone lines together to allow outside access. However, the similarity ends there. The dialer tap is an active tapping device with a most unusual nature.

To utilize this tap, the two phone lines (the access line and the target line) must be in the same proximity as with the slave tap, the normal procedure is to have both lines come into the same phone jack, one line on the ring and tip, one line on the spare pair.

For this clever unit to function correctly, one must be able to order single digit speed dialing

from the local telephone company. This speed dialing is set up on the access line. The dialer tap is then installed across both phone lines. When the target telephone line is in use, either by an incoming or outgoing call, the unit will automatically prompt the second line to call whatever number you have selected and place the conversation or data going over the target line, on the access line.

In simple terms, when the target goes to use his telephone, you will receive a phone call anywhere you so desire, local or long distance, that will put a one-way tap automatically on the line allowing you to listen to the conversation. This feature can dial long distance, can have an answering machine installed at the other end instead of a telephone and will automatically dial-up and record all calls on the target line, or can be sent to one phone and then call-forwarded to any other number you so desire.

This allows the listener to access the information at one location (say his office), and then automatically continue the access at another location if necessary (such as his home) without requiring additional access to the area in which the tap itself is located.

LISTEN ELECTRONICS sells an example of the dialer tap which works quite effectively, packaged in the ubiquitous small plastic box for $265 (at the time of this writing) or stashed in the 2500 series phone for $50 more.

A true example of a telephone reaching out and touching someone.

LOOP EXTENDERS

Suppose one wanted to tap a phone wire but couldn't get direct proximity access to the wires, or maybe one wanted to tap in from 50 miles away, passing through telco CO's and ancillary equipment.

Or, for the sake a hypothetical argument, maybe you want to activate a slave or a DTMF register from this distance, or just start an automatic recording process (remember one must actively dial-up a slave to initiate the eavesdropping process), what to do, what to do...

Loop entenders are compact electronic generators that place a tone, usually audible, on the target phone's line when it is ON hook. An LE is bridged across a target line from any distance and the output is passed to a leased line which usually also supplies the power for the unit.

When the target phone is lifted off hook the tone is broken and the leased line will begin to accept all subsequent audio (including DTMF tones) from the target line.

LE's can be combined with matching receivers (COI) that permit direct dialout without a separate telephone instrument (dials out until a handshake is received and redials if connection is broken) easy connection to pen registers.

Some LE's (BARTEC's LP-2) will work on "dry" (non powered) lines which extend their usefulness to various pairs other than telco leased cables.

LE's are pretty much law enforcement-based, although a clever person could make use of this technology to remote a listening post or a dialed number recorder.

DTMF TONES AND PEN REGISTERS

DTMF tones are the signal tones produced by a touch tone phone when dialling another number, operating Telco-signalling equipment, or accessing anything that can be controlled by a touchtone phone such as an answering machine, WAT's extender, computer, etc.

Each touchtone phone is capable of producing 16 DTMF tones. These 16 tones are the numbers 1–0, the #, the * (or star) button and 4 additional tones incongruously labeled A, B, C, and D. In most U.S. phone systems only the first 12 tones are involved in voice or data transmission, but the other 4 tones are available and are used in various military phone systems as well as some electronic proprietary systems.

Each DTMF tone is actually a combination of 2 separate tones, there are eight individual tones available for this mixing process.

DTMF tones are important to us for several reasons, the most important probably being that even if a phone line is tapped and the resulting conversation recorded *there is no indication of who the call was made to except for the recorded touchtones at the beginning of the call.*

In order to find out the callee in a recorded conversation, the DTMF tones must be run through a device that will translate them into a phone number, either after they are recorded or in a real-time format as the call is being made. A special device known as a pen register is designed to make a numerical record of all outgoing calls on any telephone line. Pen registers analyze the tones, store the resulting data in memory and/or print out a record of each call.

Pen registers in the past were an extremely important piece of surveillance gear because unlike taps *they did not require a court order to place on anyone's line as there was no expectation of privacy in a dialled number.* Police, agents, and phone security people were notoriously easygoing with their placement of pen registers on a suspect's line, often before procuring a court warrant. The sequence of numbers tells an awful lot about what sort of conversation might have been occurring and could be used for evidence as well as securing a legal warrant to install a tap to record the actual conversations.

The use of pen registers have recently been redefined to fall under various security acts and now, in most cases, they are treated much the same as is a phone tap under the law. Pen registers are still a popular law enforcement product manufactured by such surveillance greats as AID, HDS, and a company called Voice Identification Incorporated, Somerville, New Jersey. Probably the best known enforcement pen register source is Mitel Corporation which offers a variety of single and multi line dialled digital recorders that will interpret both dial pulse and DTMF tones.

Law enforcement pen registers are normally equipped with a variety of bells and whistles that do such things as run internal automatic test sequences, produce alarms and/or start tape recorders when certain numbers are dialed, and automatically record the time and date of each call.

They also average about $5,000.00.

The best civilian counterpart to the pen register has long been the Doufone, CPA-1000 computerized phone accountant. This lovely device attaches to any phone line in a parallel fashion and automatically senses all outgoing DTMF tones, prints these tones on a calculator-like print list, gives the duration and time of the call, and also records any tones made after the call is connected. The Doufone is a marvelous unit that runs off house current or will operate for a number of hours off of internal batteries. It is compact in size, works like magic, and best of all, runs about $90.00 from your friendly neighborhood surveillance supplier.

Of course, I mean Radio Shack. The bad news is that Radio Shack is talking about phasing out this wonderous device and if they haven't by the time you read this, take Uncle Lee's advice and go out and buy one. You never know when you're going to need a good pen register and besides they make ideal stocking stuffers at Christmas.

If and when Radio Shack pulls the plug many spyshops sell a similar unit for about three hundred bucks and SIERRA DESIGN (supplier's section) makes a nice little unit which reads all 16 tones and displays them on an LED readout. The unit will store numbers in a buffer and works from phone lines, recorders, or receivers.

ANI, ANÁC, & A TOUCH OF CLASS

OBTAINING CONDFIDENTIAL PHONE COMPANY INFORMATION

All phone companies in the United States possess a means of Automatic Number Identification on calling party numbers. ANI or ANAC is used by telephone company personnel so they can check to make sure they have the right line when installing equipment or new service requests, by emergency service providers, (this translates as 911—when anyone calls 911 their name, number, and address is automatically displayed at the police or fire dispatcher), and for telephone company security services to trap nuisance or illegal calls.

ANI and ANAC are valuable to folks in our line of work because either will allow the instant identification of any line appearance or termination point in a cable run making it easy to insure that a tap or dialed number recorder is sitting on the correct line.

ANAC, the more popular system, is the automatic number verification system, there's no operator involved. One simply dials the local ANAC number and a computerized voice reads back the telephone number the call's originating from. This call can be placed with a telephone set or a lineman's handset. The computer doesn't know the difference.

Hackers enjoy this feature because it will allow one to verify the number of any dial tone that can be grabbed such as: pay phones, privately-owned pay phones, or corporation phone lines. Besides it's fun to impress your friends at parties by dialing up the secret number and having a computer read the return echo off to them.

The phone company changes ANAC every so often to avoid curious folk like us but new ANAC's can be gotten from the proverbial friendly phone repairman or from publications like *2600*.

The following is a list of the current ANAC numbers in the United States. This list is up-to-date as we go to press but will be changed in the not too distant future.

ANAC GUIDE

205–908–222–2222	414–330–2234	615–830
212–958	415–200–555–1212	615–830–222–2222
213–114	415–211–2111	617–200–xxx–xxxx
213–1223	415–2222	617–220–2622
213–61056	415–640	618–200–xxx–xxxx
214–970–xxxx	415–760	618–290
215–410–xxxx	415–760–2878	713–970–xxxx
217–200–xxx–xxxx	415–7600	714–211–2121
217–290	415–7600–2222	716–511
305–200–222–2222	502–997–555–1212	718–958
309–200–xxx–xxxx	509–560	806–970–xxxx
309–290	512–200–222–2222	812–410–555–1212
312–1–200–5863	512–970–xxxx	815–200–xxx–xxxx
312–200–xxx–xxxx	516–958	815–290
312–290	517–200–222–2222	817–211
313–200–222–2222	518–997	817–970–xxxx
317–310–222–2222	518–998	906–200–222–2222
317–743–1218	602–593–0809	914–1–990–1111
401–222–2222	602–593–6017	914–99
403–908–222–2222	602–593–7451	914–990
404–940–xxx–xxxx	604–1116	914–990–1111
407–200–222–2222	604–116	915–970–xxxx
408–300–xxx–xxxx	604–1211	919–711
408–760	604–211	
409–970–xxxx	612–511	

A TRICK

> In many areas of the country a sort of manual ANI can be achieved simply by calling the operator from any phone line and asking for the number of the line you're calling on. In the past operators would not give this out but a new feature, privately-owned coin phones—which are basically private lines that some unscrupulous S.O.B. has stuck an expensive paybox on one end of—no longer show up on the operator's boards as pay phones.
>
> Simply tell the operator that you need the number because you are calling from a pay phone and some dastardly type has scraped the number off the dial and you want to tell your friends where to call you back. If the operator says it does not appear you are calling from a pay phone, tell her that it must be a pay phone because it required 50¢ just to call her, at this point she should realize that it's a private pay phone and read you off the number with no further trouble.
>
> As of press time, a national ANI identifier is also available to the curious by dialing 800–933–3258.

CLASS

CLASS, or Custom Local Area Signaling Services, is coming to a neighborhood near you. Because of the inception of Signaling System 7, network and associated databases, a certain class (no pun intended) of services are being offered to various telco customers around the country as this is written and phone companies are desperately trying to perpetrate these expensive little ad-ons across the U.S. Although some states are, for the moment, effectively blocking them through various maneuvers in the courts.

CLASS will do several different things, the primary one being what is known as CND, or as some people call it CNID or CNI. The idea used to be known as ANI, but the acronym seems to have settled down somewhat to CND or CNID, these standing for Calling Number Display and/or Calling Number ID respectively.

What CNI does is allow the customer to rent or purchase a little black box that looks like a hand calculator, which displays the number of the calling party after the first ring *whether or not the phone is answered.* A small LCD display provides the caller's phone number including area code, the current time, and the date.

Most of the units also store about 70 numbers in memory so if the operator is not home one can still see who called even if the answering machine is stressed out. In fact, with a little creativity one can figure out who called and *didn't* leave a message by comparing messages on the answering machine or voice mail with the incoming call register numbers.

CND's have generated an enormous amount of interest in the press and the media because of the apparent violation of privacy involved. The justification for this service is to stop obscene phone calls as well as letting the caller decide with whom he wishes to speak at any given moment. The down side includes several things, first and foremost being that it will: (A) cost money to rent this little box or purchase it from the phone company, (B) cost more money if one doesn't want one's phone number to be displayed on out-going calls,

effectively letting the phone company collect revenues on either side of the transaction.

People who are concerned with their privacy are notably aghast at this situation. Why should I have my number displayed if I call someone to inquire about a product or ask about a service or even return a call? Think some sleazy salesman won't call back? Think I won't immediately be placed on a mailing list and probably on a dial-out marketing list that will be sold to other vendors who want to find suckers who respond to a particular pitch?

Bet your ass...

CLASS also allows a number of other options including a customer originated trace, which means by dialing a number i.e., *57 the last call one receives will be immediately traced and recorded at the phone company. Of course, the phone company charges (at the moment, a buck) for this service and to complete the transaction one must call the phone company and ask for the number.

This feature is designed for harassment-type callers and the phone company is probably going to want to know why one wants the number requested.

A sidebar here, if one has call-waiting one can do an interesting thing with the CLASS concept. When you hear the call-waiting notification buzz, simply tell the party you are talking to that you will call them back and immediately hang up the phone. They will be disconnected and the phone will begin to ring for the person who originally clicked in. After the first ring your display will light up and translate the data that was sent from the calling party, letting you trace a call on call-waiting without ever talking to the person.

Other items that will come along with CLASS are things like Selective Call Acceptance or Rejection, which allows you to automatically reject calls from certain numbers. Distinctive Ringing which will invoke a particular ringing pattern so you can tell if it's a good or bad call before even looking at the display, and CND

Blocking, which means the called party can program a que of people into his phone so when they call the number they get a recorded message from the phone company that says, "Party you are tryin' to reach don't want to talk to ya, bro," or perhaps a more politely phrased message with the same meaning.

CLASS services are of interest to our business for a variety of reasons, the first being they can be used in a manner similar to an ANI trace or with some creative plumbing, one's personal call display box can be wired into a target's number where it will act not only as a reversed dialed number recorder, but actually show where all the calls to the target number are coming from...

The calling number display feature of the CLASS system DOES trace unpublished numbers as well as published numbers. It's up to the individual phone company whether they will be displayed on the user's display or not. There is no way to use a display box on a particular phone system that does not have the CLASS feature installed, both components are necessary for the system to function.

Beating the class

If one doesn't want one's phone number to be displayed at the other end, one can: (A) purchase a call-blocking service from the phone company, (B) make all one's calls from a pay phone, (C) go through the operator to place a call, or (D) use a service some entrepreneurs have come up with where the caller dials their 900 number and dial out on their dial tone for an additional charge. The other possibility is a creative placement of a call forwarding box.

I don't know, Yogi, everybody on the side of law and order, not to mention telephone employees with an eye towards their profit sharing plan, seem to think the CLASS system is the greatest thing since sliced bread, but it seems to me that it's just another step in the direction of 1984. Oh, hell, that was years ago, wasn't it? I guess there's a moral in there.

CNA, DEPAC's and MUR's

CNA's are undergoing major changes even as we write. Well, actually, I write and you read. At any rate they're being centralized, modified, and eased out of existance. Phone companies are billing each other for them and getting nasty about sharing the wealth.

CNA, if you're new the game stands for Central Names and Addresses. It is a phone company office that exists to serve telco employees by identifing the owner of any phone line in their area code.

CNA's exist in every area code and are staffed during regular office hours. In the past the only form of access control on these delightful services were the actual phone numbers of the offices. When a person called the local CNA and said something to the effect of, "This is Joe from frames, I need 415–382–0127 or just, "I need a hit on 415–382–0127," the nice Bell employee would read back "that number is listed to a Warren Beatty." In the real good and real old days they would also give out the address but that concept is going by the wayside.

CNA's are still around but procedures have tightened down to stop non-telco employees from using the offices as convenient ways to track down people, numbers, addresses, and lines to tap. First of all CNA's no longer deal with phone stores or telco business offices and most now employ password security in the form of a code or account number that is required before they will give out the info.

When faced with a request for a badge number or code a wise choice is to manufacture a 6 digit number. It doesn't cost anything to try...

CNA phone numbers are themselves changed far more often than they used to be. In rare instances they change codes as often as every week althuogh at least a couple of telcos have taken the open approach, and simply give out the information to anyone who calls, but this is the exception rather than the rule.

If one has a friendly lineman or a relative who believes in sharing the wealth one can still procure these numbers and working codes.

CNA's, ringbacks and other "inside" numbers are also hacked by phone and computer hackers who use "war dialing" programs to dial every number in an entire exchange to find the interesting digits. They are published on bulletin boards and in phone newsletters like *2600*.

DPAC's are telco offices which exist to service installers by assigning the actual telephone number to the line pair. DPAC's (pronounced dee-pac) are sometimes easier to elict information from then are CNA's.

DPAC numbers can be gotten from friendly (or bribed) repairmen, or sometimes by calling the customer service number for billing information and sucessfully pretending to be from a nearby phone company.

This requires a combination of chutzpah and timing. Customer service billing people do have access to DPAC's for their area and will give them out if they believe the caller is a lineman or frames worker from a nearby area BUT this too, is getting more and more difficult.

DPAC's are also useful because, unlike CNA's, they have both listed and unlisted installations listed with no notification as to which is which.

Once an "installer" has the DPAC number he simply calls in and ask's for the listing at "77 Sunset Strip" The nice DPAC person will read back the phone number of that site.

Other ways to find who belongs at a certain number? The old standby of calling the customer service billing office (available from 411 or 555–1212) and disputing a "call" on your phone bill that no one at the house remembers making will often have the owner of the number instantly identified, still works.

Some companies will check the bill to see if the number was actually dialed before handing out the name, some will not.

A method that doesn't require any social engineering is to use one or more of the compiled data bases that will search on phone numbers. Most of these bases access both phone book listings as well as numbers that have come from folk filling out loan apps. and credit card forms.

If this is to be an often required service, pay the fee and join one of the investigative data bases listed in that section of this book, if it's just a one or two shot, use one of the "mini-markets" listed that will access the bases for $15–$20 per number.

A TRICK

One base that is easily accessible is CompuServe's phone file. This can be accessed by anyone with a computer, modem and a CS membership. If a small search script is pre-written the search will cost about fifty cents in search time. The file does a pretty good job of coming up with hits on a nationwide basis and seems to get an occasional unlisted, although, to be fair, it also seems to miss an occasional listed.

Business searches can be done through DIALOG as detailed in the database chapter.

Entire toll listings can be obtained by informing customer service that the bill was misplaced and a copy will be sent, often to an alternate address ("send it to me at work please") if the person making the request is the person on the bill.

UNLISTED TRICK

One method that has enjoyed some success in breaking open unlisted (unpublished) phone numbers is to call an operator from a pay phone with the story that it is a matter of life and death that Mr. Warren Beatty, who happens to have an unlisted number, be contacted immediately. With a convincing enough lie, (of course this is illegal and shown for the purposes of information only), the operator will dial up the party in question allowing the phone number tones (dtmf tones) to come down the line in the clear. If one had a tape recorder set up to record these tones they could be played back through any dtmf detector/pen register to give an instant readout of the unlisted number.

Murs

The previous tricks deal with toll listings but phone companies also keep records of LOCAL, non-billed calls which can be called up and printed by their computer on a moments notice.

These records, called MUR's, are not handed out without a warrant but they are available. Most phone companies also have a few people who supplement their incomes with an infor-mal retirement plan known as "selling informa-tion to a private detective."

Good, connected, investigators can often get MUR's, something to remember when you are making those little local calls that should be kept private...

Or when you need a copy of someone's calling iteniary...

CNA NUMBERS (Valid at press time)

202 304–343–7016 Wash. D.C.	203 203–789–6815 CT
204 204–949–0900 Manitoba	205 205–988–7000 AL
206 206–345–4082 WA	207 617–787–5300 ME
208 303–292–3370 ID	209 415–781–5271 CA
212 518–471–8111 NY	213 415–781–5271 CA
214 214–464–7400 TX	215 412–633–5600 PA
216 614–464–0511 OH	217 217–789–8290 IL
218 402–221–7199–MN	219 317–265–4834 IN
301 304–343–1401 MD	302 412–633–5600 DE
303 303–292–3370 CO	304 204–244–8041 WV
305 912–752–2000 FL	306 306–347–2878 Saskatchewan
307 303–292–3370 WY	308 402–221–7199 NE
309–217–789–8290 IL	312 212–796–9600 IL
313 313–223–8690 MI	314 816–275–8460 MO
315 518–471–8111 NY	316 816–275–2782 KS
317–317–265–4834 IN	318 504–245–5330 LA
319 402–221–7199 IA	401 617–787–5300 RI
402 402–221–7199 NE	403 403–425–2652 Alberta
404 912–752–2000 GA	405 405–236–6121 OK
406 303–292–3370 MT	408 415–781–5271 CA
409 713–861–7194 TX	412 412–633–5600 PA
413 617–787–5300 MA	414 608–252–6932 WI
415 415–781–5271 CA	416 416–443–0542 Ontario
418 514–394–7440 Quebec	419 614–464–0511 OH
501 405–236–6121 AR	502 502–583–2861 KY
503–206–345–4082 OR	504 504–245–5330 LA
505 303–292–3370 NM	506 605–694–6541 New Brunswick
507 402–221–7199 MN	509–206–345–4082 WA
512 512–828–2501 TX	513 614–464–0511 OH
514 514–394–7440 Quebec	515 402–221–7199 IA
516 518–471–8111 NY	517 313–223–8690 MI
518 518–471–8111 NY	519 416–443–0542 Ontario
601 501–961–8139 MS	602 303–292–3370 AZ

CNA NUMBERS (continued)

603 617–787–5300 NH	604 604–432–2996 British Columbia
605 402–221–7199 SD	606 502–583–2861 KY
607 518–471–8111 NY	608 608–252–6932 WI
612 402–221–7199 MN	613 416–443–0511 Ontario
614 614–464–0511 OH	615 615–373–5791 TN
616 313–223–8690 MI	617 415–781–5271 CA
618 217–789–8290 IL	619 415–781–5271 CA
701 402–221–7199 ND	702 415–781–5271 NV
703 304–344–7935 VA	704 912–752–2000 NC
705 416–443–0542 Ontario	706 706–685–0042,5906 Mexico
707 415–781–5271 CA	712 402–221–7199 IA
713 713–521–8988 TX	714 415–781–5271 CA
715 608–252–6932 WI	716 518–471–8111 NY
717 412–633–5600 PA	718 518–471–8111 NY
801 303–292–3370 UT	802 617–787–5300 VT
803 912–752–2000 SC	804 304–344–7935 VA
805 415–781–5271 CA	806 512–828–2501 TX
807 416–443–0542 Ontario	808 212–334–4336 HI
809 212–334–4336 Caribbean	809 809–429–5050 x313 Barbados
812 317–265–4834 IN	813 813–228–7871 FL
814 412–633–5600 PA	815 217–789–8290 IL
816 816–275–2783 MO	817 214–464–7400 TX
818 415–781–5271 CA	819 514–394–7440 Quebec
900 902–676–7070 Dial–It Service	901 615–373–5791 TN
902 902–421–4110 Nova Scotia	904 912–752–2000 FL
906 313–223–8690 MI	912 912–752–2000 GA
913 816–275–2782 KS	914 518–471–8111 NY
915 512–828–2501 TX	916 415–781–5271 CA
918 405–236–6121 OK	919 912–752–2000 NC

ANSWERING MACHINE AND VOICE MAIL VIOLATIONS

A unique method of phone tapping is not to tap the phone at all but rather to retrieve messages that other people have conveniently left for the target on his answering machine or his voice mail. Answering machines offer the best opportunity for this type of information retrieval requiring only a certain amount of active participation to play back stored messages, erase messages, or even change the outgoing message.

Most telephone answering machines are now known as "beeperless remotes." Earlier machines required a physical beeper that sent a coded series of tones down the wire in order to retrieve messages but most modern machines have foregone this operation in favor of a simple touch tone (DTMF tone) to activate any of their functions. Early answering machines utilized a simple one digit code to play back, erase, change, reset, turn off, or skip messages. In fact, some answering machines have a built-in bonus in the form of a room monitoring system which acts as an infinity transmitter, allowing all audio in the room to be transmitted down the phone line to the waiting receiver upon activation of a one digit code.

If an agent has access to a target's answering machine, even for a moment, he should check the brandname, and model number of the machine. This facilitates any attempts at code cracking. With the manufacturer's nomenclature in hand, it's a simple matter to make a phone call or visit a showroom in order to read the instruction manual as to what sort of codes protect each particular machine.

If the model type is unknown, the first and simplest step is to try all 10 touch tone codes. Press one and then wait for the reaction before moving on to the next one.

If no activation is encountered with the one digit method, a good operator will move to try two digit access codes. Amateurs will press all 200 digits in order to crack a machine's code. Professionals know that answering machines

normally disregard any tones received after their activiation tones and take advantage of this by entering 101 digits in this order:

> 0112233445566778899 1
> 3579024680369258147 1
> 5937049483827261605 1
> 7395062840852963007 4
> 1975318642098765432 10

Many machines utilize only a few digits for the code thus limiting the operator's selection. Panasonic is infamous for utilizing 3's, 5's, and 6's. Some Radio Shack devices use 2's, 4's, and 6's. In either case a quick tryout sequence can be put together such as 3355663653 for Panasonic machines.

Modern machines tend toward 3 digit access codes because they are harder to violate but certainly not impossible since three digits squared is simply 999 codes. These codes can be broken in sequence but canny agents will try simple codes such as 123, triple repetitions; i.e., 111, 222, 333, home addresses, birth dates, etc. before spending the time needed in sequential cracking.

Many answering machines do not have battery backup or their operators may not have inserted batteries. This is important because it means if there is any power loss, the machine will reset to a default code; many use the reset access code 000, always try this code first.

Once an answering machine responds to the agent's inserted digits, it normally presents a 1 to 10 or 1 to #,* menu that consists of rewinds, repeats, skip forward, fast forward, memory playbacks, room monitor, etc. It is a simple matter to sort through these 12 options to discover the operating menu of any answering machine.

Voice mail is a bit more difficult to hack as most voice mail systems require at least 4 and sometimes 5 digits as the operator code. The options here are to sequentially crack or at first try the usual relative personal data numbers.

A TRICK

A number of consumer electronic stores and companies now sell handheld credit card-size automatic dialers designed to dial numbers or access modems via a telephone handset. Many of these low-cost dialers incorporate speed dialing programming. For a small monetary outlay, an agent can procure such a dialer and program in the obvious numerical codes, as well as the sequential numerical tryout numbers, reducing by far the exposure time required to violate any answering machine's security precautions.

CELLULAR TELEPHONE OPERATIONS AND INTERCEPTIONS; FIRST OF ALL...

In a recent best seller, (*Clear And Present Danger*) Tom Clancy, one hell of a fine wordsmith, based much of the tension in the plot on the fact that the good guys (government agents in this case) could not follow the bad guys, even on their cellular telephones because cellular phones are "impossible to monitor."

Tom, Tom, lack of research or just trying to be nice to those agents who helped you out on the book? Let's face facts, it ain't exactly impossible to eavesdrop on cellular phones.

In fact cellular phones are just about the easiest type of communication to monitor without major equipment expenditures or committing grievous felonies. Ah, let me qualify that last one just a bit, it is against the law to monitor cellular conversations because they, unlike cordless phones which also transmit over the radio, give the "expectation of privacy."

Or it is against the law until some good ACLU type lawyer takes the first case to court, but that is neither here nor there. It is against the law to monitor these conversations without the correct legal documents and I am writing this section secure in the knowledge that none of you would break this law, and that anyone who uses these techniques has a legal right to do so. Right?

So please ignore the fact that anyone with a halfway decent scanner, (and they don't make many without cellular coverage anymore) can just turn on, tune in and drop, ah, in.

Some scanners won't allow this illegal listening. For instance, Radio Shack, that paragon of poor man's eavesdropping equipment, although they designed their scanners to receive these calls, made it impossible to do so after the laws were changed.

Unless you take a pair of scissors and clip one little wire...

But it's the intent of the law that is at stake here; suppose you don't have a scanner? God forbid you should look at the frequency chart and realize that some cellular channels can be received on an unmodified UHV television set.

Don't touch that dial!

A TRICK

If you have a scanner which brings in the 800 MHz band, a good, inexpensive improvement is to purchase an antenna especially designed for that band. Cellular Security Group (4 Gerring Road Gloucester, MA 01930) sells a good one for 20 bucks.

The two problems with either of these drop in monitoring systems is that A. One doesn't know who one is listening to, and B. As the target moves about in any area covered by CP's his signal will be automatically "handed off" to new cells as the signal strength of his transmission falls off. These frequencies are random on the basis that they are available on the system not in use, and do not interfere with other conversations already in progress.

Pandora's box?

Hardly. Here is how cellular telephones work and how everybody who has any desire to tune in on the world's greatest party line can do so with a minimum of effort from those with $40,000 budgets to those equipped only with a scanner and a sense of adventure...

OPERATING SYSTEMS & TRAINS THAT FLY

Cellular systems consist of a number of individual "cells" that contain a number of individual frequencies for the transmission of audio information. A certain number of other frequencies within the cell are allotted to channels that transfer the data necessary to set up and maintain the call.

Every area covered in the U.S. has at least two cellular phone companies in operation: One is a wireline company, meaning it is, or was, depending on whose lawyers one believes, owned by Bell. The other operator is a non-wireline, an independent rep. Both adhere to the same operating standards.

When a particular phone reaches the outer limit of a particular cell's power, the equipment automatically senses this and "hands off" the call to an adjacent cell to continue the conversation with no noticeable loss in signal.

The hexagons usually used to illustrate cells are really only symbolic. Graphic artists and other PR types use these shapes to describe the system but the real boundary of a cell is a jagged line that represents a point where the power level falls off to about –100 decibels relative to a milliwatt of radio power hitting the receive antenna.

At that point the system doesn't work very well because it's about equal to the regular noise input to the receiver and it becomes very difficult to get a good signal in there so somewhere in the range of –85 to –100 DBM is the point where one would no longer use the radio in that cell and the signal is handed off to another cell.

The decision of where and when to hand off is also mitigated by other factors, for instance, are there any available voice channels in that cell would be the preferred choice for the handoff target? If so the decision is simply to take the frequency in that cell and command the mobile to change its frequencies to that particular frequency in order to carry out the hand off.

In real life, cells do not come out to perfectly drawn symbols but rather jagged areas of signal which are influenced by hills, buildings, and other natural factors beyond the control of the cellular company.

There are hills in every city and every hill will create a signal shadow in the area behind it. Tall buildings will create the same effect. If the cell includes streets with buildings that have highly reflective windows, like silver glass or enameled coating, this tends to form a wave guide and will cut the power down a long distance along that street if it's in line aside an antenna.

The waves begin bouncing back and forth and side to side, reflecting energy like two parallel mirrors on opposite walls, so suddenly there are a lot of strange things that weren't included in the original symmetrically-shaped pattern. But that's life in the big city.

Literally.

The combination of particular antenna placements plus buildings and shadowing in the service city creates areas which need to be overlapped. Phone companies want some overlap with the boundaries, which requires a little leeway about where to make handoffs occur. They have to cover the whole city to give good service. No area can be excluded.

Some operators employ an engineer on a full-time basis to go out and make constant measurements. Others will bring in a consultant and have them make measurements locally every other month or two depending on the rate of growth. If a tall building goes up right on an existing antenna, they may go out and survey it while it's still under construction in order to do some modeling and field prediction to correct the problem before it happens. This means cell site boundaries and handoff points are in a state of flux.

The mobile phone operates on one frequency, sending out one side of the call and the cell operates at another frequency 45 MHz less than the mobile. The cell itself broadcasts both sides of the call.

In the cells themselves there are basically two sets of channels—the original channels were just the ones allocated to two different competitive carriers in the world's metro areas. Of these 333 channels in each of these two groups, 21 which are near the boundary and 21 on the other side of the boundary, are used as the so-called set up channels. All the other channels are available for voice.

Recently the FCC allocated an additional 83 channels to each of the two carriers. The wireline carrier, which is a former Bell operating company, got it in one nice big chunk of 83 channels in every area. The A carrier, the non-wireline carrier in each district, (Cellular One, for example) got the new access in two chunks that were split apart, say 33 in one place and 50 in the other. This is important because the FCC has said they are not going to give out any more channel allocations until the end of the century.

How Calls Are Placed

The overhead train, a continuous stream of data (on a data channel) that is constantly sending out loads of information of who is where and with what will be occasionally interrupted by a specific starting message, called a page. This is a message that mitigates the telephone number of the call of the mobile, indicating there's a call for the mobile.

At this point the system doesn't know where the mobile is in the city so this page is sent out in every cell in the whole city. The mobile, if it's there, will respond in one of the cells as it has been watching one particular frequency in the setup channel. It will go to another channel and if that fades out, it will scan and find another one so it's always watching one particular frequency and responding in the same frequency.

If located the mobile will be rung up or a pre-recorded message will be issued saying that it is busy or off hook. The caller will then be disconnected whether he wants to stay on or not. He can dial again immediately but with get the same result, because they are trying to limit the amount of air time that's consumed without producing any revenue if the subscriber is out of town or has his mobile turned off.

What happens when a user goes to make a call? The setup channel in every cell transmits a sequence of minor data in a certain frame in the overhead train, which includes things like the actual number of the phone involved. Every system in North America has a 3 digit number along with some other data which tells the mobiles if they are from outside the local system, if they should identify themselves or not. If a phone is visiting the city should it identify itself or should it wait until the switch has a call for it?

When a mobile starts up cold, it begins scanning. It starts scanning the supervisory channels. It only has 21 to look at so it scans all of them until it finds the strongest one and locks onto it and looks for the overhead train. As soon as overhead train is grabbed, it waits and watches. If the train fades away, the mobile will go back and start scanning all over again.

If a mobile operator wants to originate a call, the operator enters all the dial digits into a display register on the mobile and hits a key labeled "send." This causes the mobile to transmit a call setup message on the reverse frequency part of the supervisory or setup channel before it identifies itself and gives the telephone number to be dialed and it listens to see if the train wants any more information. The telco may only request 7 of the 10 digits of the mobile number or it may demand everything including the electronic serial number, but all the systems are capable of asking for everything and the only reason some companies reduce the amount of information is just to save transaction time when they're very busy.

The response contains all the same information. The actual switch, which is located at the cell site, has to have 3 types of radios: Voice channel transceivers are for actually talking in duplex covering about 45 usable channels per cell unless the expanded spectrum has been put into use where it goes up to 56 channels per cell. At least one control or setup channel transceiver is also required but most companies will install a spare for that in case of failure because it's role is a crucial one. If it's dead, everything's dead, calls can't be set up in either direction.

In addition, at least one locating receiver is required to measure radio signal strength indication because when a handoff occurs there's always a question. If the signal strength in this mobile is getting weak, where is it? Is he driving north, is he driving east, west or south, which cell is he getting closest to? The system, prior to the handoff, has to request all the locating receivers in the nearby cells to tune to the frequency of that mobile in order to measure the signal strength and report the strongest one.

The actual switches are called either an MTX or MTSO depending on the manufacturer. MTX means Mobile Telephone Exchange and MTSO means Mobile Telephone Switching Office.

The central switch is pretty much a standard telephone switch. Almost all the modern ones are digital in nature with some type of a switching network which connects calls from one port to another. There is also some kind of a control complex involved in the central processor similar to a computer. There is a digital trunk controller and some sort of interface which is used to connect to other telephone central offices in other parts of the city.

When the call gets into that switch mechanism, the signal is handled like a regular telephone call. All the same technologies about pen recording, intercepting, tracking and taping all the conversation can and will be intercepted by the carrier at this point without special equipment.

In addition to that, all the records exchanged produced by like automatic number identification and billing and all the call records, (MUR's) can be subpoened, so everything applies pretty much the same as it does in the regular telephone system.

There's also some type of a control connection to the central processor, usually run through a voice frequency channel which leads to a controller of some type which is another microprocessor system at the cell site that's connected to both the radios to tell them to go on and off and then back into the locating receiver in order to process the change to get the frequencies and take measurements.

This is the format of one cell site. A city may have as many cell sites as necessary. U.S. systems range from the minimum of one cell site to as many as about 70 or 80. Los Angeles has about 80, New York runs a close second.

ROAMING AND ROVING

All of North American cellular operators have uniform technical standards and in theory, if there's no business reasons not to, a set can roam anywhere in the continent where there's radio coverage. The operator can at least originate calls even though he may or may not be able to receive them, depending on whether inter-connections exist for data transfer between the various cellular systems, but technically there's no reason why one can't originate a call.

Any mobile set has several options. If it can't find any supervisory channel at all—if it's suddenly situated out in the country where there's no cellular service—the local will scan and scan and eventually, after a few tries it give up and indicates that the caller is SOL.

If the operator scans all the channels but the system number showing in the overhead train doesn't match the one in the memory of the telephone set, the mobile set, it will keep watching it in the roam mode, understanding it's outside of its home system. In most sets one can also switch to the other carrier in the area.

The business arrangement is that most U.S. wire lines have some kind of cross-billing contracts. All of the former Bell operating companies subsidiaries have almost uniform cross billing contracts and many, but not all of the non-wire line people have cross-billing contracts, plus there are many cross-billing contracts between wire line and non-wire line because there are lots of cross ownership, so almost every place the phone goes there is about a 95% chance to place a call which will later appear on the operator's phone bill.

General Telephone operates a clearinghouse that automatically bills the correct party no matter where he happens to be at the time of the call.

If the city the call is being originated in overlaps coverage with a neighbor, the handoff can occur between cities. In a few years the entire U.S. is expected to be included in a system of mass coverage.

This knowledge can be, and is, used to protect oneself from law enforcement intercept orders as follows (borrowed from the ah, well, a group of Italian businessmen):

If someone wants to protect his location and his number from intercept, he registers on a non-wire line system and then "roams" in whatever city he's located in, so, in order for his customers to reach him, they will have to dial the local roamer number, then punch in the area code and phone number to connect.

The transmitter could be 10' from the receiver, it makes no difference. This technique protects the caller's location and it protects the location of the "customer" because he can't be isolated from the roamer truck, making it effectively impossible to place intercept equipment to track and record the unit's conversations.

The roam feature knocks the caller out of the regional system that normally covers north, south, east or west in any area. Of course, the user is paying the price of a toll call, and roaming calls are always more expensive than non-roamers. But still...

By choosing the other wire/non-wireline system the phone will automatically operate in the roaming mode. Something to remember, just in case that, well, that your uncle from New Jersey drops in for an unexpected visit...

CELL CONSTRUCTION
AND INTERCEPTION TECHNIQUES

Law enforcement types can purchase sets to monitor, track and record cellular phone calls. These sets are damn expensive from suppliers like HDS and are usually just test sets designed to monitor cellular operations for a carrier.

They're still damn expensive.

If someone tries to intercept a call with a test, the results will be printed out (including new handoff frequencies) and the sets can manually switch to it almost as fast as the mobile does. That's because a certain signal is transmitted in the voice channel just before the handoff containing the mobile change frequency.

This means, among other relevant tidbits, that a person, hopefully a person in Law

Enforcement, who has a monitor that will read the overhead train (usually a modified IFR service monitor, $25–$35K) can actually tell if a subject is in a certain city and follow him from cell to cell *even if he doesn't make a single phone call,* as long as his phone is turned on...

In some systems.

These sets are out of the reach of *most* police departments at this time, but many big cities are purchasing some sort of auto-record equipment and trust me, the Feds do have them, my friend.

Test sets such as those produced by IFR will reveal everything going on. It's their job, after all. A good test set will not only listen to the audio, it will display all the monitor data in the proper form and anything else asked of it.

The test set, whether sold to telco suppliers or with a value added (say $10,000) and sold to law enforcement as an intercept station, can mimic a base station or it can metamorphosize itself into a mobile unit. It can follow every handoff via the ESN or phone number automatically.

Test sets are programmed to become a certain mobile at any given notice and record what calls it receives, when it changes to a different frequency and so on. Although originally designed for sorting through a system they are ideal for interception within any metropolitan area.

Some cellular operators now maintain a certain portion of their switch physically in the open so law enforcement folks (armed with a warrant) can hook up their recorders right at the switch without disturbing the phone company's personnel or equipment.

The telephone companies have only a certain number of spare ports to hook on to. A few government agencies, like the Bureau had a habit of grabbing them up, making it difficult for other companies to get them. For quite a while the telephone companies were lying, saying they didn't have the ports available, forcing them to use a service monitor. However, so many cellular intercepts came through that telephone companies are required by law to give the minimal cooperation necessary. In the State of New Jersey, for instance, there is a new phone building in North Jersey that has a separate room to house the intercept equipment with space for any law enforcement goodies (slaves, etc.) to live and work.

New cellular switching stations are putting an appearance outside for empty TSO's so the cops don't bother them all the time. The routine is: Show me some paper—go hook up.

It does happen.

By understanding the concept of cellular placement and frequency allotment *it is very possible to monitor cellular phone calls.* Author Bill Cheek in his fine book *"Scanner Modification Handbook,"* published by CRB Research Books Inc., describes cellular layout and how it can be tracked with a scanner. This system is absolutely right-on and we are reprinting it (with permission from Mr. Cheek and Tom Kneitel of CRB Research) here in full as our first find 'em technique.

Table 3–1

CELLULAR BAND FREQUENCY ALLOCATIONS

Wireline (telephone company) cell sites (bases): 880.020 – 889.980

Wireline (telephone company) mobiles (car phones): 835.020 – 844.980

Non-wireline company cell site (bases): 870.030 – 879.990

Non-wireline company mobiles (car phones): 825.030 – 834.990

Since cellular systems are computer controlled and operated, the digital data channels are always going full blast with an annoying buzzsaw sound. These control frequencies are shown in Table 3–2.

Table 3–2

CELLULAR MOBILE TELEPHONE COMPUTER CONTROL FREQUENCIES

Wireline (telephone company) cell site (bases): 880.020 – 880.620

Wireline (telephone company) mobiles (car phones): 835.020 – 835.620

Non-wireline company cell site (bases): 879.390 – 879.990

Non-wireline company mobiles (car phones): 834.390 – 834.990 With 30 kHz channel-spacing, in a typical 870 to 880 MHz, or 880 to 890 MHz system, there are twenty-one computer control channels and 312 channels for voice, for a total of 333 channels for each service provider. This, then, breaks down into what might be considered several voice bands for cell sites and mobiles:

Band #1 870.030 to 879.360 MHz (Non-wireline cell sites)

Band #2 880.650 to 889.980 MHz (Wireline cell sites)

Band #3 835.650 to 844.980 MHz (Non-wireline mobiles)

Band #4 825.030 to 834.360 MHz (Wireline mobiles)

The bases (cell cites) use more power than the mobile units, and have antenna systems that are higher and more formidable than the mobile units. As a result, the cell sites present strong signals. Moreover, in almost all instances, the cell sites transmit both sides of all conversations inasmuch as they repeat the received signals from the mobile phones with which they are in communication.

You might wish to refer to Tables 3–3 and 3–4 which depict the unique frequency layout for up to seven cells. This is a complete cellular system frequency layout plan for wireline and non-wireline systems. Visualize a system this way: In order to avoid adjacent (side-by-side) cells from having the same frequencies to interfere with one another, seven cells are required; one at the center and six more surrounding the center cell. There is no particular pattern as to how Cells "A" through "G" have to be laid out. That is, Cell "D" can just as readily be a center cell with the others circling it, as could any other combination. In a metro system consisting of many cells, there isn't any such thing as a "center" cell, because every cell is, in effect, a "center cell" with respect to six others which surround it.

Generally speaking, two cells can (and do) operate on the same frequencies when they are separated by at least one different cell. Actually, the seven cell system unit as depicted in Figure 3–1 is used over and over. Two or even more adjacent cells on different frequencies are located between any two cells on the some frequencies. The cellular concept thus takes advantage of low powered, short range 800 MHz propagation to reuse the same frequencies at several different cell sites in a large metro region. If this weren't possible, then only 312 simultaneous conversations could take place at any one time, as it is thousands of simultaneous conversations could be accommodated within a large cellular system, thanks to frequency reuse.

Another factor here is the unique side effect of Frequency Modulation (FM) where an FM receiver exclusively "hears" the stronger of two signals presented to it on the same frequency.

So when cells on the same frequency are separated by one or more cells, even though a mobile might be positioned to detect signals from either, it actually will accept only the strongest one. The odds are very slim of the mobile being located precisely where the two signals are exactly equal. But even in that case, the odds against interference are improved even more because chances are virtually certain that the mobile would be under the control of a stronger third cell site signal on a different frequency.

Not only do two adjacent cells use the same frequencies, but no two cells use adjacent frequencies. For example, a given cell (Cell "D") that transmits on 880.950 MHz will not transmit on 880.980 MHz nor on 880.920 MHz. Likewise, mobiles within any given cell will not transmit on adjacent frequencies. This arrangement prevents adjacent channel interference in receivers located at cell sites and mobile units. FM receivers are not very selective to begin with, and the use of adjacent channels would cause interference within a cell.

The scheme depicted in Tables 3–3 and 3–4 was created to minimize the chances of adjacent channel interference throughout the entire cellular system. Note that each cell is allocated 47 or 48 frequencies, with a spacing of 210 kHz (seven channels) between each assigned frequency. In that manner, adjacent frequencies are not used in the same or adjacent cells.

DISCUSSION OF FIGURE 3–1:
Figure 3–1 illustrates the concept of a very large cellular mobile telephone system. Cities and metro complexes are rarely symmetrical due to geographical and other considerations, so Figure 3–1 is elongated to simulate the configuration of a realistic cellular network.

Cities tend to grow along railroads, rivers, and major highways, so the cellular system here is designed accordingly. Most are not this large, with the typical system consisting of three to seven cells. Small communities might even be served with a single cell, while metro areas like Los Angeles and New York City might consist of a number of interconnected systems fanned out to form a huge network. Frankly, size doesn't matter, because of low power, short range, and frequency reuse. The potential size of a cellular system is unlimited, so let's use Figure 3–1 to discuss how a "typical" system is structured:

FIGURE 3–1.
TYPICAL CELLULAR SYSTEM LAYOUT

1. Cells of the same letter operate on same frequency groups. See Tables 3–3 & 3–4.

2. Numerical designator distinguishes cells of the same letter/frequency group—otherwise there is no difference.

3. Two companies are permitted to operate cellular systems in any given metro area. The two systems will be laid out functionally as shown above, even though the physical layout will be different.

1. A hexagon is used to depict a cell's coverage territory, but the actual coverage wouldn't be that shape; it would be more-or-less circular, depending upon terrain and geography. However, circles don't illustrate the cellular concept as well as hexagons, and that is why hexagons are usually used in diagrams of cellular systems.

2. No two adjacent cell cites use the same frequencies. In other words, two Cell "A's" are never side-by-side, nor two Cell "B's," nor Cell "C's," etc. At least one cell site on different frequencies is always located between two other cell sites that are assigned the some frequencies.

3. No two adjacent cell sites are assigned adjacent frequencies. So, Cells "A" and "B" are never located next to each other. Neither are Cells "A" and "G," or "B" and "C," etc. At least one different cell site is always located between two other cell sites that are assigned adjacent frequencies.

Summary: Each cell site is always assigned frequencies that differ by 60 kHz or more from cell sites that are adjacent to it.

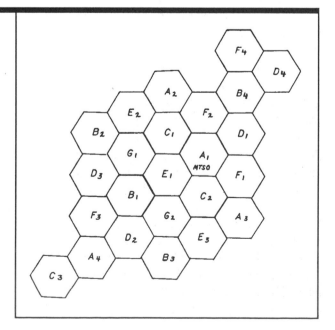

FIGURE 3–1

TYPICAL CELLULAR SYSTEM LAYOUT

This information, while perhaps boring to lay readers, might be very useful or handy to persons such as law enforcement officers performing court-warranted electronic surveillance on cellular conversations of a drug dealer— in-as-much as DEA and other enforcement officials have long been aware that cellular phones have become heavily used by drug traffickers.

So, let's say that an authorized surveillance is taking place and the suspect is monitored on 880.740 MHz, which is depicted in Table 3-1 under Cell "D." Everything's fine, and the suspect starts to advise his party to meet him at — —, and then right at the crucial moment, the suspect's car enters the control of a different cell site, and presto, the channel goes dead.

Putting the scanner into "Limit Search" mode in an attempt to track the conversation would bring only frustration; might as well have a cup of coffee and call it quits for the night. Chances are that the suspect's resumed conversation will not be encountered. The "Search" mode tracks in a linear, consecutive-frequency order, either higher or lower. If the suspect's conversation should be relocated, it would certainly take a while.

There would, however, be a way of increasing the chances of zeroing back in on the suspect. First, the scanner would have to be programmed with each individual cellular frequency in order by cell sites as depicted in Table 3-3 or 3-4. For such an operation, it would be highly beneficial to be working with a Realistic PRO-2004/2005 that has undergone the 6,400 channel memory modification outlined in this book (ed. note-Bill's book) (MOD-16) so that wireline and non-wireline cell site channels could be programmed.

There wouldn't be any reason to program any of the data-only control channels, but the scanner could be programmed with Channel 1 = 880.650 MHz; Channel 2 = 880.860 MHz; Channel 3 = 881.070 MHz, etc. Channel 40 would have 888.840 MHz, then continuing with Ch. 41 = 889.050 MHz and ending all Cell "A's" programming with Ch. 45 = 889.890.

Then, all zeros would be entered into Ch. 45 to 50, with Cell "B" programming as: Ch. 51 = 880.680 MHz; Ch. 52. = 880.890 MHz; through Ch. 95 = 889.920 MHz. All zeros would go into Ch. 95 to 100, and Cell "C" programming would start in Ch. 101 with 880.710 MHz. Get the picture?

When completed, the wireline company's 312 voice channel's would have been programmed into the agency's scanner, organized by cell sites and frequency allocations.

This would be particularly useful to the surveillance officer because, as noted earlier, when a mobile unit passes from one cell to another, the new frequency will not be in the old cell's assignment nor will it be an adjacent frequency!

Therefore, one could logically eliminate the frequency assignments of three cells from any consideration. So, when the suspect's conversation gets handed off from one cell to another, up to three scan banks that are known not to contain the call are deselected.

The scanner could then check for the resumed conversation on the remaining sites and probably locate same rather quickly, as in the example following the frequency tables.

Table 3-3
WIRELINE COMPANY CELL SITE TRANSMIT & MOBILE RECEIVE FREQUENCIES

	CELL A	CELL B	CELL C	CELL D	CELL E	CELL F	CELL G
	889.890	889.920	889.950	889.980			
	889.680	889.710	889.740	889.770	889.800	889.830	889.860
	889.470	889.500	889.530	889.560	889.590	889.620	889.650
	889.260	889.290	889.320	889.350	889.380	889.410	889.440
	889.050	889.080	889.110	889.140	889.170	889.200	889.230
	888.840	888.870	888.900	888.930	888.960	888.990	889.020
	888.630	888.660	888.690	888.720	888.750	888.780	888.810
	888.420	888.450	888.480	888.510	888.540	888.570	888.600
	888.210	888.240	888.270	888.300	888.330	888.360	888.390
	888.000	888.030	888.060	888.090	888.120	888.150	888.180
	887.790	887.820	887.850	887.880	887.910	887.940	887.970
	887.580	887.610	887.640	887.670	887.700	887.730	887.760
	887.370	887.400	887.430	887.460	887.490	887.520	887.550
	887.160	887.190	887.220	887.250	887.280	887.310	887.340
	886.950	886.980	887.010	887.040	887.070	887.100	887.130
	886.740	886.770	886.800	886.830	886.860	886.890	886.920
	886.530	886.560	886.590	886.620	886.650	886.680	886.710
	886.320	886.350	886.380	886.410	886.440	886.470	886.500
	886.110	886.140	886.170	886.200	886.230	886.260	886.290
	885.900	885.930	885.960	885.990	886.020	886.050	886.080
	885.690	885.720	885.750	885.780	885.810	885.840	885.870
	885.480	885.510	885.540	885.570	885.600	885.630	885.660
Voice	885.270	885.300	885.330	885.360	885.390	885.420	885.450
Channels	885.060	885.090	885.120	885.150	885.180	885.210	885.240
	884.850	884.880	884.910	884.940	884.970	885.000	885.030
	884.640	884.670	884.700	884.730	884.760	884.790	884.820
	884.430	884.460	884.490	884.520	884.550	884.580	884.610
	884.220	884.250	884.280	884.310	884.340	884.370	884.400
	884.010	884.040	884.070	884.100	884.130	884.160	884.190
	883.800	883.830	883.860	883.890	883.920	883.950	883.980
	883.590	883.620	883.650	883.680	883.710	883.740	883.770
	883.380	883.410	883.440	883.470	883.500	883.530	883.560
	883.170	883.200	883.230	883.260	883.290	883.320	883.350
	882.960	882.990	883.020	883.050	883.080	883.110	883.140
	882.750	882.780	882.810	882.840	882.870	882.900	882.930
	882.540	882.570	882.600	882.630	882.660	882.690	882.720
	882.330	882.360	882.390	882.420	882.450	882.480	882.510
	882.120	882.150	882.180	882.210	882.240	882.270	882.300
	881.910	881.940	881.970	882.000	882.030	882.060	882.090
	881.700	881.730	881.760	881.790	881.820	881.850	881.880
	881.490	881.520	881.550	881.580	881.610	881.640	881.670
	881.280	881.310	881.340	881.370	881.400	881.430	881.460
	881.070	881.100	881.130	881.160	881.190	881.220	881.250
	880.860	880.890	880.920	880.950	880.980	881.010	881.040
	880.650	880.680	880.710	880.740	880.770	880.800	880.830
Digital	880.440	880.470	880.500	880.530	880.560	880.590	880.620
Control	880.230	880.260	880.290	880.320	880.350	880.380	880.410
Channels	880.020	880.050	880.080	880.110	880.140	880.170	880.200

Table 3-4
NON-WIRELINE COMPANY CELL SITE TRANSMIT & MOBILE RECEIVE FREQUENCIES

	CELL A	CELL B	CELL C	CELL D	CELL E	CELL F	CELL G
Digital	879.900	879.930	879.960	879.990			
Control	879.690	879.720	879.750	879.780	879.810	879.840	879.870
Channels	879.480	879.510	879.540	879.570	879.600	879.630	879.660
-|-					879.390	879.420	879.450
|	879.270	879.300	879.330	879.360			879.060
879.090	879.120	879.150	879.180	879.210	879.240		
|	878.850	878.880	878.910	878.940	878.970	879.000	879.030
|	878.640	878.670	878.700	878.730	878.760	878.790	878.820
|	878.430	878.460	878.490	878.520	878.550	878.580	878.610
|	878.220	878.250	878.280	878.310	878.340	878.370	878.400
|	878.010	878.040	878.070	878.100	878.130	878.160	878.190
|	877.800	877.830	877.860	877.890	877.920	877.950	877.980
|	877.590	877.620	877.650	877.680	877.710	877.740	877.770
|	877.380	877.410	877.440	877.470	877.500	877.530	877.560
|	877.170	877.200	877.230	877.260	877.290	877.320	877.350
|	876.960	876.990	877.020	877.050	877.080	877.110	877.140
|	876.750	876.780	876.810	876.840	876.870	876.900	876.930
|	876.540	876.570	876.600	876.630	876.660	876.690	876.720
|	876.330	876.360	876.390	876.420	876.450	876.480	876.510
|	876.120	876.150	876.180	876.210	876.240	876.270	876.300
|	875.910	875.940	875.970	876.000	876.030	876.060	876.090
|	875.700	875.730	875.760	875.790	875.820	875.850	875.880
|	875.490	875.520	875.550	875.580	875.610	875.640	875.670
|	875.280	875.310	875.340	875.370	875.400	875.430	875.460
Voice	875.070	875.100	875.130	875.160	875.190	875.220	875.250
Channels	874.860	874.890	874.920	874.950	874.980	875.010	875.040
|	874.650	874.680	874.710	874.740	874.770	874.800	874.830
|	874.440	874.470	874.500	874.530	874.560	874.590	874.620
|	874.230	874.260	874.290	874.320	874.350	874.380	874.410
|	874.020	874.050	874.080	874.110	874.140	874.170	874.200
|	873.810	873.840	873.870	873.900	873.930	873.960	873.990
|	873.600	873.630	873.660	873.690	873.720	873.750	873.780
|	873.390	873.420	873.450	873.480	873.510	873.540	873.570
|	873.180	873.210	873.240	873.270	873.300	873.330	873.360
|	872.970	873.000	873.030	873.060	873.090	873.120	873.150
|	872.760	872.790	872.820	872.850	872.880	872.910	872.940
|	872.550	872.580	872.610	872.640	872.670	872.700	872.730
|	872.340	872.370	872.400	872.430	872.460	872.490	872.520
|	872.130	872.160	872.190	872.220	872.250	872.280	872.310
|	871.920	871.950	871.980	872.010	872.040	872.070	872.100
|	871.710	871.740	871.770	871.800	871.830	871.860	871.890
|	871.500	871.530	871.560	871.590	871.620	871.650	871.680
|	871.290	871.320	871.350	871.380	871.410	871.440	871.470
|	871.080	871.110	871.140	871.170	871.200	871.230	871.260
|	870.870	870.900	870.930	870.960	870.990	871.020	871.050
|	870.660	870.690	870.720	870.750	870.780	870.810	870.840
|	870.450	870.480	870.510	870.540	870.570	870.600	870.630
|	870.240	870.270	870.300	870.330	870.360	870.390	870.420
|	870.030	870.060	870.090	870.120	870.150	870.180	870.210

EXAMPLE:

Suspect is on a frequency in Cell "D" when the call is switched. The officer immediately knows that the new cell will not be "C," "D," or "E," so those are deselected and the scanner does not bother with them. The suspect will be on only one of about 180 possible frequencies, which the officer could locate within thirty seconds or less if he knows what to do and can react quickly enough. If he had unsuccessfully used the "search" to look for resumed conversations, there were more than 300 frequencies to check through that way. Note: If the suspect was originally in Cell "A," then Cells "B" and "G" can be eliminated as possibilities. Likewise, if the original call was in Cell "G," then calls from Cells "A" and "F" would be eliminated.

Remember: Cells of the same and/or adjacent frequencies are never physically located next to another! A judicious law enforcement surveillance expert would use both the "scan banks" and the "search" feature as tools to relocate a handed-off cellular conversation.

Note: Cellular handoffs occur quite rapidly, especially when a mobile goes from one cell through the fringe area of a second and then soon after into a third cell. The two handoffs could take place within seconds, and a search for the first handoff could well be in progress when the second handoff takes place. That's when a cell map of a particular area or system would come in handy.

Since the time Bill calculated the above information, new frequencies have been allocated to cellular companies as follows:

824.010 – 834.990 Mobiles non-wireline	A
835.020 – 844.980 Mobiles wireline	B
845.010 – 846.480 Mobiles non-wireline	A
846.510 – 849.000 Mobiles wireline	B
869.010 – 879.990 Bases non-wireline	A
880.020 – 889.980 Bases wireline	B
890.010 – 891.480 Bases non-wireline	A
891.510 – 894.000 Bases wireline	B

It would be a simple matter to create the same frequency-cell tables with these new frequencies.

OUR OWN REFINEMENTS:

I sat in on a cellular phone interception project with a couple of law enforcement types during the writing of this book using an offshoot of Bill's idea. Here's how they did it:

The target was operating in a major metropolitan city in the U.S. with a number of hills and dead air valleys. The LP was situated in a house on a hill that overlooked much of the city.

The LP was equipped with an ICOM 7000 receiver and a non-directional 800 sensitive antenna. The ICOM had been modified slightly by clipping an internal lead which allowed it to receive a baud rate of 9600.

The receiver was connected to an IBM PC clone that was loaded with a frequency scanning program called Program 801. The local frequency banks were programmed into the computer and we had a colleague watching the target's residence.

When the target left his residence, the watcher called us on his cellular phone and so informed us—we began scanning.

Within a few moments we had identified the subject by both his voice and the subject of the conversation on a certain cell. When a handoff to another cell occurred, the F4 key was stroked on the computer and it began to look through the logical frequencies.

Did it work? The intercept was conducted on a weekend so, admittedly, the traffic was light but in every case we found the target within a few seconds. The maximum conversation loss was at most, 20 seconds.

The ICOM and the elevated listening post followed the target through each and every cell as he changed position. There was NO cell that he accessed that we could not receive from our stationary LP.

INDIVIDUAL CELLULAR TAILING

Another system tested for this book which proved quite invigorating was to take a Motorola bench frequency counter and equip it with a directional 800 antenna. This set up allowed me to follow a particular subject from a distance of 100–200 feet and simply read the operating frequency of his cellular whenever it was put into use.

The keys to this system are to use a 12 volt bench counter with high sensitivity and a gain antenna. Omni direction cellular antennas are limited by a 3 dB gain. Use at least a 5 dB gainer from the 800 business band, or, better yet, a Yagi transmit/receive antenna from one of several antenna suppliers.

This will make it directional but will make the entire concept viable. Remember, although the car phone only broadcasts one side of the conversation, the cell rebroadcasts *both* at a frequency of 45 MHz lower than the mobile channel.

When the frequency counter latches on to a

frequency, a handheld scanner is manually programmed to the correct frequency and the entire conversation is monitored.

When a handoff occurs the new frequency is quickly acquired in a similar manner and the monitoring resumes with only a minor loss of conversation. It is possible to drop back from the 200 foot limitation until a handoff occurs at which time the LP car must move back into position, but only long enough for the counter to read the new frequency. *And now folks, there's a brand new tool about to come onto the market as we speak which does a much better job than on individual intercepts.*

A TRICK

Say hello to the OPTOELECTRONICS Pre-selector APS 104, a device which comes close to duplicating the SCANLOCK counter surveillance receiver for "de-bugging" an entire area in one or two passes and has another very, very interesting use.

From a distance of a couple of hundred feet the Pre-selector will lock onto the signal of a mobile cellular and "track" it, displaying the frequency in use on an OPTO frequency counter. When a handoff occurs the unit will instantly display the new frequency.

By punching these numbers into a scanner, it is possible to follow any nearby cellular phone conversation.

A directional antenna will increase the range of this unit...

Besides the previously-detailed cellular system there used to be a pattern in use that involved 12 cells. This gave no adjacent frequencies in any adjacent cells, but most cities have given that up and gone to above, more compact 7 factored pattern because it offers more frequencies in each cell (1 of 7 instead of 1 in 12). The current system is likely to remain around a while because it's about as down as it can be taken without bringing in directional antennas.

Techniques

FOR INCREASING CELLULAR DENSITY

It is possible to use a 320 degree directional antenna by having a heavy signal lobe to avoid pickups of signals from the back side from that particular antenna segment. This gives the option to the frequency right behind it fairly close in so we get a little more density in a particular system.

Another approach to get more capacity buries some low power channels in the middle of a particular cell which are so low in power that they don't really get out to more than half way of the radius. It is then possible to use these same allocations somewhere else because they interfere less than the channels that run full power.

PHONE NUMBERS AND ESN's

The actual phone number is stored in a programmable chip known as a NAM. In most parts of the country this chip must be pre-programmed with an available number on one of the local companies before the phone can be sold, or at least before it can be put into use.

The NAM is a 16 digit chip which contains the phone number plus other info—in older style phones they are programmed in an EPROM. New phones have programming capability built into their handsets.

The ESN or electronic serial number (sometimes referred to as Electronic Identification Number, EIN) is not stored in the in NAM chip. At the moment there are about 125 different phones being manufactured and they all store the ESN in a different place in their memory in either an EPROM or a ROM. Each company can, and does utilize separate locations and different methods of coding.

NAM's themselves can be programmed at such mundane points of purchase as Radio Shack stores. NAM programmers are openly available for about $1,000. What is to stop someone from cloning a phone so their cellular will ring every time a target's does? or even so when the cloned phone makes a call, the target would be billed?

Several things, the first being the law of the land. No clones allowed. A larger barrier is posed by the inclusion of the (usually) nonprogrammable electronic serial number that is often accessed with the phone number. If a set is stolen this number is put on a computerized hot list which shows up immediately when the unit is used. Some new switches are also rumored to be able to tell if more than one phone with the same number is on line at any given time by comparing the serial numbers in a real time situation.

Does this mean no clones?

Well, not exactly. See early phones, before somebody in power decided the ESN's should be a permanent part of the unit, allowed both NAM and ESN programming. When researching this article, I was offered a series 1 or 2 Novetel mobile phone cloned to any set of numbers I required for $600.

This is to allow busy executives the option to have an extension mobile but it could also be rigged to act as an unscrupulous clone, ringing and recording every call made to the target number.

I have also been told of black market chips that can replace the ESN chips in modern phones. The FCC doesn't like these, the phone associations don't like these and even, yes, the FBI don't like these...

Although most people don't realize it, cellulars broadcast a super audible ID tone along with the normal audio. The operator will not hear this because it's filtered out, but it provides three choices for security, helping to make certain that only one phone is on the system at any one time. The system listens to what id tone is offered and if it's the wrong one, it'll disconnect the offender.

This feature is designed to protect against radio propagation faults wherein the signal comes back to the base too strong and over-powers the desired signal but it is also a factor in cloning because the system will allow 5 seconds for the proper signal and then it will disconnect the "wrong" signal automatically. Not a perfect system, but one that must be taken into account for any cloning attempt.

In fact, there are modified cellulars on the black market that the various government agencies like even less than they do clones. I was also offered a modified phone *that would come up with a random and different ESN and serial number every time it was used for $2500!*

This option lets the user put the phone into the roam mode so it would access this "traveler's" feature on every call but bill it to a different number each time.

At first glance this seems to be the ideal (criminal) way to beat phone charges since the unit will bill to a different number on every call the operator will not be bothered by those annoying little notices from the local telco every month.

But the real selling feature of this type of phone is that *it cannot be legally monitored.* If a law enforcement agency gets a court order to monitor a particular telephone (identified by the phone number) it will not be valid, and in fact will not work if the unit in question changes its identity like some sort of maddened electronic chameleon every time it is used...

Bet the farm I ain't the only person who has been offered one of these phones...

In fact, one basic cellular flaw is considered to be the existence of fraud. The rules of the FCC and the Canadian Department of Communication require portable phones have an unchangeable identification in a read-only memory in the set. The wording says it should not be possible to modify the identification without rendering the set inoperative. One industry study recently reported that it was possible, with varying degrees of difficulty, to change the identification in about 80% of the sets which are now out in the field.

Fraud, fake, and oscillating ESN numbers are estimated to account for somewhere between 4–8% of the industry's gross billing.

One of the inducements to fraud is that when a mobile identifies itself, the local system has to decide if it should query the mobile for the full 10 digits or only 7 of the actual phone number? Should the ESN be required? Sometimes the operating company, to save on transmission time, cuts down on the number of digits that are transferred in these operations, especially at rush hour.

Regardless of the saturation ad campaigns for cellular use, the systems are filling up fast and most claim to operate at only marginally profitable levels, yet corporations are always interested in purchasing cellular companies. Why?

They're buying future potential. Capacity limitation will become a thing of the past when digital cellular comes into play (scheduled to be the norm within five years) because digital systems can multiplex 3 or more conversations on each channel.

The technique has been standardized already. There is digital equipment on the market available for use with the proper support equipment already although all the in-place equipment will be continued to be supported for several years, probably until the end of the century, but digital will gradually take over the market as surely as color television edged out black and white.

Digital has several appetizing features for cellular users. It involves using a digital code technique for speech to use 16,000 bytes per second per radio channel, per conversation. This, plus 3–5 different conversations on each channel, simultaneously will make the format secure from casual eavesdroppers.

Without a doubt scanner adaptable modules will be marketed to decipher and demultiplex digital cellular, but from the point of view of security, the important thing is that when digital speech coding is present one can take advantage of these superior techniques inherent in encrypting digital signals as opposed to the problems of scrambling analog dialogue.

Systems are now available (see the scrambling section) which will lock out almost everybody but are still not considered military level secure. Digital suppliers will probably offer a option for secrecy levels than it is to constructively distort voice transmissions.

If you need to have a sensitive conversation during a mobile situation you have two choices, use a digital scrambler, or stop and use a coin phone by the side of the road.

Remember this fact.

At one point I took a mobile phone and made a call to a friend and for about 15 minutes, in the middle of a normal business day, drove around running a tape asking anyone who was listening in on a scanner to give me an anonymous phone call for a research study.

In the city of San Francisco I got three calls from casual listeners.

And these were just the people who bothered to call...

DATA AND FUTURE MODES

Because cellular was designed for audio and, at this writing, uses analog FM transmission, it is difficult to transmit data over the system even though mobile faxes and modems are available.

Using an ordinary data modem of the type that would be utilized on a landline telephone, provides less than normal service. One problem is that as the position changes the mobile passes through a combination of direct and reflected radio waves which can get out of phase with each other and produce a phenomenon called multipath which means that the RF signal is going constantly up and down like an elevator. The resulting conglomerate is okay for speech but for data it's a no-no.

In most cases the solution to this is to stop the car. Immediately the quality will improve and reasonable results will occur AS LONG AS A LOW BAUD RATE IS MAINTAINED. This is important in digitally-scrambled transmissions, as well as in data swapping, as well as with mobile FAX transmissions.

Any rate over 2400 is likely to cause some problems.

A new possibility for increasing the availability of cellular channels has already been brought before the FCC. This new system is microcellular in design and uses spread spectrum technology.

The company that requested a license for this technology (Millicom) has requested a frequency band in the 1710–2290 MHz region.

Great Britain is testing out a very short range RF-based system known as Telepoint. This concept gives the user a small, portable unit for a base fee of $12–$15 per month that can be used as a wireless/cellular phone only when the operator is within 300 feet of a clearly marked base station.

Many base stations can be located in any given area because they cost only a fraction of a cellular site and they are extremely low in power.

TAPPING CELLULARS

At first glance it seems to be an oxymoron— why tap a cellular? I mean the damn things broadcast over the public air waves with 600 beautiful milliwatts of power. Who needs to tap?

Some people, that's who. Someone out there needs to tap anything and right at this moment there are about 32 readers wondering how to tap a cellular.

The quickest method to hear at least one side of any conversation is simply to secret a VOX activated tape recorder in the car. And hope the driver doesn't play the stereo too loudly...

Saul Mineroff offers a car caddy, you know, one of those things that holds a Big Mac and a drink and slips over the transmission console, with a great little stereo recorder built right into the unit.

It would make a nice gift for, say your wife...

Olympus Corporation markets (available from C.I.A., the company, not *the company*) a series of drop out recorders for cellular phones. These little boxes connect between the handset and the phone and operate just like a regular record both sides of the conversation when the phone is taken off hook.

These units, called Woodbury Interfaces, are not designed to be hidden but are supposed to be used to record one's own conversations (legal in one-party states) for later study.

They can be used somewhat surreptitiously by stashing them, along with a mini recorder, in some sort of camouflaged unit like the Mineroff car caddy, or even installed under the phone itself or under the upholstery.

Two elements necessary for success here are access to the target vehicle and a not overly observant driver.

AID makes a bug that is concealed in a rechargeable Motorola-type battery for portable phones. This unit works off the battery, which still operates the phone, and picks up and transmits local conversation.

It would be possible to design some sort of infinity transmitter for a cellular, although each make of phone is different enough to require some uptown design work and when the transmitter was in operation, all the air time would be billed to the target, allowing him a nice printout of the connection.

A wiser move would be to employ some sort of hookswitch bypass so the phone would be hot on hook and broadcast the local audio. However, even this technique has problems because it could easily cause interference problems with other phones and might alarm the switch because more than one phone would be on a single channel.

A quick thought: You want to record a cellular conversation that you are part of without alerting anyone else in the car? Think ear mic's (devices that receive and transmit *inside* the user's ear and look like a miniature earphone) put one in your ear and have a conversation.

The DEA recently bought 1,000 of these from, well, from an unnamed New York supplier.

A cellular phone can also be "accidentally" left operating after a call is made to a recording phone. If left behind in a business conference, it will work as a long distance bug. Some portable cellulars are now made with a hot switch so they will broadcast to a nearby receiver for the same sort of "forgetful" bugging.

"CELLULAR PHONES ARE IMPOSSIBLE TO MONITOR" — RIGHT.

PAGER, FAX, AND DATA INTERCEPT TECHNIQUES

One can only imagine the internal trauma of being a paging company owner—it would be sort of like owning a company that made little glass vials, hell, business has just suddenly shot through the roof over the last few years making enormous profits for everyone lucky enough to be in the business of manufacturing little glass vials, but sometimes, late at night, the owners must wonder exactly why people are buying millions of little glass vials...

So it goes with pagers, the popularity of the common pager has exploded concurrently with the drug trade. Pagers are so popular that in America 7.2% of the *entire population* carries a pager.

In the good old days, wearing a pager meant you were a doctor or maybe a car thief, but certainly nothing more disreputable than that. Today doctors, and let's face it, even car thieves, like to hide their pagers under jackets or tend towards those new little pagers that masquerade as ballpoint pens so people don't assume they're drug dealers. At this writing, one state (Virginia) actually has a law prohibiting pager use on school grounds and several other states have tried to pass bills (unsuccessfully) demanding licensing of pagerized individuals.

Not to say that pager companies don't have some kind of conscience, they do. In fact, have formed a group known as TELOCATOR, the Mobile Communications Industry Association. Telocator promotes paging/police cooperation and attempts to keep their individual members informed on the latest laws and procedures as they apply to pagers. However, to be frank, their primary success seems to be cute little stickers they say "MOBILEized" for the war on drugs for pager companies to stick on their doors along with nice little laser-written posters that remind perspective pager renters that the "use of a pager in a commission of a felony is prohibited by federal law and carries a penalty of up to four years imprisonment and/or a fine of up to $30,000 for each offense."

One can only wonder exactly how effective these efforts are in shaping the morals of the pager industry, especially since the subscriber base is expected to continue growing and is estimated to reach *21 million* users by the mid-1990's.

Pagers operate in the clear on radio frequencies that can be received with any standard receiver or a scanner. The information transmitted on pagers can be of interest to anyone from law enforcement to business competitor groups. There are several interesting ways of extracting said information.

TYPES OF PAGERS

Although numeric display pagers constitute more than half of the pagers in use today other types are also in use. Here's a list ordered by popularity:

NUMERIC DISPLAY—This service lets one receive numbers sent from any touch-tone telephone. The pager beeps and shows telephone numbers, previously agreed-upon codes, parts numbers, stock prices, purchase orders, and so on. Limited information may be sent along in the form of numbers that stand for initials, or simple codes.

TONE—The tone pager emits a beep telling the user to call back a predetermined location such as an office, home, voice mailbox, or telephone answering machine.

TONE AND VOICE—This paging service gives an audible tone followed by the message in the caller's own voice. There is no operator, and no need for the user to call in. The pager delivers the *complete* message.

ALPHANUMERIC DISPLAY—This latest development is actually a miniature message center that beeps and displays messages in words and numbers. Messages are sent through an input device or dispatched by a live operator.

PRIVACY LAWS AND PAGERS

For each type of pager, different legal requirements must be met for intercepts. On the federal level, the easiest pager to deal with is the simple tone-only device. The U.S. Justice Department had long held that interception of a tone-only pager was not a search, since there is no expectation of privacy in a device that only beeps or vibrates. Therefore, the Department has maintained, interceptions raise no Fourth Amendment issues and require neither a warrant nor a court order.

This policy was certified by Congress when it passed the Electronic Communications Privacy Act of 1986 (ECPA), which excludes tone-only pagers from its provisions.

Although the information conveyed by intercepting a tone-only pager is limited, such intercepts can be helpful in documenting patterns of behavior by suspected criminals. Since they are the cheapest and easiest to use of all pagers, tone-only units may be most commonly encountered in connection with drug activity, at least among lower echelon criminals.

Federal and state laws treat privacy interests in display and tone-and-voice paging communications. Under ECPA, for example, the police generally cannot intercept a tone and voice or a display pager without first securing an appropriate court order. This restriction stems from Congress' conclusion that subscribers using such pagers have a reasonable expectation of privacy in the paging communications they send and receive. A similar conclusion is also reflected in state privacy statutes, which often impose stricter requirements on carriers and law enforcement officials than does the ECPA.

As requirements for legal protections increase, so do the rewards for intercepting display pagers. A numeric display pager displays a 10- or 12-digit number, usually the phone number of a person who desires a return call. More sophisticated drug dealers, however, use the digits as code, with, for example, a "1" at the end of a phone number meaning "the cocaine is not in."

Obviously, police and others intercepting such messages with monitoring devices or cloned pagers can harvest considerable worthwhile information.

The recent increase in the use of alphanumeric paging is beneficial to law enforcement due to the added bonus of text messages. Theoretically, exact details of drug transactions could be made available to law enforcement if the deal was conducted via alpha paging and an intercept was in progress.

There are several ways in which paging carriers aid law enforcement in preventing illegal use of pagers for drug transactions including leasing pagers which are cloned to police, assisting in intercepts of paging communications and providing the police with information about paging subscribers.

Federal and state privacy statutes, however, generally require law enforcement agencies to secure appropriate authorization before enlisting the aid of paging carriers. Specifically, most privacy laws prevent the police from using a cloned pager or intercepting a paging communication unless they have first obtained a court order, a special emergency request or the subscriber's consent. Similarly, law enforcement agencies may not gain access to information about paging subscribers (such as transactional records) unless they secure either a subpoena, a warrant, a court order, or the consent of the customer.

INTERCEPTIONS, AN OVERVIEW

Successful pager interception is dependent upon several factors:

1. Frequency of the paging service. Law enforcement agencies or detectives are advised to simply call local paging carriers and ask them for their frequencies. This is public information and usually will be given out without any problem. Books are also available on this subject from CRB RESEARCH.

2. Paging number. Some intercept techniques require the actual phone number that activates a particular pager.

3. Cap code. A cap code is a seven or eight digit number that is the actual EIN, or Electronic Serial Number of the pager. This digital cap code is what the pager looks for in the stream of paging messages before it locks onto a message and notifies its wearer.

4. Some interception methods require the paging format. There are a number of proprietary formats engineered by pager manufacturers.

Most paging systems operate in the FM band normally from 35 MHz to new super-high microwave pagers in the 931–932 MHz area. These signals can be received on any receiver but they will come in as frequency shift data signals, nothing that is intelligible to the normally equipped listener. Most paging systems have a local coverage area determined by the number and placement of their transmitters, the average area is probably 40–60 miles in size although many companies are now expanding their coverage by adding additional transmitters or making deals with other companies to give statewide coverage.

A new paging system actually gives nationwide coverage. The system known as Wide Area Paging and is typified by CUE Paging Corporation. The user rents a "Cue Pager" which is actually not a fixed receiver but rather a scanner that scans the FM commercial radio band. Cue (and other companies) rent space on one or more commercial FM stations in most cities in the United States. In fact, Cue boasts of over 200 FM stations in their nationwide network. The paging signal is carried on a sub-carrier or, SCA portion of the broadcast signal that is inaudible to standard receivers.

No matter where the subscriber finds himself, his unit will scan until it finds the paging sub-carrier signal and then lock on to that signal, waiting for its own cap code to appear. To page a subscriber, the caller dials an 800 number and then plugs in the specific pager identity code. This data is flashed by an uplink by a satellite where it is transmitted across the country to various downlink stations and then land lined or microwaved to FM radio transmitting towers.

In a Cue-type system, it is not necessary to know where the subscriber is, simply the fact that he is in the United States gives a very high probability of reaching him on his pager. The pager itself is no larger than a standard Motorola-type paging unit.

These wide area systems normally offer some sort of echo back or voice mail system to let subscribers retrieve messages from an 800 number in case they happen to be between SCA stations when a message comes in.

There are a couple of ways of intercepting pager messages. One of the niftiest is through the use of a clone. A cloned pager is simply a pager which operates on the same frequency and has the same cap code as the target's pager, in short, the paging system has no way of knowing how many receivers are actually listening at any given time so any message that is transmitted will be received simultaneously by all identical pagers.

Traditionally this has been the favorite method of law enforcement to intercept a suspect's messages, paging companies will cooperate with departments who have authorization by issuing them details on the owner of any pager or by physically manufacturing a cloned pager and giving it to a detective.

One narc I know uses the vaguely dubious trick of "borrowing" a subject's pager during a body search, popping out the EIN chip and replacing it with a non-programmed chip. When the pager is returned to its owner it will, of course, no longer work.

Disgruntled owner takes pager back to company and complains. With any luck the company will program a new pager to the same cap code on the spot and give it back to the suspect.

The cop simply pops the EIN chip into his own pager and now owns a non-registered clone that will duplicate the perp's messages...

A TRICK

> Most pagers have their cap code written on the bottom of the pager or the pager's belt clip. If a person can get momentary access to a pager, he will find two interesting factors: A. the paging company (and therefore the operating frequency) and B. the cap code of the unit. Both Motorola and Panasonic manufacture synthesized pagers that are both frequency and cap code program-mable. This means that anyone can set up a clone for any pager simply by employing a unit such as Panasonic's Vanguard pager.

The second paging intercept option is to purchase one of several software packages that work in conjunction with a scanner or a receiver and an IBM or a Mac PC. These soft-ware packages "listen" to the scanner which is set up to listen to a certain paging frequency. In this type of operation, the potential inter-ceptor only needs to know either the cap code *or* the call number—nothing else.

Assuming one has the phone number to activate the target pager, one simply turns on the receiver, initializes the software and then dials the pager sending a unique code (for some reason 6666 seems to be in vogue with most law enforcement agencies), and then watches

the computer monitor to see when the code is broadcast. The program will immediately display the cap code of the pager and, if it is an alphanumeric pager, the text message.

Once this has transpired, the program will set up an automatic file in the computer to grab any and all further messages to that pager, storing them as to time, date, and phone number or text message to be called. Most systems will take any of the paging formats including the POCSAG format. Case files can be printed immediately or printed when reviewed or stored on floppy disks and reviewed at any time. Most of these systems will monitor from 1–32,000 pagers at any given time and set up a file for each individual pager.

These systems began as proprietary systems to be used by paging companies to monitor hacking attempts, traffic patterns, and system problems but have spread to law enforcement and now civilian intercept markets.

Do these systems work?

Yes, I've tested the INTERCEPTOR—LE system and it pretty much does what it says it's going to do. The system grabs and displays incoming messages simultaneously or in many cases faster than the pager receives them and works with all existing paging formats as well as has the capability to use new formats as they are introduced. The LE system sells in the $4,000 range at the time of this writing but, folks let's face it, it's just a little software package and lower-priced clones are going to appear on the market if they haven't by this writing. LE is available from SHERWOOD COMMUNICATIONS.

A second paging intercept program is avail-able from TGA Technologies in Dunwoody, Georgia.

What to do if you think your pages are being intercepted by some nameless force? One gentleman I know (damn but I do know a lot of interesting people, don't I?) got a "666" page on his pager in the middle of the night. He had reason to suspect he was the target of a non-warranted police surveillance as a close friend of his had just been popped on a weapons charge (later dropped).

My friend spent the next two days calling himself and entering 30 or so "interesting" return numbers including CIA, NSA and FBI offices around the country, plus international suppliers of anything interesting, phone numbers of various embassies and even a White House "inside" number he happened to have on hand.

It may not be a cure all, but the satisfaction of knowing he was driving several detectives crazy did provide a certain amount of satisfaction.

FAX INTERCEPTION

Alexander Graham Bell must be turning over in his grave at the spread of the ubiquitous fax machine. Fax machines are rapidly replacing telephones as the primary method of communication for many businesses and some individuals. I personally know of at least two people who have impulsively ripped out their telephones and replaced them with a fax machine, the implication being, of course, that my time is too valuable to waste talking on the phone.

Many people who should know better think that faxes are a safer method of data exchange than is the telephone because no words are transmitted, simply data. As one might suspect, this data can be intercepted and logically regurgitated to "bug" fax machines.

There have been a couple of problems associated with fax tapping that have just recently been solved; faxes trade data by means of frequency- or phase-shift keying at speeds of 300 to 9600 baud. This type of data transmission does not lend itself to recording and playback on most audio tape recorders, as the speed is too high and the frequencies are too close together. Any distortion renders the transmission unintelligible.

Faxes fall into several groups depending on what type of transmission perimeters they employ. The most common one at this time is called Group III. The particular protocols for

Groups I, II, III and IV, are set by something called CCITT and are available in a $25.00 booklet.

Faxes trade setup information at the beginning of each call in something known as the handshake period. During the handshake the sending fax will set itself to the highest possible group protocol that the receiving fax will accept before it begins transmitting data. The sending fax requires acceptance and confirmation of this handshake before it will begin the actual transmission. Some faxes offer limited security by reading the phone number of the receiving fax and comparing it to an internal list before sending the data, but this should not concern anyone who is tapping into the line because if they use a high impedience phone tap (just a simple .01mfd capacitor in series with 10k ohm resistor and perhaps a NE-2 neon lamp across the line between the two components), the sending fax will not notice the "invisible" third party on the phone line.

Let's examine the handshake protocol of a typical fax machine. What happens when one presses "send" on a fax machine?

The answering fax machine transmits a 2,100Hz tone for three seconds, and then begins a negotiating process at 300bps including a single high-pitched tone, followed by a lower, warbling tone. The second tone is the 300-bps receiver capabilities packet.

When the warbling ends, there is a brief pause, and if the calling fax hasn't responded, the process is repeated. The first step is to send a digital identification signal (DIS) that tells the answering machine what it can do including: What is the maximum transmission speed possible? Does the sending unit support modified read compression? Does it include error correction?

The sending fax transmits a digital command signal (DCS) that tells the called unit which of the operating parameters described in the DIS will be used. This signal turns on these features in the receiving unit.

The sending fax transmits a test signal to help the receiving unit lock onto the proper signals.

The receiving fax transmits a confirmation-to-receive (CFR) signal to tell the sending unit it is ready to accept the first page.

The first page of the fax message is sent from the originating device.

When the end of the page is reached, the sending unit transmits an end-of-page (EOP) signal and waits for a message confirmation (MCF) from the receiving unit.

This process continues until the final page is sent and the calling fax transmits a disconnect (DCN) signal to sever the connection, freeing both telephones.

Note that the initial handshaking that establishes the capabilities of each unit in the connection is conducted only once, at the beginning of the link. Once the sending fax starts transmitting pages, there is no need for this handshake again.

Commercial fax interception devices are made by a number of companies including HDS and STG, aimed at law enforcement but, in some cases, sold to anyone with the bucks. Commercial facsimile taps are based either on an IBM PC equipped with a fax modem which intercepts and receives the protocol signals and the fax message, writing it directly to disk and then reprinting it out on the screen or on a printer or by employing a special tape recorder to save messages for later playback through a modified fax machine.

These devices do work and have been used in courts on numerous occasions. *They also average about $28,000 each*. If money's no object, hey, I say give 'em a call.

In reality there's very little difference in tapping a data transmission than there is in tapping a voice transmission. Here's how to do it for about $27,000 less:

1. Intercept the data stream by use of a good dropout recorder or high impedience capacitor circuit as described above. Record the entire transmission on a digital audio tape recorder. DAT's are now commercially available for about $800 but this will drop soon and may have dropped by the time you read this.

   DAT's use a high sample rate to record the audio in the form of boolean digits. There is no distortion, noise or error introduced in playback or recording. What you hear is what you get. Therefore, DAT's are the ideal and perhaps really the only method of recording fax transmissions.

2. Once the transmission is on tape, there are two choices: either feed it into a fax modem and into a computer where it can be stored and manipulated, or feed it directly into a fax machine. In either case the information should come down a phone line.

   The simplest way to do this, if one has access to two phone lines, is to unscrew the mouthpiece and clip a jumper cable from the output of the DAT directly into the telephone line, dial up the other phone line and run it into the computer or fax machine.

   However, a very nice alternative is to employ your own central office in the form of a VIKING Phone Line Simulator. For about $100 this little device provides a carrier that makes any phone think it's hooked up to central office and another telephone. Signals, voice and data can be fed into the simulator and will come out at line level at the output.

(continued next page.)

If the resulting signal is to be fed into a computer, the carrier on the modem should be turned off so it will not respond with a carrier of its own when receiving the target's communications resulting in interference.

If a Hayes equivalent modem is used, the signal sequence to put it into the monitor mode so it will still receive data without a carrier are as follows:

FOR ORIGINATE: AT CO S10=255D
FOR ANSWER: AT CO S10=255A

This turns off the carrier and sets the modem to ignore the carrier loss.

3. The output of the DAT can be fed into a fax machine, and with a little bit of practice one can use the pause button in order to time the handshake sequence setting up the fax machine to receive the intercepted transmission just as if it were the receiving end fax.

As long as the machines sync up with regard to baud rate and protocol, it will reproduce the fax communication.

This procedure will also work for data communications between two computers. Instead of feeding the result into a fax, simply feed it into your modem. In fact, modem transmission which is frequency shift keying and less subject to distortion than phase shift keying, can often be reproduced, by a high quality reel-to-reel tape recorder.

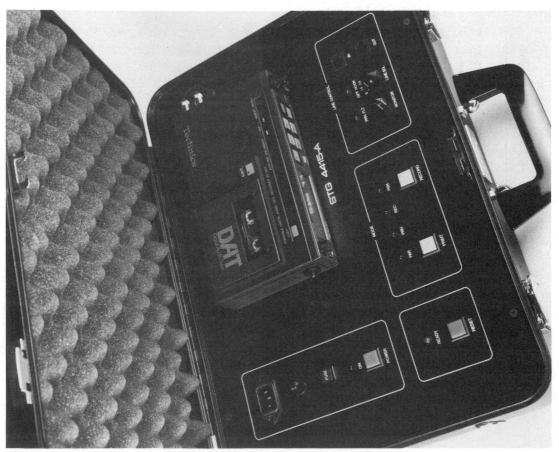

STG Commercial FAX intercept device.

VIDEO SURVEILLANCE

The field of video surveillance has probably come further over the last few years than has any other single area of surveillance. It would not be an exaggeration to say video is exactly where audio was 7 years ago.

Prices have dropped and technology has leapt forward. Ideas that were unheard of a short time ago are not only on the drawing board but in practice. How much would you pay for a complete, low end, medium range wired video surveillance system that will transmit a clear black and white picture for several hundred feet?

$300? $250? Wait, suppose we included a small camera that could be hidden almost anywhere? Don't answer yet, that's not all! Add power down the same cable as the signal feeds back on and we'll throw in, absolutely free, an audio path as well!

How much would you expect to pay for this little voyeur dream? $200? Would you pay $150? How about 100 even...

And how about for almost the very same money a *wireless* system that will throw the signal a couple of hundred feet? Examples of both are on the market as this is written.

Video surveillance is the ability of putting the operator's eye into a remote area, and recording the signal. It is no more difficult than is audio surveillance; connect the correct cables to the correct equipment and you'll be laying on your couch sipping a Coors watching as the bad guys have a board meeting in no time at all.

The whole key to video surveillance lies in being creative. Walk into any room and look around. A number of potential camera locations should be immediately apparent. Book-

shelves? Hide the camera behind, or better yet, in a book. Curtains? Behind. If it's an office it probably has a dropped ceiling which is about the ultimate place to conceal a camera or a recorder.

If one needs to violate a sterile space, an office or a conference room that just doesn't offer any viable possibilities, insert a briefcase and leave it there. Just lock it and leave it. This works in many otherwise secure situations.

If it's a large room, the floor of a plant for instance, a number of other options open up.

As we will see, lenses come already concealed in sprinkler heads and smoke detectors, cameras come in radios, and already installed track lighting, or entrepreneurs can put them there themselves.

Or simply go to the rear of the room and drop a camera over a ceiling pipe with a long range lens. One trick that works is to put it in a box clearly marked "security camera." People are used to seeing this type of housing and quickly forget the unit might be used for other reasons.

In this respect it's even easier to use than audio is, would you feel okay about a little black box on your desk clearly marked "transmitter?"

I think not.

Sitting at my desk idly rummaging through several surveillance video catalogs, a sudden thought occurs to me: Wouldn't it be great if there was a way to commit *passive* video surveillance?

A method of placing a video camera and maybe a transmitter so an entire room would be under surveillance without committing any form of trespass to plant (or recover) the electronics...

Then I looked up at the telephone line running on the pole outside my front window and noticed the nice rubber splicing boot that hung on the line at what would be the perfect angle to peer through the window.

My God! A nice, weatherproofed housing with access to power and, if needed, telephone wiring. A nice stash spot that no one would think to question... Why hasn't someone...

Five minutes later I picked up TRON-Tek's brochure to see a gorgeous, pre-assembled camera, lens, and transmitter installed in a regulation telco splice boot. All set to mount on any convenient cable and broadcast away.

For those irritating subjects that live in areas with underground telephone wiring TRON-Tek offers a regulation splicing pedestal complete with "buried cable don't dig here" sign.

And camera and transmitter.

The same set-up also comes packaged in an electric company pole can for those really hard to reach subjects.

And you wonder what happened to the best minds of our generation?

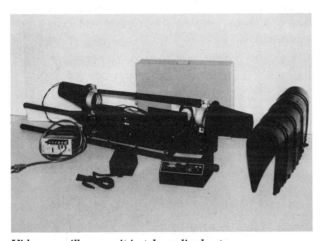

Video surveillance unit in telco splice boot.

Video systems can consist of five items, and must consist of at least four of them: lenses, cameras, transmitters, receivers, and recorders. It's possible to mix and match anything you want from these individual components to make the application work.

CAMERAS AND MONITORS

Video cameras traditionally use a tube to convert light into an electrical signal. These tubes can be 1", ²/3", or ¹/2" in diameter with the larger sizes usually providing a better picture. Surveillance cameras generally utilize a ¹/2" tube in order to keep a lower overall size.

The tubes types generally found in our applications are vidicon, ultracons, and sometimes newvicons. The most common tube is the vidicon because it is also the most inexpensive.

The other two tubes have several advantages over the vidicon, most notably they require much less light in order to operate successfully.

With this in mind, the best buy would seem to be one of the newer tube cameras.

It's not.

In the last few years solid state chips have been replacing tubes in cameras. These chips have many (usually 360,000) "holes" or pixels that each capture a small piece of the scene and then dump it out to the camera circuitry many times a second.

Chips have many advantages over tubes; they do not "burn in," they last years and years, they start up instantly and will not break if the camera is subjected to rough treatment. They do not bloom out or smear as much as their tube cousins do and are small enough to allow sub-miniature camera sizing.

Chips also thrive into the IR area. The same thing is true for the more expensive tubes, they also thrive into the IR area, so if one can interject any sort of extra light, such as an IR light source in the target area, the camera will work better.

How light sensitive are these cameras?

If one puts an IR light source out there, and the target is dealing out of a corner that he thinks is dark, with either a newvicon or chip camera focused on this guy, it's like daylight. That camera will see better than the human eye would in daylight conditions.

Chip resolutions are getting better, the quality of the chips is getting better, and the prices are coming down rapidly.

The real hot news is the fact that several companies have intensified chips on the market including Phillips, Honeywell and Panasonic's Nighthawk. These are Starlight NVD level devices coupled to the chip for viewing in the most faint light imagineable. RCA actually has an intensifier built into the chip itself.

These are still expensive BUT chips are coming in right now from Japan that will take a light level of .093, and instead of $8,000–$9,000, they're down in the $900 area. They do an excellent job and they're completely passive.

As prices fall even further on these cameras it may become more economical to utilize a small camera and handheld or eyepiece camera monitor in place of a normal Starlight scope.

Build your very own NVD for a few hundred bucks, or buy a ready made version from VMI for $1500.

Chip cameras are rapidly replacing tube types and I don't see any reason to consider the purchase of anything else.

Most of the cameras used in surveillance applications are black and white only because there really is no need for the extra expense and bulk of a color unit.

Be sure the camera comes with the lens you want or better yet, it should be equipped with a C mount which accepts almost any video lens.

Most miniature cameras advertised are actually brought in from a couple of Japanese manufacturers—the little circuit board mounted unit sold by almost everyone is in reality a Chinnon, made in Japan. The closer one gets to the source, the better the price, both SHERWOOD and VMI seem to offer good deals on these and other tiny units.

It should also be noted that because this camera is actually mounted directly on a foldable circuit board, it is the unit most often used in expensive re-proportioned camera units like PK's body pack where the boards are unfolded and worn in a hidden belt or vest.

Camcorders are starting to appear in surveillance work, especially the smaller 8 mm based units. Consumer camcorders are really not applicable to this type of work because they do not have interchangeable lenses as do the professional C-mounted camcoders. If one attempts to mount a pinhole or other specialized lens on a fixed lens camcorder the light gathering ability drops off rapidly.

**4.3 mm/3 mm
VERSIONS**
ACTUAL SIZE

**C-MOUNT
VERSION**
ACTUAL SIZE

Monitors and Receivers

Monitors and receivers are being marketed in various sizes including: 1", 2", 3", 4", 5", 7", 9", 13", 14" etc., both in black-and-white and color. Most people like a 9" monitor. It sits right in front of the operator, works well, and is cheap. The 9" monitor is the work-horse of the industry.

Smaller, 2"–4" monitors are also good and can be easily carried onto the job site to help with camera placement. Look for a loop-thru capability so the video can be checked at the site and passed on to the LP.

Tiny one inch monitors are also available for about $100 that are really video camera viewfinders. They also work well for set up, but are a bit small for extended viewing.

One reason these tiny monitors are so good is that they are battery powered. When one's up in the ceiling or setting up something out in the field with the camera, just plug in the monitor, point the camera and focus it; what you see is what you get.

Whenever the signal is hooked into any sort of a transmission device, whatever appeared in the monitor is what will appear back at the homefront. It makes for a nice and easy set up.

Have it in one's kit, put it here, adjust it, check focus, check angles, unhook, run it out.

If the monitor employed does not have look-thru, put a T connector on the back of the camera and wire it into whatever transmission mode is in use. If the camera needs to be rechecked, just go out there and check it without having to unplug anything.

Monitors can be purchased from video suppliers but many people use Sony-like receivers or even Radio Shack units.

Receivers have the ability to pull in signals from the ether, i.e., they have a tuner built in with the monitor. If one is using a wireless transmission system that works in the broadcast spectrum a Sony Watchman® or other tiny receiver handles the set up quite nicely, thanks. The thing about a small monitor is that the picture is going to look better, than on a large one. There are only so many lines and the lines tend to spread out, picture quality isn't going to be better on a bigger monitor. It's really going to be better on a smaller monitor.

Recorders

From the monitor, we need a recorder. A Macy's or Radio Shack $219 home VHS unit will work fine. Plug it into the system and it's great for two, four, six hours. If that's all it's needed for, it's a cheap way to do the job.

Time/date generators can be had for $400 which will add these elements to the recorded tape.

Next step up is a battery-operated unit. A car battery-powered recorder is going to run approximately $1,200 for about 8 hours on a single tape.

EVENT CONTROLLERS AND TIME BOMBS

One of the more important inventive concepts in video surveillance is found in a combination of triggering electronics and time lapse recorders. A video time lapse recorder takes a couple of frames of picture every few seconds (intervals are different on different systems) to effectively compress days of surveillance into hours of video tape.

This allows one recorder to function as a complete video listening post. The best unit on the market, at the time of this writing, is the GYYR. The tapes are compatible with home video systems so the operator can leave it set up, on the job, while he reviews the tapes at a fast speed at home. If something titillating appears that needs clarification he simply takes the tape back to the original machine and watches in the correct time frame.

GYYR's can be hooked up with motion detectors, which will trigger them from time lapse mode into a real time (live) mode.

GYYR's will record 10–30 days of video, and, get this, *10+ days of real time audio* (digitally recorded on a zig zag track) on *one* VHS tape.

This performance is so damn good I would suggest using it for its audio capability alone on a hot surveillance.

SONY even makes a time lapse Camcorder for those in-place, in-case briefcases.

The above units are affectionately called time bombs by those in the business...

SHERWOOD sells a similar bomb known as an event controller. Designed to control a 92-400 recorder it has 10 pin connections for recorder activation by any normally open switch such as timers, wireless activators, PIR, motion detectors, most door contact switches. After activation the unit records anywhere from 10 seconds to 3 minutes or in a manual mode, which runs as the alarm is alive. If the alarm condition ceases to exist the controller stops the VCR and waits for the next event.

These controllers have been used not only in area surveillance, but with wireless, remote starts where the operator watches the target with binoculars and switches the unit on when appropriate. Such controllers can be set up with almost any switch where a violation is expected.

Cheaper UEC's—(Universal Event Controllers)—which are designed to used with any standard VCR to catch intruders are also available. However, there's a four second lag time for the VCR to kick in, unlike time bombs which are instantaneous.

An in-place surveillance can be augmented by an event controller and a camera. Aim the camera at the door, or car to be watched and take a nap. An alarm will alert the staker when the stakee enters the picture.

Literally.

8 mm camcorders are also coming into vogue as surveillance devices because of their compact size and high quality picture. Probably the best deal for the money is SHERWOOD's X-10 unit. This is a C-mount surveillance camcorder with time and date generation. Comes equipped with a 10–140 zoom lens, and a bunch of optional accessories including 12-volt car cords, tapes, pinhole lenses, and a night surveillance module, although the camera itself is extremely sensitive to low light conditions.

VIDEO CAMERA CONCEALMENT

Video cameras, particularly chip cameras, offer unusual opportunities for creative concealment because of their small size and low power requirements. The average size for a surveillance oriented video camera is about the size of a pack of cigarettes including a mini lens and electronic options such a variable iris and sometimes pan and zoom controls.

Cameras do exist that consist of simply one chip with a lens built into the surface, but the price break (at least as this is written) is fairly substantial between the two size category and there's really few placements that would justify the extra expense.

If extreme miniaturization is required the options are to either separate the lens section from the body of the camera or to use a pinhole or fiber optic lens.

It is possible to purchase pre packaged cameras or lens systems from suppliers like VMI, P3, and NEW YORK SECURITY SYSTEMS that arrive in such innocuous containers as, my all time favorite, a fire system sprinkler head that is designed to be mounted on a drop ceiling or will cling magnetically to an overhead water pipe and IS IMPOSSIBLE TO DIFFERENTIATE FROM A REAL SPRINKLER HEAD, a pinhole lens system in a normal car radio antenna, cameras in clocks (often with transmitters along for the ride) fire extinguishers, real emergency light systems, radios, stereos, books, briefcases, garbage cans, fence posts, power transformers, picture frames, pencil sharpeners, looseleaf binders, lamps, exit signs, radar detectors, RFD mailboxes (I realize I'm sometimes prone to exaggeration but I swear this is all true) and a wonderful little unit that is designed to be lowered out the window of a skyscraper to a window directly below where only a tiny (1/2" square) lens port "sees" the entire room in question.

Spytech's cameras come hidden in some of your favorite objects.

If the hidey hole is in anything that is normally plugged into an electric socket the camera and or transmitter will always have power and could be using the building's wiring to broadcast the signal.

AID routinely teaches government agents to hide cameras in bedposts or headboards and incorporate battery packs into the box springs.

I sleep on a futon. A very thin futon...

SPYTECH specializes in cameras hidden in animals (no, no, that's sick, how could you even think that? I'm talking about cuddly little stuffed animals that sit on a girl's bed) and a working television set that watches you back as you watch it.

You may want to consider some of these applications the next time you decide to sell an UZI in a public restroom, steal something from a factory, wonder why a car is sitting outside your window day and night or visit your girlfriend's bedroom...

Remember in the movie 1984 where the TV screen watched the viewer? Do you remember how it ended? — Did it ever end?

THE INTELLIGENCE GROUP in San Francisco makes a number of unusual video products; by disassembling tiny cameras into their component parts they offer a clip-on camera that peers out from a tiny hole in one's breast pocket or on an epaulet. This is wired to a battery powered 900 transmitter that hangs unobtrusively on one's belt.

The package is marketed for cops with an auto on feature that activates everything when a gun or baton is drawn from it's holster but works well for candid civilian videography also.

In a further burst of creativity TIG disassembles industrial 8mm portable record decks, removing the play back head and associated circuitry, ending up with a tiny black box that fits under a vest or in a body harness and records for several hours.

They also feature remote switched briefcases with pinholes lens (totally hidden) power supply and a 900 transmitter that goes a couple hundred feet sans wires. On request, for, ah, export only, they will beef up the transmitter for an extended range of 1/2 a mile.

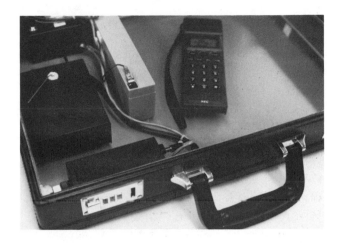

PINHOLES

A unique opportunity for covert viewing, photography or videography is provided by the beast known as a pinhole lens. PL's are tiny (1/10th of an inch to 1/4th of an inch in diameter) lenses which can be attached to the front of any camera, or in some cases, are constructed as an integral part of the camera itself.

Pinholes are designed to reproduce an entire scene through a small hole in some solid barrier. If the unit is to be mounted within the target area, applications could include radios, file cabinets, mounted above dropped ceilings or stashed inside most common appliances.

The lens can also be positioned behind a shared wall with only a minute hole opened into the actual target room. In this case the lens must be snugged tightly against the wall so its entire field of view (usually between 40 and 60 degrees) is passed on to the camera. If the lens is not mounted tightly against the wall a "tunnel" effect occurs that severely limits the FOV and also restricts the amount of incoming light.

Pinhole lenses are configured in a variety of styles, lengths, and speeds. The perfect lens would be tiny, fast and process a large field of view. In reality these factors are in a constant tug of war as the light gathering power of any lens increases times four with a doubling of the lens size.

Recently, very fast (f 1.8) ¼ inch lenses have become available on the general market which sport a good field of view and a high lens efficiency. (True light thru the lens, [t stop] not a measurement of light on the front of the lens [f stop].) These lenses are available in straight or right angle configurations.

Most PL's are fixed focus in design, allowing a reasonable depth of field and a high recognition factor. Some pinholes are now produced with automatic iris control for a variety of lighting conditions.

Most specialty lenses are set up to accept a ²/₃ inch Vidicon camera which works best with moderate to high light levels provided by sunlight or fluorescent/tungsten sources. If the application is one with a lower light level, plan on using a more sensitive Newvicon, silicon, or chip camera which will react to lower levels of light as well as to IR light which allows invisible "boosters" to be secreted in the target area.

These latter cameras do require some sort of auto iris to control the amount of light that reaches the tube/chip either in the camera (electronic or optical) or in the lens itself. A good electronic iris will have a range of 300,000–1 in order to compensate for low light conditions or day-to-night changes.

One problem with the pinhole lens concept is the length of the lens is usually fixed, allowing for little variation in the thickness of the wall that needs to be penetrated. A solution to this is the use of a fiber optic bundle which physically extends the lens to deal with barriers of varying thicknesses as well as allow a smaller (depending on the light available) aperture in the wall itself.

Fiber optic lenses come in either rigid or flexible extensions to take advantage of the territory. Fiber optics, while a wonder of modern surveillance, do not provide quite the picture quality of normal "glass" lenses; small imperfections appear where the individual optic tubes combine the light, and fibers are usually a trifle slower (f4 is average) but they make up for it in the convenience department.

Flexible fiber optic bundles can be twisted around and through obstacles as if they were a double jointed snake with no degradation to the picture quality.

The fastest pinhole lenses (in video applications) are usually those that are built into the camera itself, but the most appreciable will often be an external unit. Pinholes are also available for direct connection to 35 mm still cameras as well as to most film cameras.

One of the very best mounting techniques is to have lens installed next to an overhead light, looking down at the target. When one looks up at a bright light it blurs around the edges because the eye closes down and a person can't see a little hole even if there is a hole there.

If a lens is built into a lamp with some light shining out of it, it will never be seen because the target's eye will shut down every time it goes to the lamp.

The physical drilling of the hole should follow the same techniques as explained in the thru-wall section for audio gathering. If the unit is to be mounted above a dropped ceiling a tiny hole can be quickly made with any sharp object. Pro's will first tack up a hankerchief to catch any particles of ceiling material prior to puncturing the ceiling.

One of the easiest ways to punch a pin hole is to use a nail. In a dropped ceiling push a nail through, put a hankerchief on the ground, crawl up above the panels with a little pen knife, chip around that nail, extract it, move the camera into position, check the monitor, pick up your shavings, and off you go.

Pinhole lenses are constructed with different angles and degrees of fields of view, pick the lens with the correct FOV for any application. A number of charts, including one from VMI, will show exactly how much of a certain room size will be covered with any lens.

This allows one to pre plan the installation by drawing the target room, on a piece of paper and detailing the area to be observed.

Is it towards the far end of the room? A narrow FOV is probably called for, maybe the best place to put the camera is at the other end, using a dropped ceiling approach. One can now place the chart down and find which lens best one for the job and how many degrees it should be angled.

Because the exact placement is already calculated, time in the target room is minimal. Place the camera in the ceiling and it will work.

It requires a very close physical search to uncover evidence of a correctly installed pinhole lens equipped camera.

A wide variety of pinhole lenses and cameras can be obtained from VMI (Visual Mehods Inc.) and SHERWOOD COMMUNICATIONS.

VIDEO TRANSMISSION

Once the camera is in place we still have to get the signal out to our monitor and/or recorder. There are a number of approaches that work well with any camera configuration.

The most common method of transferring a video signal is to use a coax cable. This is the standard video cable that brings Ted Turner and friends into your house. Coax is good because it loses little signal even over long distances. It's also shielded from interference.

Two main types of coax are available for your perusal-RG59 and RG11. RG59 is the smaller diameter of the two and will easily run 800' with most signals. One can just run it, plug it in, and turn it on.

It's possible to go a bit farther but there may be some loss.

RG11 is a very heavy duty cable. It will take a run of about 1500', but it is much heavier to lug around and much more obvious of a transmission medium. It's also expensive.

Other options include 24–22 cable which is like the same size as a microphone cable, in fact, basically it is almost microphone shielded cable. Use it under carpets and around walls. Most people aren't too concerned about it because it really doesn't look like a video cable.

There is a brand new cable out—a mini cable that's extremely thin. It looks like 18 gauge microphone cable ending in some twisted pair. It's not a video camera any more when people

look at it. It's twisted pair so no one expects to find a camera at the other end.

This cable will transmit about 75'.

A TRICK

To get more distance a good trick is to run the mini for a short distance through any sensitive areas and then splice it off about 5–10' away and switch to RG59 and the possible distance will jump up to 500'.

The next way to transmit stuff is with fiber optics. FO's are a marvelous invention, tiny, hair-like plastic tubes that can be bought in pre-cut lengths and the excess just coiled up at the receiving end because the loss rate is so minimal.

Fiber optics will not transmit video signals, they transmit only light, so a transmitter and a receiver unit are needed for both termination points. These units convert the video signal into light by modulating an LED, usually a LASER LED and then pumping the light waves down the tube to the receiver.

Fiber optic cable be run damn near anywhere, on the roof of a building or through a lake, it's will still work. The result is going to be a good picture at the other end, no matter what traumas it has to endure to get there. It works *very* well.

A fiber optic transmitted signal will go for several thousand feet with a good transmitter and receiver. It's a great material to weave into any other cabling run be it telephone, data, or even real power, because these other signals will not interfere with FO's as they might with coax.

Fiber optics transmitter mounted on surveillance camera.

Next we can consider twisted pair. This is the type of "bare" wiring that an intercom or other audio system utilizes. Video can be sent for a relatively short distance over this type of wiring with special transmitters and receivers.

This means one can appropriate available wiring, impose a video signal on it and then splice it off into coax after it leaves the target area.

The coax runs for the distance, so to speak, and the operator lifts the signal off at a safe listening post. Very hard to find; very hard to recognize.

Twisted pair signals can also be transmitted on a dedicated phone line, but this requires the cooperation of Ma Bell. A dedicated line must be specially ordered that doesn't go through normal audio processing equipment which would kill the video component.

Sometimes this works on the first try, sometimes the telco gives you whatever they have available and charges you for a dedicated line.

This does not work so well...

The last possibility is to use normal quality phone lines. Phone lines as they exist right now will simply not deal with the bandwidth of video. The only way around this is to go slow scan. A slow scan transmitter sends a still picture down the wire every couple of seconds, an experience sort of like watching a VCR that is just about to go tits up.

The good news is that SS is an infinite method. We can actually place a camera in Iran, God forbid, if there was any reason to do that, dial the phone number there, open up the connector, sit back and enjoy the show, but in slow scan. Each separate picture takes, depending on the quality, say from 5 to 30 seconds.

Slow scan is available and it's just a matter of using the phone. If one has a camera in Columbia that needs watching, pick up the phone, dial the number, open it up, put the monitor on top of your TV, and while you're watching the 49ers kick the shit out of somebody, you can use the remote to follow your own show.

This is done all the time...

Remember our Radio Shack wireless baby-sitter that uses carrier current to send the little darling's voice through the wall wiring? Now it's possible to transmit video on carrier current arrangement.

Take the CC transmitting unit, BNC it to the camera and, assuming one is on the same side of the power company transformer as is the target, the picture appears on the monitor. It's very easy, works well, and produces a pretty good picture.

VMI sells a carrier current camera and transmitter built into a outlet strip. A common outlet strip. Picks up the signal, tosses it onto the wiring and transmits to the LP. Really a tricky arrangement.

WIRELESS VIDEO

Wireless video surveillance can be accomplished in a variety of ways and means depending on the operator's budget parameters. The FCC has recently okayed the use of the 900 MHz band for low (100 milliwatt) powered video transmission.

This new crop of systems are generally FM in nature and offer quite good transmission qualities as well as strong building penetration and interference rejection characteristics.

These 900 units offer a low cost alternative to super high (GHz) commercial surveillance systems and by mixing them with available VHF units most applications can be easily satisfied. By choosing components, or complete systems, from one of these groups a wide variety of size, power and range requirements can be met.

VLP SYSTEMS

In this case I am referring to that all important electronic term, very low price.

1. Free. Or just about. Put an antenna on the output jack of your VCR. This will radiate the RF signal for a short distance. Some units can achieve ranges of several hundred feet with a good receiver. A camera can be hooked up to the unit to provide "live" action.

Broadcasts on either channel 3 or 4 of the VHF band.

2. Cheap. Use a Radio Shack RF modulator ($30) to modulate the output of a camera, will transmit a short distance.

3. Better. Purchase a 6 meter power amplifier from ham radio suppliers that can be driven by 100 milliwatts of input power and produces several watts of output. Feed the output of one of the above units directly into it.

   This, notably illegal set up, will transmit for several miles, and is also a nice system for use as a signal repeater for low powered transmitters. Do realize that anyone in the vicinity who happens to tune across that channel will also be a party to your impromptu broadcast.

4. Any one of a number of "video distribution" transmitters on the market. These are kind of gray in legality, usually operating directly to a normal television set tuned to a UHF channel, but they are still widely available in consumer mail order catalogs (I believe Sharper Image was induced to stop selling them but some other companies still list the units). Find them in the source section or read the classifieds in *Radio Electronics* and *Nuts and Volts magazines.*

   Battery or AC adapter powered, these units accept composite video from cameras, camcorders or VCR's. Separate audio input. Range, about 100 feet in most environments, range increase of 2–3 times possible by employing a gain (Yagi type) antenna on the receiver.

5. One of the new, legal, 900 MHz transmitter/receiver combinations now on the market. Early entries are the Video Dispatcher from Carol Products, featuring two channel capability, an optional battery pack and a gain antenna for the matching receiver for about $175.

Add another $70 for a high gain antenna for the receiver.

Second choice from VMI simply, yet elegantly titled the wireless video link, it appears very similar to Carol's offering. About $195 or available pre-packaged in a complete point-and-shoot system that the major networks would envy including the transmitter/receiver pair, sub-miniature b/w camera, a wide angle pinhole 6 mm auto iris lens, magnetic camera mount, SONY Watchman® receiver and a choice of 110 or 12VDC power supplies for a mere $795.

Both the above units are a little larger than a pack of cigarettes (transmitter and receiver respectively) and transmit a very clean signal for an unenhanced distance of 120–200 feet. They are not subject to accidental audiences and can be mounted in any of the false front units mentioned in the camera section or directly in radios, TV's, computers, or whatever is at hand.

VMP SYSTEMS

Very Medium Priced systems include more sophisticated technology that still falls in the now legal 900 band and legal low power or legal-if-you-apply-for-a-license higher frequency microwave systems, and a gray area unit or two...

1. AVCOM OF VIRGINIA INC. Offers a very professional microwave transmitter that will be set to the customer's choice of frequencies (in the 4–8 MHz region), transmits color or b/w NTSC video with studio precision and will be "physically recon-figured for concealment in an article of the user's choice."

   The standard xmitter kicks out 100 milliwatts (but can be ordered at higher power levels) which they figure is good for 1/2 mile with a top receiver.

   Experiments have shown that by utilizing a dish and a Yagi antenna on each end of the system it will actually cover several miles of unobstructed, line-of-sight operation. $1900 transmitter only.

The receiver recommended for this system is AVCOM's PSR-1000 ($2450). Rather than a receiver it is actually a 17 pound package which includes a receiver, internal b/w monitor, FM demodulator, signal strength meter, rechargable battery pack and charger.

This unit sports such sophisticated features as continuous, AFC governed tuning and adjustable gain, and a video output to feed large screen monitors. It will run about 2 hours on the internal battery and can be enhanced by outside 12 volt batteries or AC.

A great receiver that produces a signal of such quality that it can be, and is, used for broadcast electronic news gathering organizations.

2. Go to the library and dig out June and July 1989's issues of *Radio Electronics,* build, or pay someone to build for you, their very pleasant 2 watt video transmitter (which requires a license to operate legally) but transmits an easy 2–3 miles on selected channels.

This is also availabe in kit form from North Country Radio, POB 53, Wykagyl Station, New Rochelle, NY 10804 for the extremely reasonable price of $105!

In fact this would rate this unit as a cheap "best buy" by far except it still has to be put together and tuned—not a major, major, job but requires equipment, time, and some knowledge.

Even if construction is farmed out, this device is a deal.

HP TO VHP SYSTEMS

Commercial systems that are designed for surveillance applications include:

1. TRON TEK (law enforcement only, some used units around), offers matched transmitter/receivers operating in either the 400 MHz or 900 MHz ranges. Both units operate approximately the same with the correct antennas although the 900 units require

only half the antenna length of their smaller cousins. The TRON TEK unit pictured is equipped with their flat gain antenna.

Prices are between $2K and $3.4K for the transmitters, the former being a 50 milliwatt b/w unit, the latter a 1-8 watt full color PLL (crystal) unit.

Matching receivers run $1,850.

2. SHERWOOD transmitter, operates on standard television frequencies, 3,000+ foot range. About $4,500.

3. WIRELESS TECHNOLOGY INC. 900 MHz units that feature encrypted signal so only the intended receiver can decode the signal. Expensive.

4. Law enforcement and foreign suppliers like PK and Micro and Security Electronics.

5. P3 video systems that include a number of receivers, gain antennas, one belt mounted transmission system, a video transmitter and receiver mounted in a picture frame, transmitters in books, briefcases, and so on.

An item of passing interest is that law enforcement, or good non LE video transmitters seem to average about $1.00 per foot of range.

6. LASER units. Atmospheric transmission of video and audio signals over LASER beams is now available and offers several advantages over RF systems. LASERS require no license to legally operate and will not interfere with any other form of transmission.

They are also very difficult to locate from a countermeasures standpoint.

The basic LASER system used a beam of infrared (about 820 nm is the average) light which is then focused through a lens system to produce a slightly cone shaped signal to allow for some divergency in aiming.

The transmitters typically use a solid state laser diode to produce the beam which is then modulated by the camera (or microphone). The receiver's lens focuses the received beam on a photo detector where it is demodulated.

Disadvantages include line-of-sight operation with a narrow beam transmission that will be affected by heavy rain, snow or any solid object that comes between the transmitter and the receiver.

Good units are sold by LASER COMMUNI-CATIONS INC. Inexpensive units can be configured from DIJIRO's components.

7. APPLIED SYSTEMS CORP offers a "two domino" sized RF video transmitter that operates from X band to UHF and spreads the signal over a 20MHz wide channel so standard television receivers cannot demodulate it.

Transmitter can be battery or mains powered and operates in the low end of the power scale (around 20 mW) and requires its own receiver to pick up the signal.

Tron Tek law enforcement video transmitter and receiver.

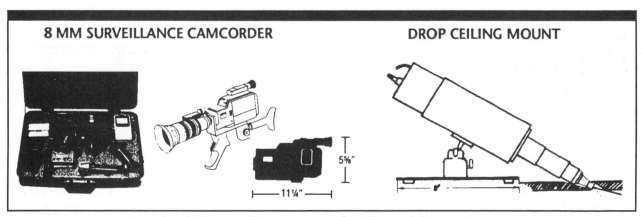

Samples of video surveillance equipment from Sherwood Communications.

NIGHT VISION

Simply stated, the problem is to see in the dark. Humans have limitations imposed by our biology, and we're able to see things only at a certain light level. To do otherwise requires a system of electronic enhancement.

The person responsible for the idea behind night vision devices (NVD's) was none other than the man who gave us the idea of curved space and the atomic bomb, among other things—and the survey says—Alfred Einstein.

He discovered that if he took a piece of matter, and if hit it with a ray of light, it could be induced to give off electrons.

Atoms consist of both positive and negative particles and when a ray of light strikes some atoms they take on the extra energy provided by the light and free up an electron. After this theory was discovered someone else decided it might just be possible to actually start a flow of electricity using light energy.

The people who came up with the very first infrared devices tested materials until they got an element with this property. Next they were able to find a wave length of light that was particularly useful in this application, and they were able to cause electrons to jump from one spot from a negatively charged electrode to a positively charged electrode. At the positive electrode a phosphorescent screen was added and the first infrared device was born.

Hook a battery up and charge the screen to a positive value and the electron gains energy when it bounces off. When it runs into a phosphorescent screen it actually gives off light.

In this process light energy being transferred to electrical energy and then as it hits the phosphorescent screen it back to light.

The first practical uses of this old infrared technology dates back to the time of about the second World War, it is now known as zero generation night vision.

Some of these early goggles are still available from several suppliers. They are advertised as Israeli surplus night vision goggles, and sell for about $400. The only way these things are able to function in today's environment is if the operator provides a very bright IR light source.

Next the engineers came up with a better device by changing the metallic substance. Some substances, when placed on a photo cathode changed all light, include the visible variety, into moving electrons.

They were then able to activate a phosphorescent screen, and see the other image on the other side.

Two major areas of concern remained: Most light, even in daylight, was too weak to kick loose enough electrons to make the unit function, a system for amplifying the available light was required.

The other problem was that as the electrons bounced around they acted incoherently, scattering their energy unless the plates were placed almost on top of each other or the electrical potential was dramatically increased.

Easy in theory, this proved difficult off the drawing board. When the engineers put too much electricity in, they got an arcing effect that obliterated the whole night vision system.

Next they tried a system using a couple of different photo cathodes.

If one could take these electrons and take the light energy and convert it to more moving electrons one could actually take these electrons and use them to daisy chain the effect by knocking off more electrons which in turn could be used to knock more loose from another plate and cascade into a large stream of electrons.

The first generation of actual night vision devices used a cascading effect and several image intensifying phases combined—a three phase system. This provided a system that had an incredible gain factor of some 65,000+ times.

These units we packaged in the late 50's and early 60's and allowed a human eye to actually view objects in near darkness, hence the nickname starlight scopes. An amplification factor of 75 or 80 thousand times will turn medium level starlight into daylight as surely as magic.

The main problem in this technology was in keeping the electrons straight as they bounced off the multiple photo cathodes. With each subsequent hit the electron's spatial relationship tended to deteriorate. In order to cascade and still maintain an actual image rather than just a gathering of electrons coming out the other end, a way had to be found to make each of these little electrons run a straight line.

Not to say these early starlight scopes were useless—far from it. First generation units performed several duties quite well.

A first gen unit allowed the operator to see infrared just like the zero generation systems but it also translated and amplified white (all color) light by the same factor of 65,000–100,000 times. First generation night vision devices are characterized by this outstanding gain. They are also characterized by a three phase intensifier and resolution problems.

Another problem with first gen units is the tendency to bloom. If all the electrons emanating from one collision initially in the photo cathode are suddenly made available, and if a bright light suddenly appears, say a car headlight, both a resolution and a blooming problem become quickly evident. When something overloads the system, there's nothing to compensate and the image is wiped out.

These units were widely used in Vietnam Nam and did provide some help in dark situations because they amplified both IR and normal light to a great degree even if they were bulky and had some built in problems.

The early success of these units cast the die for the next step. Enter generation 2—a very significant leap in the idea of night vision.

Several government agencies, partially funded by the military, coordinated their efforts in order to maintain the high amplification factor while losing some of the negative aspects of the three stage, first gen, units.

The concept that won out was to guide the electron inside a very small tube as it passes from the photo cathode where it was created all the way to the phosphorescent screen where it would be viewed. This would seem to maintain objective coherence of the image by taking each electron in hand, so to speak.

This idea was tried and a new factor came into the fray. The tubes could actually free up additional electrons. If one electron went in it bounced against the glass wall, and actually liberated several more.

All of a sudden, in this little glass tube where one electron entered there would be 20,000 exiting the other side. The down side was the problem of keeping these little glass guides perfectly straight, but small enough to be practical.

The solution came in the form of a micro channel plate. This is a doughnut shaped piece of ground, very hard glass. In the center, in the hole, there's a very soft chemically active type of glass inserted. The two are heated together, and they start to flow they are drawn out. At this point the glass can be pulled down into very fine pieces of glass "wire."

Bear in mind that the two types of glass maintain the same integrity even in the fine fiber optic wire as they did in the original relationship. Next one puts about 3,000 of these are put together in a hexagonal shape. After that's done, 3,000 of the finished product are put together in another hexagonal shape and it's drawn again.

In a finished micro channel plate there are 1-1/2 million of these tiny single draws.

The micro channel plate is then polished and treated with a aluminized substance for electrical contact.

The target gives off the electrons just like before but now they go into our micro channel plate where each one brings out many more. Each one of the little holes in the micro channel plate is offset about 5 degrees in order to guarantee a collision every time an electron goes inside.

Put a phosphorescent screen at the end and there's a visible image with good gain and high resolution.

This is what constitutes a second generation unit. A photo cathode that is very sensitive to all the different colors of the spectrum including infrared and a micro channel plate that maintains the spatial relation between all the different electrons while creating an amplification factor of about 20,000 times.

Second generation devices were small enough to put in night vision goggles with one image intensifier in front of each eye and create a system that's much more compact than their first generation counterparts, but it won't quite produce the gain that the first generation device was able to offer. Okay for viewing, but not great for photographic purposes or sighting a rifle accurately.

About 1980 the FBI decided to tackle the problem head on.

The designers went back into the laboratories and figured out how to increase the electrical potential involved for more gain and more collisions in order to end up with brighter images on the phosphorescent screen.

These are known as 2 ½ generation units.

So what's the cutting edge now? Third generation is almost a copy of the second generation types except that the photo cathode, the thing that actually produces the flow of electrons in the first place is galieum aluminum, arsenide.

When a photon of light comes in and hits this new and improved photo cathode, it gives off more electrons resulting in more gain, and greater sensitivity.

What is the true electron gain? In second generation plus figure about 18,000–20,000, in third generation there is around 25,000–28,000, figure an increase of nearly 35%.

What is the actual light gain between what the naked eye would see and what the NVD will allow?

Maybe 2,000 times…

Why do these numbers seem weak compared with the ads for units with their gain figures listed as 65,000 or 70,000 times?—They lie.

Litton, the largest manufacturer of light amplification tubes lists their products as follows: Second plus—actual light gain of approximately 1,800–2,000. Their second generation pocket scope, boasts a true gain of approximately 1,800–2,000 times. The image that you see in your pocket scope is approximately 1,800–2,000 brighter than what you would see without the night vision pocket scope.

It is possible to have an ELECTRON gain in the multi thousands as the electrons elicit their mirror images from the micro channel plate tubes, but the actual LIGHT gain is limited to 1,800–2,000 times.

As this is written third gen is still new, read expensive, but they are available. However, one might find that a third generation device is overkill fo rmost applications unless one is operating in an environment that offers NO ambient city lights, no moon, and only faint starlight. Under normal surveillance activities the additional cost may just not be justified.

The two standard tube sizes are 18 millimeter and 25 mm.

Besides tube gain, another oh so important factor is that of resolution. If a tube does not maintain the spatial relationship between the loose electrons in the micro channels the operator will simply not be able to make out the resulting image.

Resolution is listed in line pairs per millimeter. This is gauged by looking at a video line pair chart until the lines run together. The resulting number is the resolution of the unit.

In a good second or third second gen tube one should be able to differentiate between 28 - 30 line pairs per millimeter.

The most practical piece of equipment for general, non-photographic, nocturnal viewing is a pair of night vision goggles, these units offer a "hands off" approach to nocturnal viewing. Unlike most handheld or front end acquisition units, goggles do not offer a choice of lenses or any image amplification. One to one. In other words, what one would see with an unaided eye distance-wise is what is seen with goggles. This is the reason they can be used for driving or walking.

The "hot" goggle system is the Ambus system of aviator's night vision goggles. These are designed to allow pilots to fly helicopters in almost flat-out darkness and come in both third and second generation configurations.

A third generation type of Ambus system at military spec levels will set the household budget back between $15,000 and $16,000. Second generation plus runs $9,000–$10,000.

Goggles are composed of three separate sections: the objective lens, the tube, and the ocular lens. The front end is an objective lens which takes the light in. The tube, or tubes are buried behind the lens then there is an ocular lens that one looks through to see the image. Most NVD's utilize a green colored screen simply because the original phosphor used was green in color and it worked.

Besides this sense of nostalgic inertia, green happens to be the easiest color for the eye to work with, the easiest and most pleasant color for the human eye to assimilate.

One of the first things one will notice after using a pair of goggles for a few minutes is one's eyes don't seem to function correctly when the goggles are removed.

When wearing night vision goggles at night it's like having two little TV screen lights right in the eye causing the iris to close down to accommodate those little lights. When the goggles are removed it takes about 20 minutes for the eye to adjust to the dark and open up again.

Goggles do have a built in depth perception conundrum. The human eye has the ability to automatically adjust from near to far but a static lens does not. Lenses simply cannot do a running adjust when the operator looks up, down or from a object close at hand to infinity.

Goggles offer two adjustments to compensate for the human eye—the first adjustment is simply an ocular adjustment—eye glass adjustment. It's called a diopter adjustment and will compensate for the operator's need or lack of need for eye glasses. It is only set once for each operator.

The second adjustment is on the front end and is for distance. To look anywhere beyond six feet, one sets it to infinity but it's impossible to go from distance to close up without making an adjustment. This can initially cause a bit of a depth perception problem if one is attempting to walk and suddenly looks up into the distance. Once one becomes used to this phenomenon one can drive a car, a tank, or a plane without too much difficulty.

There is talk about bifocal goggles appearing in the near future.

Original night vision goggles used two of everything—two tubes, two lenses, etc. The new stuff runs both eyes through one tube in a single tube biocular arrangement. There are several advantages to the new system, the first being the fact that it is considerably lighter than the double tube version.

There's really no difference in resolution between double and single tube goggles, nor any difference in FOV. What there is is a difference in redundancy. If a tube goes out and it's a two-tube goggle, there's still one left. On a single tube goggle, you are sorta outta luck. The single tube goggle was strictly a cost saving device that was evolved by the United States government because they wanted to buy a lot more goggles on the same budget.

Both types of goggles offer the same field of view, 40 degrees. This is a bit limiting for some people but it works well enough after the operator becomes used to dealing with the narrow viewpoint. The military likes to employ three people at once on patrols with NVD's so they share a common 120 degree FOV, however 40 degrees is quite sufficient for most purposes.

Remember, first gen was the Vietnam era scopes and goggles. Second gen brought miniaturization as well as improvement with about the same gain. Next came 2 1/2 units with automatic brightness control and other advantages, now we have gen number 3.

There *is* a difference between gen 2 ¹/₂ and third gen at night, no question about it. Whether the price is justified remains to be seen. On the darkest nights there's about a true 10% difference between gen 2 ¹/₂ and gen 3.

This makes 3 worth every cent as far as complicated tasks like flying a helicopter are concerned but most people can drive a vehicle just as well on either model.

In photography, nine times out of 10, at this point gen 3 equipment will not justify the price.

When one wears goggles or any other night vision device, there are times when some areas that are absolutely too dark to see. There has to be some available ambient light for any starlight type scope to work.

IR ENHANCEMENT

To combat this problem modern goggles come equipped with an infrared light source. A little infrared LED that can be switched on when extra light is required. This will effectively illuminate a distance of about six to ten meters in front of the operator. This LED is an active IR source which means if someone else had an NVD it would literally be like the other person had a flashlight turned on, highlighting his position. This is an important factor in using an IR source in any situation where someone else may be looking back for one reason or another.

A more efficient IR source is an infrared laser. It can be mounted on the NVD, or utilized separately but it will enhance any NVD like magic. Dark Invader systems come with their own, personal, IR LASER. It projects an infrared beam, a very tight light, to a distance of about 1 and one half miles. This means it is possible to illuminate a target at night and see it better with goggles than one could on a clear day.

If one were to use a sighted LASER correctly mounted on a rifle, one could, hypothetically speaking, shoot more accurately than one could in daylight.

A LASER dot will increase its size with distance, a good feature for observation or photography. A typical beam will be about six inches

wide at 100 meters and a full 30 inches at 500 meters. Double the distance, double the size.

It's quite easy to adapt a commercial IR laser for NVD use. Fairly powerful lasers are available from a number of listed sources.

A second option is to use a very bright, non-coherent light source.

Very powerful (in the millions of candle power) dedicated IR spotlights are available from PEAK BEAM and MEGABEAM companies and used by the military among others.

Most infrared lights have a red eyeball. If someone lines up directly with it, it's going to be visible, especially in dim conditions. If a target is looking for it, he's going to spot it.

The other option is to use an interference filter which passes only the IR spectrum. These can be put over flashlights, spotlights, or just about any source of white light. That is a good way to do enhanced photography of specific items like license plates.

Years ago most military vehicles had IR headlights attached. They had an extra set of headlights that were infrared and the operator wore an old time pair of goggles and "saw" at night.

It's also possible to mount an IR strobe (for still photography) in a room and trigger it just when one needs to snap a photo or even trigger it occasionally to provide a quick enhanced glimpse of the room without too much chance of discovery. Take a hint from the DEA and the FBI, both of whom will do just about anything to get a guy inside a room or a building rather than outside where they can access an enhanced IR source.

Another trick drug agents use, if they know an outside meet is going down, is to go out rig IR lights to illuminate that street corner in advance and not have to bring the equipment along, then they use a radio signal to turn the source on when needed.

It is quite possible to get conviction level photography with an NVD-equipped camera and an IR source. It's just a question of getting set up for it.

For the widest variety of applications one should consider a modular NVD. This type will break down into elements. Most systems will use a variety of camera lenses, by employing a C mount or an adapter to mate with common camera lenses to allow any degree of image amplification. If normal is 25 millimeters, 50 will provide two power, 100, four and so on.

The middle section of a modular NVD unit is the light intensifier tube itself. The backend can be an eyepiece or a screen for direct observation or a relay lens directly to a video camera or onto most popular still cameras.

For any photographic application bear in mind that the quality of the lenses is extremely important. Stay with the fastest lens you can afford—for photographs that need to be ID'ed the lens should have a speed of under 2.5. Sometimes it will be necessary to get down around 1/15th of a second or 1/30th of a second of exposure, and the unit will have to be steadied or tripod mounted.

Do NOT use fast film in a NVD camera—the backend image, the one to be photographed is actually quite bright.

There is no magic to night photography—understand that there has got to be some ambient light, if enhancement is needed one can hook some type of infrared light to the camera.

THERMAL OR FAR IR...

There is a second type of IR viewer that is rapidly coming into vogue, the thermal viewer. This device detects and displays changes in heat (far IR). Sensitive units will show differences of 1/10th of a degree.

Thermal measures minute temperature differences to 1/10th of 1 degree but not light. It will not see through anything solid, but if a target is hiding behind a rock or a bush, his heat signature may radiate around the edges and through the gaps in the foilage.

In fact in the latter application the body outline can usually be seen and a thermal camera can be used in day or night conditions.

How effective is thermal imaging? Remember a few years ago when the Israelis were able to shoot tank rounds at terrorists in a building without destroying any other part of the structure?

Today M1A1 tanks no longer shoot with anything except a thermal sight and the Israelis have stopped night patrols in fire zones. They simply bring tanks up, turn the thermal sights on, and anything moving out to 2,000 meters gets killed. If it moves, they shoot it. An operator can tell if it's an animal or a human being by its thermal "fingerprint."

Both the U.S. and British armies use a hand-held thermal unit that will detect a human at over 1 mile from the operator. While the unit will not allow individual recognition, it will show if the person is holding a weapon.

These units will also show where a person was, or a hot vehicle was operated until the area returns to the ambient temperature level. It is actually possible to take a "picture" of a person 10 minutes after they have left the area.

How to Tail Anyone, Anywhere

The technique of tailing a subject, either on foot or in a vehicle, really hasn't changed too much since the movies of Bogart and Bacall. The first and most important rule is simple: don't get burned.

Any pro will tell you it is better to lose a subject than to have him realize he is the object of surveillance. This is true in 98% of all surveillance, moving or stationary.

Successful single tailing requires extreme caution and quite a bit of practice. Carry enough money on your person to cover any unexpected transportation hassles and always bring along a grab bag of identity-alternating paraphernalia such as:
— Quick removal ties
— A reversible jacket
— Wig
— Glasses, sun glasses
— Wig, hat
— Bright tee shirt, plain dress shirt
— and so on…

Tradecraft includes avoiding eye contact with the subject at all costs, using any means possible (such as the reflections in store front windows) to watch the subject without exposing yourself.

The only way to learn to follow someone is to follow someone. Start on unsuspecting subjects and concentrate on blending in with the crowd, note the difference in following someone in a fast (busy) area as opposed to a slow one.

Practice using space and time concepts, i.e., gauging the distance a particular subject will cover in a given amount of time. If he turns a corner and is no longer in sight you must be able to judge whether he had enough time to cover the space to the next corner.

If not, chances are he turned into a building on the block in view and the correct procedure would be to stop and wait for him to reappear.

Practice with "live" subjects. Have them walk a route that has been planned in advance and have them decide afterwards if they were indeed being followed. Can they describe their shadows? Where and how did they spot them?

The key to telling if someone is following you is to act naturally but use selected vantage points—windows in a building, high bridges, hills—anything that allows one to observe the route just taken in order to see if anyone is duplicating movements, if anyone is waiting for someone to come out from the viewpoint building…

If one or more of the same faces seem to be around after you have covered some distance and checked at least two vantage points, break the coincidence factor by getting on a bus or taking a taxi somewhere and immediately look back from a new vantage point.

At this point familiarty breeds contempt.

The actual mechanics of tailing include the A,B,C method favored by government agencies where two watchers tail the subject and one parallels him. If the operation is via automobiles the parallel can actually be on the next block. Exchanges are made at natural break points, or when the subject stops or slows down. The watcher in the rear position moves up to cover the immediate rear while the in-place man drops back to distance himself.

If and when the subject turns or crosses an intersection the parallel watcher switches places with the back man.

With practice this method can become quite fluid and a good team can box in any but the most elusive subject.

In that case the team should revert to a completely parallel operation, matching the target's speed one street over, and speeding up to catch a glimpse at intersections, following the target directly only when absolutely necessary.

Some form of radio communication is almost mandatory for ANY kind of successful tailing mission. Portables are preferable to automobile console models because they will allow watchers to be shifted in and out of cars as required.

For years the G-Men used handhelds with a separate microphone taped to their wrists just under a jacket sleeve, running the earphone wire under their clothes, exposing it for just a few inches between the collar and the ear.

Today there are several good types of wireless (usually bone conductive) earphone/microphone combinations that fit directly INSIDE the ear itself. Coupled with a VOX operated radio this allows hands-and-microphone-free communications.

Large watch teams combine auto and foot surveillance to avoid detection. If the subject takes evasive action, or turns a corner and stops to see what follows, a jogger or bicyclist is unlikely to generate the same attention as a brown Plymouth sedan with two antennas on the roof.

This system requires a number of watchers, radios, logistic considerations and at least one chase car to pick up any watchers who have pulled foot duty and need to be moved forward to keep the general scheme alive and working.

If a vehicle is to be used for auto surveillance a simple set of switches can be rigged to turn off various lights on the outside of the car to make it appear to be several different vehicles, at least at night.

Another useful trick is to mark the subject vehicle in a manner which will aid the track team. Quick and simple methods include adding reflective bumper stickers or pieces of reflective tape to the rear of the vehicle or damaging one of the tail lights.

Night tailing can be greatly enhanced by secreting a miniature IR flasher ($50, the batteries last a couple of days) under the vehicle or even behind the bumper and then using a night scope to pick up the IR spotlight effect of the flasher.

Although most effective in the dark, this method can be used in the daytime by using an IR viewer instead of a starlight scope, or by stopping the iris of the more sensitive viewer down, or using a neutral density filter to let very little light into the tube. No flasher handy? Keep a couple of CYLUME IR chemical light tubes in your kit. Shake and break and the result is an IR dye marker that will easily be "read" by a 'scope.

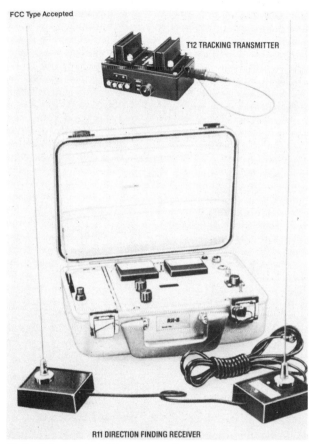

Typical electronic tailing system from COI.

An inexpensive and throughly ingenious system of following a vehicle is illustrated below.

The concept is a sure fire winner—a mechanically- or electrically-stimulated tank of some nice water-based paint that is allowed to drip onto a rear tire when the vehicle is in motion, leaving behind a trail of footprints that even Hansel and Gretel could follow.

While the intent involved is A1, the follow-through on this particular project was a little weak. The device was marketed by a company before its (the company's not the product's) time had come. Checks were cashed, bills not paid, and orders, were, apparently never filled.

It wouldn't take a mechanical genius, however, to bolt a couple of magnets to a can containing watercolor paint or even IR cylume liquid with a small hole drilled in the can to allow the substance to drip out at the crucial time. A small drawstring cork taped to the wheel could initiate the process at the first sign of motion.

In a quick spot an oil can could be taped in the wheelwell to at least provide an assist.

If a particular subject needs to be followed to a particular place that he frequents it is possible to follow him/her for a short distance every day, picking the tail up sequentially each day until the final destination is reached.

This progressive surveillance is only for the patient but is effective and quite hard to detect.

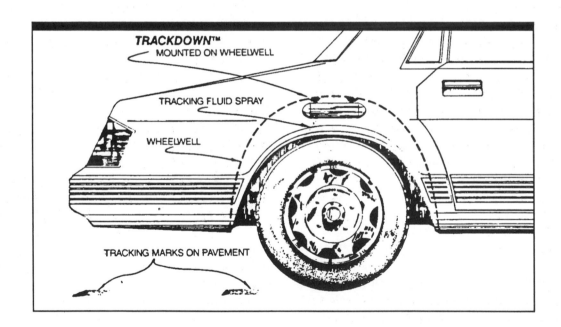

TRACKDOWN™
MOUNTED ON WHEELWELL

TRACKING FLUID SPRAY

WHEELWELL

TRACKING MARKS ON PAVEMENT

A TRICK

If a watcher needs to know the exact time a vehicle leaves a parking spot, a cheap mechanical watch can be placed under a tire where it will be mashed when the car moves, recording, permanently, the time of departure.

The following section is a re-printed article, by permission of the author, Steve Uhrig, because, frankly, it's the best article I've ever seen on the subject of electronic tracking systems, and Steve (dba SWS Security) is one of the top experts/ consultants on this type of gear in the world.

VEHICLE TRACKING SYSTEMS, ARE THEY FOR YOU?

Bumper beepers, bird dogs, tracking systems, direction finders, homing devices, whatever name we know them by we're all talking about the same thing. Though the name is misleading (I'll explain later), around here we refer to the generic line of tracking systems as bumper beepers. Bear with me if I unconsciously default to that name even where something else might be more appropriate.

What are we talking about? In a nutshell, bumper beepers are electronic packages that assist you in following successfully a vehicle under surveillance. A quality unit, specifically designed for covertly tracking a moving vehicle, and operated by someone who knows what he's doing, will let the operator hang a considerable distance behind the target vehicle and indicate what direction to travel in order to stay behind him.

If you're an active investigator, in either the public or the private sector, these devices are one of the most useful investments your agency can make.

How do YOU run a vehicle surveillance? Two investigators (money), two cars (money), two radios (money)? Somebody either within sight of the target, or both of you at either end of the street covering two possible directions of travel?

If the Target leaves and one of you has to turn around, what happens if you get stuck behind Mr. or Mrs. Elmer Grope or their grandmother, all of whom are going to cop a prima donna attitude that the whole rest of the world is also going to observe the 20 MPH residential speed limit?

Suppose the target is suspicious and uses the rear view mirror that God and Detroit (or Japan?) gave him? You have your choice of either being made or dropping back far enough to where the subject might be lost.

Forget the entire concept if you get caught at a long light, involved in heavy traffic, complicated intersections, or if the target cuts behind the 7-11 for a few minutes to evade any possible tail.

Underground parking? Residential garage? Evasion? 90 MPH... Forget it, I've been there too...

Bumper beeper packages consist of a transmitter which usually is affixed magnetically to the car under surveillance, and a companion receiver which will tell you certain things about the conditions between the transmitter and the receiver. Cheap units, usually the imports selling for $500 to maybe $2500, will give you a tone of sorts which will tell you only if you are moving closer or further away from the target.

Better units will indicate, by either a zero center meter or a series of lights, where the target vehicle is located in reference to your vehicle. All units which indicate a bearing also will give you a relative range. Properly applied and used, a real beeper (real meaning not a toy, which comprises virtually all of the cheapies widely promoted to private detectives) will let you stay far enough behind the target to be well beyond visual range. By glancing at the receiver's meter panel every so often as you drive, you will know quite a bit about where the target is.

If the meter is hanging around center, you're doing fine. If you start to see a definite indication of right or left, slow down and pay attention to where the target might have made a turn. The closer you get to the turn the more solid will be the left or right meter indication. No longer will you have to take a chance at a 4-way intersection if you've lost sight of the target. If the target has turned, you'll see it on the meter well before you get to the intersection. The meter will start pulsing to the right (or left), ending up pinned to one side or the other as you approach the turn.

By the same token, if the target slides off behind a building or onto a side street in an attempt to evade surveillance, you'll see that in enough time to take the appropriate action.

With a beeper, you won't have to worry any longer if you get caught at a light. If you're far enough behind the target to where he has time to park in a garage-no problem. With a bit of practice, your unit will take you right up to the garage door.

Sounds great, doesn't it? As I mentioned earlier, vehicle tracking systems are one of the greatest products ever developed for investigative use.

Modern electronic investigative goodies are nice, can save you thousands of dollars and hundreds of investigator hours as well as enhance your reputation as being the man who gets things done, however to use an analogy that's usually applied to weapons, just because I give you a violin doesn't mean that you are a musician.

The same holds true with bumper beepers. The units work, and they work well, but a certain amount of training and understanding of what the system is doing is necessary in order to be successful in following a vehicle.

I have a hard time getting this across to some of the investigators who call me and want a unit shipped overnight for a surveillance starting up tomorrow.

You're NOT going to open up the box, read enough of our instruction manual to figure out how to install the batteries and go out and follow a car around town. This thing will NOT tell you the direction to the transmitter.

It doesn't know that. What it will indicate is the direction(s) from which it is receiving the signal. Due to numerous factors involving physics and radio propagation characteristics, you can hope that the signal is arriving from the same direction as the transmitter but you can't count on it, the point I'm trying to make is that, regardless of what many salesmen of these devices would have you believe, a certain amount of training is mandatory in order to get the most out of your new tracking system.

If you do buy a unit, plan on spending several hours reading not only the technical manual for the unit, but some information on radio direction finding in general. Knowing just a bit of the theory of direction finding (which is what the bumper beepers really do) will help you get much more out of the unit.

Don't try to use a tracking system, without cracking the books or you'll be disappointed with the results and probably blame the equipment. Remember we have a relatively pipsqueak transmitter (pipsqueak due to low power, less than optimum antenna and a crummy location buried underneath steel just a few inches from ground) trying to squeeze a signal into the twin antennas mounted on the roof of your car.

The signal from the transmitter bounces off every natural and man made object. Imagine a flashlight in a hall of mirrors. If the light is weak, and there's many mirrors to reflect the signal, you'll see hundreds of images.

The only way to find your way to the flashlight is to walk towards the strongest reflection and hope you can pick out the actual flashlight from there.

So it is with tracking systems. In busy downtown areas, with many high buildings, overhead wires, and bridges, you will have to settle for a bit less performance than if you were in the suburbs or the country.

Fortunately in the city you can usually hang closer to the target without being spotted, so the reduction in range is not too serious a problem.

There is even a partial solution to the problem of reflections, or as they are really known "multipath."

Most tracking receivers have an audio output. Our unit (SWS) has an internal speaker as well as a headphone jack. When you're experiencing multipath, you'll hear it as a raspy tone from the transmitter instead of a pure audio note.

A pure audio tone is an excellent confidence builder that usually means you are hearing the beeper transmitter directly, and it should be music to your ears.

Raspiness is caused by several reflections arriving at the antennas at almost the same time. You'll also notice the needle on the bearing indicator acting a bit squirrely. The overall average, as shown on the meter, will *usually* be correct unless you're in a real difficult situation, maybe the target is over a hill from you, or you're in an artificial "tunnel" (at least as far as radio waves are concerned).

If a hill is in the way the signal from the transmitter will go around it rather than through it. An artificial tunnel might be a city block where high buildings surround you on all sides, and the target is a few blocks off to one side.

Again, picture a light shining and all buildings and other objects as mirrors, which they are to radio waves. In an artificial tunnel the tracking system will point to one end or the other, regardless of where the transmitter is actually located. If the signal is banging off buildings the best you can do is proceed in the direction of the strongest signal. From there you will have an excellent chance of acquiring the target directly.

By the way, if you ever lose the target and really have no idea where to start looking beat feet for high ground, maybe a bridge or hill that overlooks the area. In most cases, if you don't waste too much time, you'll reacquire the target pretty easily

If all else fails, head in the target's last known direction and start driving in a grid pattern or an increasing spiral with your unit set to maximum sensitivity and you'll stand a pretty good chance of locking on to the target again. Don't treat bearings taken when you are not moving as gospel. Many, if not most, of the multipath errors will average out with motion. Keep moving if you hear a lot of multipath through the speaker of your receiver (remember multipath sounds raspy).

Your tracking receiver should have some means of reducing its sensitivity. We have found that better results are obtained with WEAKER, not stronger signals in these situations.

A decent beeper receiver designed for investigative use will track accurately on signals that are inaudible through the speaker, so if things get difficult, keep the sensitivity at the absolute minimum necessary to get a definite indication on the meter. As long as the meter is reading, don't worry that you can't hear the beep through the speaker.

You'll have to use your unit enough to know how to tweak it for best results. In most cases even when there are a lot of reflections the *true* signal will still be the strongest, so if you keep the unit tuned down to where it only hears the strongest signals it will help keep the confusion from multiple reflections to a minimum.

If you're out of sight of the target, keep relying on the indications from the beeper receiver until you actually see the target. You will experience many false bearings towards the end because of all the strong signals. This situation can make it easy to overshoot the target.

For some reason, (*ed. note: bad karma?*) whenever I overshoot I get tied up in a maze of one-way streets, long lights, etc. By this time the target is several blocks away and there's a mad rush to reacquire and get back on track. Vehicle tracking is like anything else in investigative work, hours of boredom followed by minutes of pure terror.

Some tracking systems give 180 degree performance and some even offer 360 degree. What this means is that the 360 units will track on targets both in front of you and behind you although the 180 degree systems will only indicate correctly on targets in front of your vehicle. It is possible to make a 180 act like a 360 with a little technique—first, though, let's look at the major differences between the two.

If cost or covert operation is not a factor, buy a 360. A 360 will cost you almost twice what a 180 will and a 360 unit also requires FOUR antennas to be mounted on the roof of your vehicle where a 180 only requires two. These antennas will eventually need replacing just from ordinary wear and tear, especially if the unit is frequently moved from car to car. The coax cables always seem to go first, probably because everybody squashes the cable when they roll the window up on it or close the door on it. Remember the antennas are magnetically mounted on the roof of your car.

If you are using two antennas (with a 180 system) mount them left and right on the roof, with a single cable that enters the car on the driver's side. A 360 system requires four antennas mounted in a cross pattern on the roof (one left, one right, one front and one rear).

If you're trying to be covert, 4 antennas on the roof will not help the cause. Two antennas, with the 180 unit, aren't invisible either but two are a lot easier to swallow than 4.

There are tracking systems with low profile antennas, but they are VERY expensive and the manufacturer could care less about any clients who are not federal government with unlimited budgets. Don't kill yourself trying to spring the extra money for a 360 unit unless you really need that one feature of being able to track accurately both ahead of you and behind you. A 180 will do just fine if you understand the concepts involved. If you're totally ignorant maybe a 360 would be worth the bucks, but remember what we said about merely owning the equipment as opposed to knowing how to use it. In my business I can own anything I feel like buying, and my own personal tracking system is a 180.

That should tell you something. If you have a 180 unit, the position of the meter (left or right) will indicate in which direction you need to proceed in order to close in on the target. Remember, ALWAYS TURN INTO THE NEEDLE.

You might want to write this in red magic marker on the front of your unit. If the needle is pointing left, the box is telling you that the target is to the left of your vehicle. By steering left, the needle should approximately center as you get onto the right bearing.

Now listen carefully, this next part is important, especially for 180 system users. If you turn into the needle, and the meter starts reading OPPOSITE of what you expect, meaning you

headed left and the needle moved even more to the left rather than toward the center, then the target is BEHIND you. The meter will be also be centered 180 degrees away from the target, but the needle motion will reverse.

If you always turn in the direction the meter pointer indicates, and the needle moves BACKWARDS from the direction you turn, then you are correct. This is a very important concept as you will get really messed up if the target ends up behind you and you don't realize it.

Also, by visualizing this, you can make a 180 unit do virtually everything a 360 does, and save 4 or 5 thousand dollars in the process.

One last time, turn into the needle. If doing that tends to center the needle you are on track. If you turn into the needle and it moves away from center then the target is probably behind you. After a bit of practice all this will be second nature.

Thank you.

Any tracking receiver, no matter how good, can be confused by other antennas or objects on the same roof as its antennas. Try to keep the roof of your car clear of other communications gear while you are involved in direction finding. Unscrew the CB antenna. Work off a portable for the duration of the surveillance. If you're tracking from a vehicle that is equipped with a light bar, mount the antennas on top of it, or in front if you can't get on top for some reason. A certain private investigator of our acquaintance drives one of those Morocco Mole cars with a plastic roof. Of course the magnet mount antennas won't stick to it so he does just fine with the antennas on the hood of the car. Looks funny but does the job.

We tried attaching the antennas to a metal plate and securing the plate with bungie cords to the rain gutters but we gave up on that and just stuck them on the hood.

Antennas count on a large mass of metal underneath of them for proper performance, so range will be considerably reduced if you try to mount them on a non metal surface.

The same thing also goes for vinyl roofs. The antennas will work OK electrically, but the magnet will not hold very well through vinyl. If the antennas slide around on the roof you will get wrong bearings on your tracking receiver. In a two antenna system, one antenna should be marked "left" or coded somehow so you know which antenna goes on which side of the vehicle.

Our unit has a label on it which always points to the rear of the car. Do NOT get these reversed or the system will lie to you. Read your instructions. You don't have a 50/50 chance of getting them right, you have a 50% chance of getting them right and a 90% chance of getting them wrong. If the antennas are backwards your bearings as indicated on the meter will be backwards.

We had a case once where we did a leading tail and I purposely reversed the antennas because I knew the target would be behind us all the time. Gimmicks like this are best left to the professionals but it is something to bear in mind.

You also ought to know that cheap beeper units will vary their indication as the vehicle's battery voltage changes. This, of course, is assuming that you are running the receiver off the cigarette lighter. Smaller cars especially are affected by this. Even though the car's voltage is allegedly regulated, and all manufacturers of cheap tracking systems will tell you that the car's electrical system voltage will not affect the unit, they are lying.

In many cars, the voltage will increase with higher engine revolutions, and vice versa. As you slow down for a light or whatever the engine will also slow down and the voltage will drop slightly and the unit may not indicate accurately.

Solution? Use a top quality tracking receiver. To be extra safe, our unit has provisions for built in batteries, which will power the receiver for more than a day. This feature is primarily because our unit has been used from an aircraft with a 28 volt electrical system instead of 12 volts like a car, and we didn't want to fool with regulators.

Several accessories will make life a bit easier if you're going to use a tracker on a regular basis. Consider adding the following items to your bag of tricks:

- Narrow bladed, sturdy putty knife or similar scraper
- Strong plastic bag large enough to enclose transmitter
- Foil packages of hand cleaner towelettes
- Roll of dark colored, non glossy duct tape
- Roll of good quality electrical tape
- TWO sets of batteries, new and date coded, for both the transmitter and receiver
- Small penlight that works

Although the principle involved is the same, there is a world of difference between direction finders specifically designed for tracking moving vehicles and those originally intended for finding illegal CB radios, sinking ships, clandestine spy transmitters or meese (plural of mooses) wandering the open plain.

Unfortunately, most of the "vehicle" tracking systems widely marketed to the investigative community are converted units like the above.

Merely packaging a battery operated transmitter in a box with magnets does not a bumper beeper system make. I would suggest you speak with the manufacturer or his representative and ascertain the design purpose of any unit. Ask for a copy of the instruction manual. Does the sales literature specifically discuss investigative applications? Is the manufacturer in tune with the needs of the professional investigator? The answers to these questions should help you select a vendor, which is the first step to selecting an appropriate tracking system.

There are several technologies applied to direction finding. Based on our rather extensive research and hundreds of hours in the field using the various packages, only one is well suited for tracking a moving vehicle, the proper system, used by a man who knows what he is doing, will work fine. Remove any one of these factors and you will have an expensive, useless toy left over.

Let's delve into the theory of electronic direction finding for a moment, there are three types of direction finding receivers found in the field today. They are: Adcock, Doppler, and switched pattern.

All work, and all work well for their intended applications. Of all three, however, I feel that the switched pattern is the only one really suitable for investigative use. (Note: I am not including in the above the simple, although popular, signal strength type devices which merely tell you through a varying tone or series of lights whether you are moving closer or further from the transmitter.)

The signal strength devices sometimes also include a directional antenna (beam, or Yagi) which looks like a small TV antenna built on a broomstick and is intended to be held out the window of your vehicle and rotated for the strongest signal. The direction the antenna is pointing when the signal is strongest is the bearing to the transmitter. *Read the fine print in these ads!* A beam antenna is a giveaway to signal strength devices, which are pretty much worthless for tracking in the real world.

Directional antennas have their use, but only in the hands of a for real radio professional, and then almost never for vehicle tracking. Stay away, also, from any tracking system which only uses one antenna.

As far as I know, it is impossible to derive bearing information with only one non directional antenna. As I constantly stress, dealing with a knowledgeable supplier who will work with you is the best way to end up with the best value in equipment.

There is one rather well known west coast manufacturer of an Adcock system. This manufacturer is about as interested in your successful tracking as the IRS is in your pursuit of happiness, but both are about as equally interested in how much money you can cough up. Aside from this, Adcock has an advantage

of low profile antennas which can be disguised rather easily.

My use of the term Adcock is a generic term that refers to a technique of deriving bearing information rather than the name of a manufacturer, which I'm not allowed to mention in an open forum.
(*Ed. note: Steve's phone number, if you are serious about buying a system, is (301) 879–4035.*)

An Adcock system, uses four vertical antennas in a box pattern with a fifth antenna, called the sense antenna situated in the middle of the array. Appropriate electronics compare the transmitter's signal as received by the sense antenna to that received by the other four.

The results of this comparison are displayed on some sort of indicator that tells you where the target transmitter is in relation to your vehicle (actually, in relation to the antenna array, which is presumed to be mounted on your vehicle). The indicators are pretty much the same for all tracking systems. The system sold by the manufacturer not mentioned above is unique in that it displays bearing information on a CRT (like a small TV screen).

Your vehicle is in the center, displayed as a dot. The system draws a line from the center to the edge of the screen face, and this vector indicates the relative bearing to the target. There is an advantage to this graphic display other than bells and whistles in that certain types of multipath interference actually is shown as garbage on the display. With some practice and trial and error you can tell by looking which displayed vector is most likely to be genuine.

The Adcock system tends to be considerably larger than what is considered practical for mobile applications. Now if you're on a Coast Guard ship, this may not be a problem. If you're in a standard passenger car, it probably is one.

The Adcock technology works well for very short pulsed signals. Short pulsed signals (though they must be repeated frequently) tend to be associated with data transmissions or pulsed encoding techniques such as might be used in surreptitious transmissions to and from a satellite. Real life bumper beeper pulses are infinitely long compared to the short bursts in which the Adcock excels.

We need to digress for a moment and discuss an important factor relating to antennas. There is a term used in reference to antennas known as "polarization," briefly and approximately, this means the orientation of the radio waves leaving (or arriving) at an antenna. Vertically polarized signals emanate from an antenna that is vertical—like your car radio antenna or a handheld radio antenna. Horizontally polarized signals are used with broadcast TV—look at the TV antenna on your roof for an example of a horizontally polarized antenna. The important point to remember here is that signals must maintain the same polarization or severe losses will result—(ed. note this is true in ANY RF reception, not just BB's)—and, for vehicle tracking applications, cross polarized signals will cause unacceptable errors in bearing information. We might simplify things by saying that antennas that are perpendicular to the ground are vertically polarized. Antennas that are parallel to the ground are horizontal. And rarely the twain shall meet.

Why do we need to concern ourselves with polarization? Well, virtually every application you and I will have for vehicle tracking will be vertically polarized. The two (or four) receive antennas mounted on the top of your vehicle are vertically polarized. Ideally, the transmitter's (beeper's) antenna should be vertically polarized for best signal strength and most accurate bearing information. Herein arises a problem—many, if not most, of the tracking systems we've seen in the field use what we refer to as a "dribble" antenna. This is an extremely flexible stranded wire antenna which is left to flop out of the bottom of the beacon transmitter.

The idea of a flexible antenna, on its face, has merit in that you can't always give the antenna a clear shot to the atmosphere when the transmitter is buried in the underbelly of

the car. However, this is the classic situation where someone knows enough to be dangerous. I realize I frequently sound cynical, (ed. note: "Steve? Nah.") but it's obvious from the design of the product, along with the advertising, and occasional conversation with the manufacturers and their reps that none of them truly know anything about vehicle tracking. There is more to successful vehicle tracking than packaging a small transmitter in a box with batteries on the inside and magnets on the outside.

Forget the soapbox. A dribble antenna, by its flexible nature, will blow around in the wind, from vehicle vibration, etc., AND CONSTANTLY BE CHANGING ITS POLARIZATION from vertical to horizontal or some useless permutation of the two. This, we have found in our field trials, is a critical problem with vehicle tracking systems.

Hopefully you can understand, based on what we've just covered on polarization, that if the polarization is not constant, the signal strength and other parameters will vary, causing serious errors in what your receiver will faithfully try to tell you.

The bottom line? Any tracking system (transmitter) that uses a flexible wire antenna is probably designed by someone who really doesn't understand vehicle tracking. That being the case, you might consider whether you want to deal with such a critter. Unless you know EXACTLY what you are doing, do not buy a beeper transmitter that uses a dribble antenna.

You might even have some fun, when you're talking to the vendor, by asking him what antenna his unit has, and why.

What is the alternative? Simple. A copper wire antenna that is stiff enough to stay how you put it. Our unit uses a regular piece of #14 solid copper wire (insulated, of course). You can bend the antenna however you need to clear the underbelly of the car, even if that requires odd shapes.

The antenna length at VHF frequencies where many tracking systems operate is about 16 inches. Obviously we can't deal with that long an antenna so ours is coil-loaded down to about 6 inches. This means is that the antennas are special and can't be substituted. If you need another antenna, call us and get the proper one—they're cheap and anything else won't work right. Antennas are as critical as tires on a car—they are what couple the transmitter to the atmosphere. Everything hangs on the antenna so please don't accept any compromises.

If you have a beeper transmitter that uses a dribble antenna, we might be able to do something to improve it for you. Call our office to discuss it.

Wow! That really was a digression from a discussion on polarization. The reason I led into polarization in the first place was to mention that the Adcock technology of direction finding works very well with vertically polarized signals. It does not work very well with signals of mixed polarization, such as might be found in vehicle tracking applications. Other methods of processing tracking information handle varying polarization better than Adcock.

There are many systems out which operate on a principle called Doppler. The Doppler systems are characterized by four antennas. By their nature Doppler systems are 360 degree devices. Doppler systems (generically, not the company known by the same name), are relatively less expensive to produce than some of the others we will be discussing, and therefore find their way into some of the quick buck operations. Doppler direction finding is certainly a viable technique, and has its place—but that place is not for vehicle tracking.

Doppler receivers are characterized by a compass "rose" of lights, perhaps 36 of them arranged in a circle for all 360 degrees. Theoretically only one light at a time should be on, although with severe multipath you'll get lights everywhere and all bets are off.

We have performed extensive field testing on Doppler systems and have found that they seem to need a relatively stronger signal to

indicate accurately than their associates. Doppler systems work by comparing the transmitter's signal as received by the four antennas and deciding with intelligent electronics which antenna is closest to the transmitter.

Dopplers are quite reliable at determining bearings, but not too terrific at determining range. This does not mean that the other systems do determine range, rather that the others are able to make a more accurate extrapolation of range vs. signal strength than the Dopplers.

Dopplers are also considerably more tricky to operate in built up areas such as busy concrete jungles. One advantage of Dopplers (for spies, maybe) is that they can give accurate bearing info with a very quick transmissions. If you're DF'ing a pirate transmitter that only says one word every few minutes—maybe in the instance of a stolen radio that found its way back onto your system—the Doppler would be a good route to go. For vehicle tracking applications, though, the advantage of locking onto quick transmissions is relatively unimportant and not, in my opinion, worth the tradeoffs in other areas.

(Ed. note: Dopplers ARE used successfully to help pinpoint bugs that may be shut off by the operator when he hears a search commencing but when we asked DOPPLER [the company] to participate by allowing one of their units to be tested they informed us they did not sell their units for vehicle following and did not feel they were appropriate for this use.)

Ok. Now that we've discussed what NOT to buy, what should we use? The best type of direction finder for moving vehicle tracking is the technique known as "switched pattern." Some good tracking systems are available using switched pattern; sources include several three-letter named private manufacturers of police electronics systems.

Switched patterns involves two (or four, for 360 degree coverage) antennas which are alternately "switched" one at a time to the input of the receiver. Our unit switches 120 times each second, by the system knowing the placement of the antennas on the roof of the vehicle and the approximate "pattern" of the antenna, the signal received from the beeper transmitter will be stronger on one antenna in the system. As the system knows which antenna hears better, and where it is on the car, the receiving electronics can reliably derive bearing information.

Due to the fact that only one antenna is actually connected to the receiver at a time, multipath is easier to discriminate. Switched pattern systems excel in areas of most concern to vehicular applications. They do not care as much about polarization (even though it doesn't hurt to keep the polarization as close to vertical as possible), are usable in all types of terrain, can accurately translate signal strength into relative range (with the help of the operator's wealth of experience), and can track fine on weak signals. In fact, with our unit we have demonstrated long range tracking on signals that were too weak to be heard through the speaker. And, another major consideration, the switched pattern is one of the easiest systems to learn the techniques of vehicle tracking with.

The ORION unit that we sell displays bearings on a zero center meter. On this system when the meter reads center it indicates roughly that the target vehicle is directly ahead of you. A needle showing left or right of center means that's where the vehicle is, and indicates the direction in which you should steer your vehicle to stay on the target.

The whole receiver package is small, about the size of two reams of Xerox paper stacked, and is built into a weatherproof Haliburton suitcase. On internal batteries, the unit is good for better than 24 hours of continuous tracking, or it can be plugged into the vehicle's cigarette lighter for extended duty. If you're running a moving surveillance for more than 24 hours, anyway, you're a marathon operator qualified for the surveillance Olympics.

In addition to the meter indicating bearing, there is another large face meter which displays signal strength. With some experience signal strength information can tell you a lot about what the target is doing. A remote panel is available to mount the meters on the dash of your car if you're working alone and don't want to keep glancing down at the seat next to you while you drive.

I guess all the above can be summarized rather briefly: Buy a unit that was designed specifically for law enforcement vehicle following. Stay away from units originally designed for Coast Guard, military, tracking meese, or "public safety" and select a switched pattern tracking system. Do not accept a transmitter that has a flexible wire antenna, or if you have one already call someone like us to install a solid antenna on your existing transmitter.

Don't buy any system that uses a single antenna on the receiver, or mentions a directional, beam or Yagi antenna. DO know and trust your supplier, and make sure he is familiar with the ins and outs of law enforcement vehicle tracking applications. Make sure he can support you with training, as these systems are far too complex to be delivered in a plain brown wrapper with no after-sale support. And stay away from any system that is priced significantly below the others. There is no such thing as a free lunch. Expect to pay between $5000 and $7500 for a serious system, 50% to 75% more for a 360.

Request a demonstration if you have any question at all about either the unit or the vendor. Any vendor of a quality piece will welcome the opportunity to put his unit up against the competition.

Remember when I mentioned your bumper beeper bag of tricks? The putty knife is for scraping away undercoating, grease or other crud from the surface to which you will attach the transmitter. The plastic bag is for putting the transmitter in at the end of the surveillance, since it will be greasy and muddy. Keep the transmitter in the bag until you can clean it up, so it won't get your car all grubby. The hand cleaner towelettes are for wiping off your hands after you've removed the unit, before the grease can rub off the vehicle when you're installing the transmitter—even in daylight it helps to have some light on the area. I use a minimag or, more recently, one of the new micro streamlights that's about the size of a lipstick. The reason for a small light is that you can hold it in your mouth when you need both your hands free. And, when you're covertly installing the transmitter, you usually don't want to be seen carrying a whole bunch of stuff up to the target vehicle.

I guess we should discuss actually installing the transmitter. Contrary to the name, the bumper is usually not a practical place in which to conceal the beeper transmitter.

You want a flat surface big enough for the magnets to sit flat. Do NOT use the gas tank as the metal there is too thin for the magnets to attach securely. We've never had a transmitter fall off although it does happen occasionally. Pick an area where the transmitter will be hidden from casual view, not buried too far up in the vehicle.

The transmitter does not have to be mounted to the rear of the vehicle, although it doesn't hurt to have the signal radiating to the rear, presumably towards your car. We have had the best results with a frame crossmember, frame rail, or occasionally up inside a fender well.

Scrape the area clean with your scraper. It's not necessary to get down to bare metal, although it sure doesn't hurt. If at all possible, reinforce the mounting with either the duct tape or the electrical tape, whichever seems more practical at the time. Use several wraps completely AROUND a frame rail for the most secure mounting. Make sure you do not use one of the gaudy silver colored duct tapes.

Try to place the unit so that the antenna can poke out in the clear as much as possible. If you can, keep the antenna vertical and don't let any part of the antenna come any closer than necessary to any other metal—always keep it at least 4 or 5 inches from any metal or find another location.

Select placement and antenna orientation such that the transmitter is not likely to be "wiped off" if the antenna hits brush, a curb or crap in the street. And it should go without saying not to mount the thing on any component of the exhaust system...

With experience you eventually will develop your own techniques for installing and removing the transmitter so I won't say too much more here.

Transmitters have a certain amount of weight if they are to have any useful battery life and range. Our unit has the magnets sort of shock mounted so that the rubber shock absorbers soak up the bouncing around of the unit while the car is moving. Without some sort of shock mounting all that force is transferred directly to the magnetic coupling, which is likely to break loose and let the transmitter fall off without the buffering. Again, experience and appropriate design for the application.

Are these things legal? Well, I'll take the standard cop out and say that we don't render legal advice. Ask the State's Attorney. In this state, he has rendered a verbal opinion that no privacy is being violated, as one has no reasonable expectation of privacy in regards to one's vehicle's presence on a public roadway. And, no interception of written or spoken communications is involved. There is an incredible amount of fiction related to beepers.

(Ed. note: The Omnibus crime act and other wiretap related directives do NOT, at this time, prohibit anyone from using an electronic tracker.)

I have never heard of anyone, anywhere having the slightest problem related to these devices. Of course, don't commit a trespass to install the device.

In a domestic investigation, frequently the vehicle in question is jointly owned and the client party can give you permission to install the device. Sometimes semantics is involved. We have been hired to install "executive protection" beepers, to allow us to track and locate a subject and vehicle if they are taken. We've also sold them as "route verification" systems, to let a fleet operator keep track of the movements of his delivery vehicles. Don't do anything stupid, get a legal opinion, and you'll probably be OK.

Another aspect to investigate is FCC type acceptance of the transmitter. VERY few transmitters advertised for vehicle tracking are type accepted, and a unit that isn't is subject to confiscation and harassment of the owner by the FCC. I would go so far as to say that you probably shouldn't buy a transmitter that is not type accepted unless you are a bona fide government agency. There is an excellent chance of a supplier being approached by the FCC and ordered to turn over a list of all purchasers of a non approved device. All purchasers would then be contacted and directed to turn in the illegal transmitters.

In fact this has happened quite recently and cost some friends a lot of money. Our ORION unit, by the way, is type accepted. Call us for the FCC registration number if you need it. Any FCC type accepted device will have a permanently affixed metal tag to that effect stuck to the unit. I have seen more phony type acceptance stickers than I have real ones, so don't be afraid to ask the manufacturer for a statement in writing that his unit is approved for vehicle tracking applications.

Care and feeding—replace all batteries EVERY time the unit is issued. No matter how little use the current set of batteries has had, replace them. Keep new batteries in the refrigerator and write the date on them so you can use the oldest ones first. Batteries are insignificant in cost compared to the consequences of blowing an investigation.

Unless your unit is in constant use, I recommend throwaway batteries as opposed to rechargeables. Rechargeable batteries will save you money in the long run, but their operating life per charge is maybe a third of that of throwaways. Rechargables also require some special care to avoid problems which are especially serious in vehicle tracking operations.

Use the best alkalines you can get, or even lithiums if you need extremely long life out of the beeper. If the weather is very cold the performance of the batteries will suffer, so keep the unit in a warm car until the last possible moment. Conversely, do not let the batteries get too hot in the summer or their life will be reduced considerably. Batteries have their internal connections made by crimping, which occasionally can go intermittent under the severe vibration usually experienced by the transmitter. (*Ed. note: Again true in ALL transmitter applications.*)

To add a bit of redundancy, our ORION unit has three batteries in parallel. Should one open up, the other two will still carry the unit for 36 to 48 hours. And, of course, three batteries offer longer life than two. Replace all batteries at the same time, and do not mix battery types or use anything other than all new, similarly handled batteries. Used batteries removed from a little used beeper can still be used in radios, toys or other electronics, so they needn't be wasted. Just make sure you label them so previously issued batteries don't get cycled back into the system. Please don't compromise a five or six thousand dollar tracking system for the sake of five bucks worth of batteries.

Be very careful of the receiver antenna coax. Don't squash it in the car door or roll the window up on it. Also don't kink the coax or coil it up too tightly in storage. Coax is relatively fragile stuff and must be in near perfect condition for your tracker to work right. If (when) the coax starts to deteriorate, the entire antenna assembly must be returned to the vendor for service. For all practical purposes it is not possible to replace coax on the receive antennas in the field as the lengths, type and even brand of coax is all precisely tuned. Any deviations here and the system will not read accurately.

It would be wise to keep an eye on all connectors too, both in the antenna system and power or remote console cables. Fix anything that is not perfect.

Examine the beeper's antenna every time out, too, and be certain to tag the unit as bad and turn it in for repair if it needs it. Don't forget about it until the next clown signs it out for his surveillance. If you use a tracker regularly it doesn't hurt to have a spare transmitter around. Make sure it is on the same channel(s) as your receiver BEFORE you issue it.

As in any other surveillance equipment package, it's a good idea to have a check off sheet listing all components and accessories necessary for the job. Make sure everything is checked off before the unit is issued.

Bumper beepers are not inexpensive—but neither are vehicles, radios, video equipment and everything else in our black bag of tricks.

Don't be intimidated by bumper beepers. A quality unit from a reputable manufacturer will work well, save you many hours, and ensure more successful surveillances. The manufacturers have spent many thousands of hours and huge sums of money to produce these units for you—the investigator. Let technology make your job easier.

—Steve Uhrig, SWS Technologies.

It's also possible combine technology with old fashioned footwork—as a friend told me "You know the best way to follow a car in New York?

"You put on a good, directional beeper on the target car and then go out and hire a Puerto Rican kid with a Moped to follow the guy through the streets. When he leaves the city your kid radios you and then you turn the receiver on and start working with the beeper."

If you have the time and budget it is also possible to rent the same model of automobile the subject will be driving, put the beeper on it and spend the next day or two getting used to the signal characteristics of both the car and the area in which you expect to be working. Large, here unnamed agencies do this with good results.

If you don't believe Steve and want to try out a single antenna, field strength system, it is possible to secure a complete set up from for about $1900. It is also possible to manufacture or purchase inexpensive beepers, attach a Yagi style gain antenna to a scanner or ICOM type receiver and see what field strength following is like in real life.

Besides the system SWS sells the two most popular systems around are probably the TRACMAN, a Canadian built but FCC type accepted RF unit with a fairly good reputation that uses two meters to show direction of travel and a includes a motion sensor/indicator.

The CANTRAC 360 is one of the Cadillacs of bumper beepers, offering Doppler or Watson-Watt antennas, a microprocessor signal analyzer that helps reject multipath and even a choice of four operational modes, one of which allows voice monitoring.

Both of the above units are available from COVERT OPERATIONS INTERNATIONAL.

A super slick, super expensive tail aid is sold by DBA Systems in Melbourne, Florida utilizes a composite *video* signal to electronically follow a target. The video signal radiated by the hidden transmitter is decoded by a computerized receiver that develops the timing and synchronization signals from the video signal relative to the horizontal and vertical sync pulses.

The output of this unit is a very accurate, very precise set of coordinates including the location of the center and the edge of the target, in crosshairs.

Very James Bond. Very good...

SURVEILLANCE PHOTOGRAPHY
HIGH SPEED, LOW LIGHT, HIDDEN CAMERA
This section was written by a group of professional surveillance photographers. Ed.

This class is entitled High Speed Photography 101, also known as "the urban photo safari primer." This is a course in how to get those special shots that really, really matter. Don't worry if you have been confused by cameras and films before. No matter how much you do or do not understand about cameras now, when you are through with this lesson all you will need is a little practice. And that's where the fun starts!

To get the shot, one must prepare one's self by understanding each of the three areas we are covered here. First the camera—it's simpler than you think—know your tools. Second, the film, the latest super fast types can get the shot in limited light, and at a great distance. Finally, a few special techniques to put the odds in your favor, and how to use the subminiature camera up close and personal.

Camera's all run on just two controls; the shutter speed controls how long the shutter (door to the lens) remains open and lets light onto the film. Long lenses magnify camera shake, so to work from a distance one must have a fast exposure or the picture will be blurred, even if the subject is still. Unfortunately we need a specific amount of light to reach the film, in order to get a decent exposure.

The second camera control is aperture, which is adjusted by turning a ring around the barrel of the lens. When you turn the ring you are choking the lens. A fully choked lens only sees through its very center, it lets in less light than it would wide open. The important thing about aperture is that it also controls the range of distances from the camera where things will be in focus at once, this is called "depth of field."

For example, let's say you are "shooting" two people who are close to each other, and you are pretty close to them; no problem. But if we move the same two faces a few feet apart, and use a long lens from a distance, it may not work.

Each click of the shutter speed control is equal to one click of the aperture ring. Every time you move either control one "stop," or click, you have doubled or halved the total amount of light getting to the film. To keep the same exposure you would move, say, "one stop up" on aperture and one stop down on speed. This adjustment would put a deeper range of distances into focus but you would have more blur from anything that was moving. Don't worry if you don't hear these things click, even on the auto-everything electronic marvels the same things are occurring.

If the subject is moving fast, or is under less than ideal lighting conditions, other factors must be taken into consideration:

The Film: it needs to be very, very fast. A "speed" printed on the box, like 100 ASA or 400 ASA tells us how much light reaching this film will make a usable exposure, so we zero the camera's controls to this number. What you want to remember is that the 400 on the Tri-X box is only an average, everything depends on how one develops the film in the lab.

When you find yourself waving around 800mm lenses trying to keep it all in focus, change the film speed. The aspiring speed demon routinely doubles or quadruples the speed of a film, just by dialing in the higher (faster) setting and then having the film "push" processed. Push processing involves leaving the film in developer for a longer time. The image quality changes a little but it works.

Each doubling of the film speed buys one extra stop up of either aperture or shutter speed, your choice. Shooting Tri-X ASA 400 speed film with the ASA on the camera set to 1600 would be pushing it twice, or quadrupling it. Find the ASA setting on the camera and turn to 1600, then use the exposure control system normally.

Always bring film to a good camera shop or a custom photo lab for push processing, the people at the drug store may not understand what you are talking about. When you have exposed correctly at the 1600 setting and they process it for that 400 average anyway, you lose.

Finally enter T-Max, a "high speed" film that is more than two stops faster than "normal" films. The rating on the T-Max box is ASA 3200. What makes this film even more wonderful is that it stands up well to the rigors of push processing. Pushing increases contrast and apparent grain, image quality goes down. Tri-X can only go to 1600 before losing some detail. T-Max pushed the same three stops is so fast the ASA dial on your camera may not go high enough. T-Max can be used at ridiculous speeds but detail, especially in the shadows, suffers. Don't push more than twice unless you are sure. At the Laughing Dragon we anticipate "a high degree of martial sophistication" from our opponents, you want to be able to see those faces in the shadows.

The Fun Stuff: how to get the shot, anything, anywhere, anytime. How does it all come together? These are a few special tips from our collective experience.

First a quiet word. The laws of the United Kingdom, allow courtroom photography only by one specific model of camera. Unfortunately this very silent camera is a Leica rangefinder, which is terribly expensive and not good for our purposes anyway. If you are close enough that noise is a problem, the best 35mm you can still buy, albeit used, is the original Olympus XA compact. Newer models have flash, gimmicks and a different shutter, which is much louder. Olympus has also made some very quiet full sized 35mm cameras, that have been the choice of many documentary photographers over the years. Despite this, most serious shooters still rely on the large noisy motor driven Nikons, but it is good to have something else a little less conspicuous as well.

Auto exposure is useful when a subject moves into a shadow or a cloud rolls by overhead unexpectedly. Run the lens over your area watching closely what happens to the settings the camera is selecting, plan ahead. Think about both depth of field and shutter speed.

If you are hand holding an 800mm lens and the shutter speed dips down to 1/30 when the subject steps into shadow, you're in trouble. On a long lens, if aperture drops too low focus may become so shallow a single face will not stay in focus. This is when fast film shines. Whatever happens do not get stuck with a snapshot camera that sets the film speed automatically as this makes it tough to push the film.

Some photographers use converted telescopes for long shots, but they lack the ability to change aperture. A regular 80–200mm zoom lens, a 400mm and maybe a 600mm are what we recommend for surveillance photography. Absolutely carry a doubler attachment for the lenses. Nikons are nice, and Canon telephotos have a strong following with sports shooters, but for just recording the facts less expensive brands like Sigma and Vivitar will do. Of course if the money is available fluorite lenses offer a couple of extra fast f-stops, are amazingly sharp and even inherently scratch proof.

Lens quality is less important in black and white prints, and they are also the faster, more easily manipulated films. Unless you have a specific need, stay black and white, and remember Tri-X is safer than T-Max, particularly with details of things in shadows. Slower films like Plus-X will have even greater detail, allowing small areas of a distant scene to be enlarged and printed better, but with long lenses, changing light and moving subjects the order of the day, you will seldom manage anything slower than Tri-X at 400 ASA. If it has to be color try Kodak's latest color print refinements, they are fairly rugged. Color slide film is the most temperamental and delicate type of film, avoid it.

When time is of the essence, Polaroid is available in two forms for use with 35mm cameras. A special back is available for Nikon F-type cameras, made by Marti Forscher, that loads Polaroid pack films for instant prints. The image size is small, and the backs are only available for a few cameras.

The other way is to use Polaroid 35mm films, which do exist, in a number of types. Use the small portable processor gizmo, then digitize the slides or print them using Vivitar's equally portable Polaroid slide printer. This method is flexible, can do black and white or color, and works in any camera. Both approaches to Polaroid are using very delicate films, they do not have much room for exposure errors.

For the traditional duck blind and long-lens-in-window shot, getting the camera to follow the action yet remain steady is difficult. Normal tripods don't work well; "fluid head" systems made for video production do. The ideal unit is a Bogen 3063 Fluid Head with a 3046 or another of their medium weight professional tripods. Pre-set the camera and use an electric cable release on the motor drive. The fluid head moves smoothly, allowing the camera to track a subject and shoot without blurring the pictures. If you have to travel light use a large bean bag as a camera rest, and be glad you know how to push the film. Once again you are going to want both the fast shutter speed and the small aperture for no blur and a wide easy focus.

At night the light spilling out of bright shop windows is often enough for an accelerated film to record anyone walking by on the sidewalk. You do have to make intelligent use of the light meter; the shop window trick is one of those things that is never going to come out right on a simple auto exposure system. Learn to substitute a meter reading in one area, perhaps inside your car, for the readings you can't arrange to do directly.

This is a very useful principle when you have limited access to your subject, although it does take practice. In cars and when shooting through glass, don't forget to use a polarizing filter to remove reflections.

One way to work in low key situations is to use a very compact telephoto like the new version of the 500mm mirror lens from Nikon. Put a doubler on it, it's still so small that from a distance it doesn't look like a threat.

Use a camera body that allows the attachment of a waist level finder, or one like the Nikon F that allows removal of the prism, allowing the operator to look down into the screen.

Dressed like a tourist and standing a block and a half away, let the camera hang at your waist. You appear to be out of range, the camera is not raised for use, perhaps you are frowning over some technical problem as you manipulate the focus and sway your body... To follow the shot.

A TRICK

Take a smallish camera body, load it with T-Max pushed three times (that's 25,600 ASA) and mount a slightly wide angle lens like a 35mm. There is a mirror for the viewfinder which many cameras allow you to lock to the up position which will reduce operating noise by at least half. Set the shutter speed to about 1/60th and focus to about seven feet, or whatever is appropriate. The aperture is set for maximum depth of field and let the camera dangle lengthwise from the fingers of your right hand.

Your arm hangs naturally at your side, get to the right distance and squeeze. Often no fuss will be made when a camera is noticed, as long as it clearly wasn't being used. This is the "dead camera" technique. Practice shooting to the front and to the rear.

Minox makes the little silver spy cameras seen in all those great movies. The EC is a black plastic camera, it is smaller than the other current model which was intended more for document work. Both current models have auto exposure, making them more useful in quickly changing situations than the older cameras.

Look through the viewfinder once, then cover it and all the markings with black plastic tape. With all that extra shiny glass gone you are ready for some practice in concealed photography.

Let the closed camera rest vertically in the palm of your hand. With your arm hanging naturally at your side the camera should be

snuggled against your leg and mostly hidden behind your thumb. When there are people around the Minox is a magician's camera, open the case, make a small movement to cover the action, such as a sniff, then make an expansive motion, such as a yawn. As the body mimes the yawn the arms naturally turn out and the camera is exposed, takes a picture, and turns back into the concealed position. The empty hand may add a little misdirection by rising to cover the mouth. The head should turn away from the actual focus of attention.
— Good Shooting!
End of contributed section.

DOCUMENTS

Picture this situation—you're in the library, it's five minutes before closing time and you desperately need to copy three pages from the latest *PLAYBOY*. You rush to the only aging Xerox machine to find the "correct change only" sign is illuminated.

A frantic scavenger hunt of your 501 pockets produces nothing less than a $100 bill.

What to do, what to do...

Luckily you have your trusty Minox LX in your briefcase loaded with copy film—the perfect solution for those little unforeseen photo opportunities just like this one...

Document photography is a specialized art requiring some specialized gear, but none that is rare or unobtainable. Why do you think they invented the Minox?

One of the more truthful unsolicited testimonials in advertising history was provided by convicted Russian spy Col. Walker who praised the document copying ability of the Minox even though he "wore out a box full of them" in the course of his duties copying secret U.S. Naval documents.

To quote William White, Ph.D, author of the excellent book, *Subminiature Photography*, "there is little question that most of the Minox cameras in the world today and most of the MInox film consumed are used to copy documents."

So what features do we look for in a semi-dedicated document copier?

The first consideration is probably size—size of camera as well as the size of the film used. The former should be as small as possible, the latter as large as possible. The target is usually assumed to be an 8 1/2 x 11 inch printed page and the resulting copy will be, in most cases, a 4 x 5 positive image.

This means negative, slide type film is not in our range of options. What we are looking for is fine grained, good gray scale or stark black and white copy film that produces good resolution in a 4 x 5 print.

Start with the largest negative size possible. 35 mm will give an excellent account of itself with the further convenience that virtually any emulsion from Ortho-Litho black and white (no gray) copy film to 12,500 ASA high speed surveillance film is available packed in a 35 mm format.

The problem is that most cameras that are considered miniature utilize film smaller than the standard 35 mm format. The exception to this are a few cameras which use 35 mm film but expose less than the full frame in any shot (Robot SC, Tessina) to mantain a low physical profile and offer more shots per roll.

16 mm film is generally the next format involved with mini photography and is available in some professional emulsions.

The 9.5 mm Minox cassette film size is large enough to give a very credible performance when copying documents *except* for the fact that Minox limits the emulsions in this cassette to the standard Agfa 100-400 black and white film which is not the best film for our purposes.

The solution to this dilemma is to order specially loaded cassettes from MICROTEC which contain more suitable document oriented emulsions including Agfa Copex and Kodak recording film.

The major concerns, besides the film, for document copying is focus and illumination. As one can imagine, focus is critical when small print is to be reproduced in a readable form.

Most sub-miniature cameras do not offer SLR type lens arrangements so some means of assuring sharp focus must be introduced.

Minox (and GaMi) cameras do this by providing a method of establishing the exact distance from the cameras lens to the document to be copied. A metal chain attached to the camera has several beads incorporated in its design at intervals which correspond to settings on the focus dial of the camera.

These beads are typically at distances of 8", 10", 1 foot, and 1'6" from the camera. This system allows for quick and accurate camera positioning without taking the camera from the operator's eye.

Depth of field is not important in document copying as long as it is adequate for the job at hand, however flatness of both the image as well as of the subject is a very real factor in taking good document.

Light must also be present in suitable quantities for good photography. Handheld copying wants camera speeds of at least 1/60 if not higher. With the relatively slow lenses found on most tiny cameras (3.5 or 5.6 on the Minox) getting sufficient on-target light using only available room lighting is a just-so thing with slow film.

To overcome this situation, use medium to high speed film or push slower films. If the room light is subdued, use a top line camera with built in metering and speciality fast film, or enhance the lighting by shining two lights onto the target from 45 degrees to either side of the camera.

Some mini's now use flash cubes and MICROTEC offers a new strobe attachment for the Minox based camera system.

The very best way to copy documents is to use a copy stand that holds the camera steady at a precise distance from the target. This ensures camera steadyness, thereby allowing for slower shutter speeds, less light while maintaining complete focus. Kodak and Minox cameras have, at one time or another, had copying

stands built for them although to my knowledge, Minox is the only company to still offer one. It is a fairly simple project for the home craftsman to rig up a small stand that will hold a subminiature camera in place for document photography.

Creative stands may even include extension arms with built-in light sources.

Besides documents, CRT's also allow for unique photo opportunities. CRT's are not constant sources of information, rather they consist of separate frames and fields which are interlaced to provide a momentary "still." Frames occur at a refresh rate of 30 times a second, so a shutter speed of 1/30 will normally suffice.

CRT's are also lit internally by the electron beam which is displaying the data and tend to be brighter than they appear. William White advises a lens opening of f/4 to f/2.8 for most CRT's but one should also test a particular camera on several different displays in order to establish particular parameters.

A purely subjective list of the best cameras for document copying would be as follows:

1. MicroTec CFS covert document copying system. An modified Minox EC featuring a fixed focus (depth of field 10-22 inches), faster lens, and available strobe.

2. Tessina. Swiss made precision camera with SLR, magnifying finder and frame finder. Excellent photographs of very small objects.

3. Minox LX, Minox C (used), Robot SC models.

4. Minolta 16, II, Minox 110, Pentax Auto 110.

CRT and document copying requires particular features that other photography does not. Some of the above cameras, such as the CFS is not suitable for any other photography, while some, such as the Minox LX are more adaptable but trade off a little of their close up ability.

SURREPTITIOUS PHOTOGRAPHY

Thanks to the miracle of telephone conference calling I assembled three gentlemen whom I consider to be the best around in the field of candid camera photography and flat out asked them to tell us how.

Me—The idea is I need photos or video of a rather shy person, who, for some obscure reason does not wish to appear in image... How do I do it?

1. I was recently called into consultation for the DE...well, let's just say a federal enforcement organization, that was having a problem with things disappearing from their labs.

    Not dope, mind you, things like $2500 electronic scales. I took several miniature IR illuminators that use the new laser LED's (ed. VIKING ELECTRONICS, etc.) and stashed them behind the opaque plastic drop ceilings that cover fluorescent lights.

    The IR shines clearly, and invisibly, through the plastic covering and lights up the entire room. I used a long play VCR hooked up to a mini camera to grab three days of action at a time.

    Worked like magic, although I could have saved tape and current by wiring the suspect targets with a switch, but why screw around with perfection?

2. I like black plastic—stuff they use on the outside of the modern office buildings. The next generation of one way mirrors. Passes some light, blocks others—you can shoot right through it, light up the whole room and it looks neat.

    Always try for style, I say...

    Besides you can always have a nice Elvis Presley or bull fighting scene painted on it in order to pass it off as "art."

3. My first choice is always to use some sort of image enhancer on a camera. Flood the area with IR if necessary and pick up the image

on sensitive film. If you can't get access to the room use a mega watt IR source (PEAK BEAM, SHOMER-TEC, etc. ed.) and blast it through the windows.

    There's a guy in Washington state who gets conviction-level photos (*verified in court, ed.*) by smashing through thick curtains with a heavy duty IR source and photographing right through the window covers.
    It takes a little practice, but it works...

2. I'd rather use the mini approach—stash a mini camera with it's own IR source. The MINOX LX is a good example, if a brighter approach is available the MICROTEC Robot SC will go up to 3200 ASA will grab very dim images. Whatever works.

3. In an outdoor situation I take an IR laser and a starlight scope lens. I can get a face at 2500 feet... If I need closer I spread the beam with a lens and flood the area. Lasers are so hot you can aim the beam off center or bounce it in order to avoid the subject seeing the source.

1. I like to hide IR bulbs in regular lamps for room stuff...

2. Near IR is cheap—views and/or cameras are in the $1000 range and cheap chip video cameras can grab much of the same range.

3. Well let's talk moneyed—if you got the budget the CANCOM Knightstalker system offers twin 750,000 candlepower lights that pan and tilt to offer max illumination.

    You operate the lights and the camera from a video game-like joy stick the points the chip camera and the lights where you want them. It's really invisible in most apps and will light up an entire basketball court.

1. Great, assuming you have big bucks and want to bust the entire Salvation Army. I prefer a Robot still camera. You can use it

for IR or real light and stash it in almost anything (*comes in attache case, radio or handbag from MicroTec, ed.*) and it can be set to trigger from any kind of switch or even by radio remote.

Sources
AND SPECIFICS:
ROBOT CAMERAS
4000 Dusseldorf 13
Germany

Manufacturers of 35 mm cameras designed to obtain photos under automatic conditions. They feature the ability to take a sequence of photos at the rate of one a second and can be triggered by remote cable releases or even a specially designed radio transmitter/receiver system.

The ROBOTS have automatic film transport and motorized rewinds and, depending on the model, will accept standard film cassettes for a 48 exposure per roll or expandable magazines for up to 12,000 shots.

The units have a large depth of field, silent operation and can be packaged in a variety of unobtrusive containers.

MICROTEC INDUSTRIES
POB 9424
San Diego, CA 92169

MicroTec offers several unique options for candid photography and document copying. The Slimax-Lite is a Minox format based mini camera stashed in a working cigarette lighter.

It offers fewer options that a stock Minox, fixed shutter, fixed lens (15mm 5.6) but checks in at $125.00, cheaper than many lighters that won't take pictures...

They offer modified Minoxes such as their Covert Document Copying system which takes a Minox E.C, increases the speed from 5.6 to 3.5, adjusts the focal length down from 3+ feet to 10-22 inches which is "ideal for copying an 8.5 x 11 document or a computer CRT display."

This model is strictly for close copying and has an internal light meter that works well with super slow (25-100 ASA) fine grain copy film.

For covert non-copy photos they sport a "stealth camera"—a modified Acmel which uses the Minox 9.5 mm film cassettes but unlike the Minox does not require the push-pull motion to operate, has a silent, fixed shutter and built in infrared flash. This unit can be operated with one hand in complete darkness.

A modified Minox LX with a built in, sliding IR filter is packaged with a couple of IR light sources which allow one to take both IR and normal photos on the same roll of film.

MicroTec also offers the widest variety of Minox film cassettes I have ever seen in one place, plus all types of mini film processing and even a dedicated strobe unit for Minox cameras.

COMPUTER CRACKING

0011000010111011

ELECTRONIC METHODS

One of the most exciting forms of electronic interloping is almost unknown to the general public and even to many so-called professionals. Suppose it was possible to read the data being entered or displayed on any computer without physical access to the computer and from a distance of at least several hundred feet.

Sound interesting?

The military has reportedly known about and utilized the concept of passive data eavesdropping for quite a few years, but only recently were details on this amazing concept released to other interested parties.

The primary source of information comes from a group of Swedish scientists who began a research project in January, 1983, to see if computers were vulnerable to information theft via electronic eavesdropping. In 1985, at the Securicom Conference in Cannes, they presented some startling proof of the vulnerability of all computers to passive information gathering.

In the electronic hacker's world this has become known as "Van Eck freaking," because the scientist who wrote the report and presented most of the evidence was named Wim Van Eck.

What the Swedes proved was that it was not only possible, but quite easy to reconstruct data hidden in the radiated fields produced by computers, and did not require access to sophisticated decoding equipment. In fact, they made the case that eavesdropping on a video display unit (CRT) can be accomplished with a normal television broadcast receiver with some "minor alterations" to the unit.

Dr. Van Eck estimated "the equipment cost would be approximately $15.00 to alter a television receiver into a device that would eavesdrop on almost any type of video display unit and could be designed and constructed by an electronic amateur within a few days."

Computers generate several types of radiated electronic fields from various internal components. These fields contain many random or seemingly random factors and are subject to cross talk and resonance, making them extremely hard to reproduce from any distance, however, the video display unit itself shows the opposite predilection.

Most of the TTL signals inside a computer are extremely low level and really don't transmit to any distance; contrary to this is the video signal which is amplified to 700 volts before it is fed into the CRT display unit. The radiation originating from the video signal is the dominant component of the broad band field generated by any computer.

Radiated harmonics of the video signal show a remarkable resemblance to broadcast TV signals and it is therefore possible to reconstruct the picture displayed on the video display unit by means of an altered television receiver

Note that this unit is entirely passive in nature. It does not allow one to go inside the computer's memory banks or even visit the RAM, nor does it allow the operator to illicit queries. It simply receives the signal that is being "painted" onto the CRT unit of any computer. The CRT unit must be in operation in order for this equipment to function.

All-in-all it's still an interesting package because it's completely passive. No bug has to be planted at the site, no hidden cameras to worry about. One simply sits down at the console and reads and/or captures the data that is being displayed on the target computer. The primary modification to the TV receiver concerns the fact that there's no synchronization information on a virgin unit and the pictures displayed from a video display unit will not be very stable and quite unreadable.

The way around this is to externally generate the necessary synchronization signals to establish the beam and feed them into the receiver.

The most common method of reconstructing synchronization is with a device containing two oscillators: a. one adjustable oscillator for the frequency range 15–20 KHz to generate the horizontal synchronization signal (line sync.); b. one adjustable oscillator for the frequency range 40–80 Hz to generate the vertical synchronization signal (picture sync).

Both signals can be combined and fed into a synchronization separator. It is rather difficult to adjust both oscillators to the VDU's synchronization frequencies because both have to be adjusted constantly during reception.

A programmable digital frequency divider which can be used to overcome this problem can be easily constructed.

Once the number of screen lines has been determined, the synchronization can be restored by adjusting only one oscillator.

In order to prove that this was no mere theory, the Nederlands group carried out the following experiment:

"The equipment (dipole antenna + TV receiver + synchronization oscillators) was put in a car, which was placed in the car park of a building in which a word processor was being used. It then (sic) tried to copy the information from this word processor by taking photographs of the screen of the receiving television set. The photographs convinced even the most skeptical people in our organization of the threat of this possibility to information security."

These experiments convinced Van Eck and his associates that it's very possible to eavesdrop on CRT's in buildings from distances of several hundred feet to over *one kilometer* using a mobile listening post set up for this purpose. The group took video and still photographs of information they picked up in exactly this manner and presented them at this conference. Further refinements showed that the use of a directional antenna on the front end of the receiver made selectivity of the received signal

quite good and it was possible to isolate single computers in a target area.

The U.S. Government takes this threat so seriously that they defined a stringent standard called the NACSIM 5100A Tempest Standard and NATO followed up with their own AMSG 720B Compromising Emanations Laboratory Test Standard. Both these Standards cover the amount of radiation that is allowed to leak from government contractors, military, and government computers in order to combat just such computer eavesdropping.

How practical is computer eavesdropping? Dr. Van Eck, bless his little heart, included full plans of a device known as a "synchronization generation recovering device (SYNGARD) and an interface device to hook it up to a normal TV receiver and complete operating instructions in his original manual. Carrying this one step farther, the laboratory that did the studies (Dr. Neher Laboratories in Leidschendam) manufactured a number of their SYNGARD devices for sale to outside parties who wish to measure their vulnerability to this type of eavesdropping."

At least two commercial manufacturers (PK ELECTRONICS AND LORRAINE ELECTRONICS in England) manufacture computer readers so you can, "test your own vulnerability."

PK, who seems to have some sense of humor, calls their tester "The Computer Cracker."

Van Eck's original plans have two problems to those of us on this side of the pond; the first is that he uses European PAL television receivers which are based on a different system than are U.S. NTSC systems.

The second minor problem is that Dr. Van Eck, uh, hedged his bets in his paper by leaving out several necessary facts. When friends of mine tried to build the units they discovered several inconsistencies in the procedure. One actually contacted the good doctor who quite candidly admitted he had felt it was necessary to "alter" the actual circuits because, after all, he was in the business of protecting information not showing folks exactly how to go out and steal it...

Is there a real source for SYNGARD systems that will work with most computers?

Sure is…

An acquaintance of mine and a rather good, if slightly away from the beaten track, electronics engineer by the name of John Williams runs a company known as CONSUMERTRONICS (2011 Crescent Dr., PO Drawer 537, Alamagordo, NM 88310). He took the SYNGARD plans and re-engineered them so they actually work. Here's John's story:

"Dear Mr. Lapin,

We, too, have the original plans to Van Eck's device. Unfortunately, we have found that several of the critical parts he specified are either not clearly specified or were very difficult to find, so substantial redesign of his device was required. Our version is the SYNREST system. Also, his device requires a 5 volt power supply (in addition to the 12 volt supplies) because the poor design practice of combining TTL and CMOS circuits was used. Except for a 555, our circuit is totally MOS. Further, the upper horizontal frequency of their Van Eck device is 20 KHz, which eliminates its use for EGA, VGA, multisync, 8514, Macintosh, etc. monitors. Our upper limit is 45 KHz.

∎

The SYNREST system is basically a horizontal and vertical sync restorer. In addition to the SYNREST device, a modified TV/EGA monitor is also included. Tuning is as good as the antenna (also included), microwave amp TV/monitor's circuitry that derives the syncs is internally disconnected, and the combined SYNREST sync is injected into the TV/monitor's sync processing circuitry. Some other circuitry changes were also required to provide proper function of the TV/monitor.

∎

Directionality is primarily a function of the antenna. We supply a nominal antenna for the SYNREST. We don't sell antennas because there are many variations and some are bulky and expensive to ship. High-gain, highly directional antennas are commercially available which we have found capable of distinguishing between two monitors placed five feet apart on a line vertical to the line between the monitors and the SYNREST, 100 meters from the SYNREST.

∎

Our original design used a modified TV in conjunction with the SYNREST device. However, we now have an EGA version. The EGA version is best for observing EGA and above monitors. (But) the TV version is best for observing TV's, CGA's, etc.

∎

In our original design, tuning stability was a problem. That's because the SYNREST makes no use of the original signal's sync components (that's because they are just not available at any reasonable distance). Therefore, even a minute sync frequency difference between the monitor being observed and the SYNREST will cause observable horizontal drift. However, we have developed circuitry that much-increases stability so that horizontal sync adjustments are now infrequent.

∎

In addition to being capable of observing TV's and monitors of all kinds, the SYNREST system also ACTS as a TV descrambler for most types of TV scrambling, whether that be cable, satellite or whatever. The reason why I use the term, "ACTS" is because the SYNREST does absolutely nothing to the incoming TV signal so it doesn't literally descramble it. Instead, it simply and totally independently injects its own combined sync into the TV/monitor. Nevertheless, the SYNREST system is sold strictly for educational purposes only and we absolutely do NOT recommend any illegal use of the SYNREST whatsoever."

Van Eck devices are some of the most exciting high tech devices you'll ever run into! And they are definitely required in some lines of business. Personally, I don't see how a private investigator these days would have the nerve to even advertise his business without one of these devices tucked away in a van! Not only can computer monitors be observed and the type of information lifted, but also TV's. By being able to tell if a TV or monitor is turned on, one will know that a person is located in a certain room of a certain building. If the observed person just leaves the TV/monitor on, the fact that channels (TV) or display (monitor) are not being changed over a period of time would imply that no one is there. And by observing what the person is viewing, you can not only ascertain his habits but by knowing people's habits, ascertain who is viewing the TV/monitor.

Van Eck devices have perfectly legitimate uses. For example, you can use one to monitor another system in your business without the expense and effort of networking the systems together. And you can use one to monitor your TV. This is especially great for housewives who go in and out of different rooms of their home. They can have a master TV turned to their favorite program, and Van Eck devices in one or more rooms that automatically pick up and display whatever the master TV is displaying.

The SYNREST is $1,495.00 for the TV model and only $1,995.00 for the EGA model (the big difference is the cost of the monitor). Plus $50 shipping and handling."

Various government agencies in the military have had workable Van Eck-type units for, as one source in the know told me, "at least 15 years."

COMPUTER PASSWORD BREAKING

Most computer programs of any import are protected by a password. Said password blocks unauthorized entry and prevents outsiders from accessing or changing data stored in any of its memory facilities. In theory, a password is almost perfect protection because, depending on the number and type of characters used, it can require years of superfast computer time to break or it can be quite frankly, unbreakable.

Password access lets even a non-computer literate person into the protected system where most friendly systems provide help menus and directories to guide one around the system and help accomplish whatever is wished. A password is *gold.*

If passwords are so difficult to crack, why do we worry about them?

Because most of them really are not that difficult to dig out. There are a number of things many passwords have in common. The most important being that people select passwords with some sort of meaning or association that makes them easy to remember to the operator. This is the basis on which many passwords are hacked.

In a recent study of thousands of computer systems, it was discovered that many of the passwords fall into two types. The first variety included the first name of the operator, his spouse or children, any of their initials and on occasion, their surnames.

To attack these, one ascertains who constitute the highest executives in a company, including the sysop, head engineer, maintenance engineer and system installer. Frequently when a system is being set up and people are being trained to use it, the installer will use executive's names as passwords.

Another technique is to examine the interests of the top personnel in the company and try words that would pertain to these interests.

Such information is frequently published in the local newspapers, available from the company itself, or the public library. Good hackers search through the target's trash if at all possible.

Another successful attack is to "piggyback" a password by dialing into a company's communications lines, then enter the computer system by following a legit user who has entered the password.

Nicknames, home addresses, SSN's, phone numbers and addresses are also popular passwords. Social security numbers seem to be a favorite of many users and may be procured from credit reports or by paying a minor charge (usually about $1.00) to the Department of Motor Vehicles to get registered ownership information of any particular vehicle.

Another huge category of password names comes from—surprise—the subject's environment. That is, his computer system. THE MOST COMMON PASSWORD IN THE WORLD TODAY IS, guess what?—*PASSWORD.*

Yes, that's true. When a computer program prompts a user to come up with a password, in a great salute to the creativity to the American public (those same people who pay to put their initials on their custom license plates) many choose the word "password."

There are many other computer-oriented passwords such as: PEEK, DIAG, HELP, DISK, DIAGNOSTIC, TEST, SYSTEM, TESTER, SYSTEM MANAGER, TESTING, SYS, SYSMAN, SECTOR, SYSOP, SYSMAN, HELLO, ENGINEER, OPS, OPERATIONS, PHONE, GUEST, CENTRAL, SECRET, TOP SECRET, MODEM, IBMCE, LOVE, SEX, (THE MANY SYNONYMS FOR SEX), DATA, DEMO, DEMONSTRATION, MICRO, POKE, LOOP, GIGO, AID, DISPLAY, BYTE, CALL, CIPHER, TERMINAL, TERM, EXTERNAL, BAUD, REMOTE, CHECK, NET, NETWORK, FRED, CONFIG, CONFIGURE AND ZEUS.

Hackers write simple BASIC programs which try sample passwords against a system as rapidly as the system will accept the tries until one is verified. This process can take days, but if the machine will do this unattended it's only computer time, right?

Passwords consist normally of one or two words. If two, they are frequently separated by "." or "?"; word format and the delimiter chosen depends upon the system itself.

A password will be at least three characters in length. In a one-word system, the length is often, 6, 8, or 10 characters. In a two-word system, 10–12 characters are the most popular formats, but the words are often commonplace with obvious spelling. Letters usually are in upper case and may be used with numbers.

Although numbers are often used alone, seldom do users insert punctuation, graphics, or graphic characters that would complicate things.

People also tend to re-use passwords, one that worked on another system or has been used before, may still be valid, "carried" by the operator.

System and company instruction booklets are a fine starting place. All systems include password examples. A number of these default passwords are never negated and are still in operation. System manuals can be obtained from the manufacturer, computer bookstores, or libraries.

SOME TRICKS

A couple of password cracking programs on the market automatically test dictionary word groups against the protection gate. The best such program runs 10,000 of the most popular password choices against any target. Check with bulletin boards, computer magazines, and user clubs for the latest available.

A few programs designed to locate and produce files only by reference to one or more keywords included within the file, will, in some instances, automatically bypass any password protection, delivering the virgin file to the inquirer.

The most common examples of this type of inadvertent password bypass would be ON LOCATION (Mac) and FYI (IBM).

HYPERZAP (macPublic, 11329 SW 74 Terrace, Miami, FL 33173) is a dedicated program that automatically strips the password(s) from any HyperCard stack. Works like magic...

SUPERZAP is an IBM utility program available from several publishers which restores data on non functional disks. Superzap works directly on any sector on disk to restore and modify information and can/and will bypass both passwords and operating systems to address a disk.

This situation creates what is known as trap door or back door passwords. These are passwords which exist outside the sysops' domain. They may have been put there by the company who did the software, by a technician who installed it, someone who worked on it, or by someone who simply wanted to make sure he had a way into the system in case of trouble.

Back door passwords are often things like: HELP, GUEST, and IBMCE. These selections are especially valuable because they will often override all other protection in the system.

Some systems accept only numeric or all character passwords. It's wise to try AAAA, or words which are easily typed on a typewriter keyboard including: QWERKY, FRED, AND, ASDFG.

If the password is numeric, sequential strings such as 12345678 and easily typed quickies such as 101010, or 11111111, 22222222, etc. are used more often than one would think.

If the password syntax is suspected to be numeric, the second most likely category is personal numbers such as birthdays, phone numbers, vehicle license numbers, bank account numbers, addresses, anniversaries, ages, and ages of any children.

Another high percentage shot is anything from the CEO, or department Vice President. Try his name, nicknames, or those of his children, because there's a very good chance that when the system was set up, it was demonstrated to him, probably with a tech rep on the premises. Quick access with the officer's choice of password, was likely offered to make the system seem extremely simple.

This word may still be a valid entry.

A frequent method of obtaining passwords is through hands-on inspection: the agent secures access to a facility with computer terminals and finds passwords taped on the computer or printed on paper in trash receptacles. People who work at home often have their ID's and passwords taped to their computers, as they feel this is a protected location.

Optical aids may allow one to watch a target when he uses a computer terminal in order to reproduce what is typed, even if the output does not appear on the monitor.

ANOTHER TRICK

A high percentage password attack is simply to tap the computer's phone line and record in/out data. Playing this back through a modem will reveal any passwords involved in the transaction.

Secret passwords can sometimes be obtained by tricking the user to show them. A session on-line can be interrupted by one from a "chat" or "conference" mode wherein a hacker pretends to be a system operator and requests that the user re-enter his password.

The victim then types in his password.

In the past, a group of bold social engineers had great success by simply writing a letter that said, "Hi, I'm a computer hacker and I really need your password in order to monitor your communications. Would you please be so kind as to give it to me so I can enter your files, steal your customers, copy your R & D, and generally eavesdrop on all transactions?"

Sound silly? No. This really has worked in the past. The only adjustment is to fine tune the letter by phrasing it to read something like, "would you please tell me your password. I need it badly," in a way which can't be refused...

SAMPLE LETTER

June 19, 1995
Corporate Espionage Headquarters
1234 Elm Street
Cleveland, OH 80212

Large Conglomerate and Extortion Company, Inc.
852 Avenue of the Americas
New York, NY 10011

Dear Sir:

I'm with the security department of (Dialog, One-line, CompuServe, Local Area Network, Macwinner Magazine, Computer Security Newsletter, etc., etc.) and it has become apparent to us that the incidences of password hacking; i.e., unauthorized users determining the structure and content of passwords in order to bypass legitimate security is on the rise in your type of system. It is my job to help eliminate these breaches of computer security by increasing the security of YOUR password system.

I would greatly appreciate your returning to me the enclosed form completed. The results of our studies will enhance both corporate and personal security and be a major benefit to users like yourself.

Again, thank you for your time and consideration.

Dr. H. Hacker
V. P. Security
XXX

PASSWORD SECURITY SURVEY:

1. Relationship between the symbols of your password:
   a. Does your password contain two letters that are the same?
   yes   no
   b. Does your password contain two numbers that are the same?
   yes   no
2. Structure of passwords
   Please indicate with a cross the position of the letters in your password: _ _ _ _ _ _
3. Is the first symbol in your password a zero?
   yes   no
4. Letters making up your password
   In alphabetical order, the sequence of letters making up your password: _ _ _ _ _ _
5. Addresses of other people using the service:

   _____

   _____

Please fold this form, staple it and return it in the post paid envelope.

Thanks for your cooperation.

PASSWORD PROTECTION

Never use passwords with less than 4 characters.
The more characters the better. Use randomly generated, non-word units, even if it means a loss of user convenience.

1. Control computer access. Plug up all dial-in access ports that are not absolutely necessary; keep unauthorized personnel away from computers and areas where passwords might be found.
2. Use a maximum of characters in the actual password. If the system permits the use of two words, by all means take advantage of this feature, if not, insert non-printing or symbolic characters (a backspace, $, or % for instance) in password makeup.
3. Limit the number of password entry tries.
4. Provide only "yes/no" feedback.
5. Require a time interval between attempts.
6. Provide a system for alerting security personnel if cracking attacks occur.

7. For maximum security insist on an ancillary keying method such as a physical key, card, fingerprint reader, etc.

If possible employ an authentication method that requires the host computer to match up phone numbers. In such a system the user dials the computer, enters a touch tone code and hangs up.

If the code is legit, the computer will then dial the user back (from a list of authorized numbers) and connect him.

This system does limit field access but provides good security, and several commercial systems are available.

INFORMATION TRACKING
GENERAL DATABASES

There are literally thousands and thousands of commercial databases on-line that can be accessed by anyone with the correct gateway, a computer, a modem, and some knowledge of how databases work in general as well as a few techniques for the database or the database provider that will be utilized.

Why do I recommend the use of on-line sources?

1. One can get the facts in the shortest period of time. Rather than tracking down people for interviews, pounding the pavement, visiting libraries and county registrars for needed information, one can access what has already been collected by utilizing a computer search.

2. Obtain the most current data available. Newspapers, journals, newsletters, and many legal briefs and federal reports are updated within 24 hours of their publication. Some resources such as stock and business quotes are actually listed in a real-time format.

3. Research information otherwise inaccessible. Access to data such as newspaper morgues that are impossible to crack for most investigators as well as reach data housed at distant sites such as books in the Library of Congress, major data banks and card catalogs at major universities.

4. Research large amounts of data quickly. Computers can scan huge amounts of data; i.e., years of back newspaper articles or legal records with one search statement and without requiring huge file cabinets to store insuing information.

5. Build a dossier on any issue or any person. Some on-line files can be searched by key words, others by names, organizations or subjects, allowing quick background compilation.

6. Identify relationships by searching seemingly unrelated events, people, organizations, dates or locales. One can define new associations and identify new leads which can then be followed up on-line or offline.

Investigative reporters have discovered the phenomenal accessibility provided by these commercial databases and any good newspaper now runs a database search as a prerequisite to writing any important story. This search may turn up important information that can be used to research the story or it may in fact turn up the bare bones of the story itself by simply expending a few minutes of the investigator/researcher's time.

In days past this material could only have been gotten by extensive on-site research which is limited by the proximity of good libraries and research facilities. At the very least a competent researcher will pull out a number of facts, often including people's names and references to items that will be used as leads and followed up upon by more conventional techniques such as telephone interviews, social engineering, or in person visits.

There have been a number of Pulitzer prizes awarded to reporters; i.e., Mary Pat Flaharty and others at *The Pittsburg Press*, found and investigated their prize-winning stories solely through the auspices of on-line research. A number of top notch investigative reporters who I interviewed admitted that at least 50% of their stories, would not have made it to the print stage if it had not been for computer research.

The same concepts and techniques utilized by investigative reporters can be put to good use by private investigators, security consultants or intelligence collectors. One does not have to be a computer hacker in order to burrow through the maze of data available but some basic understandings of the system must be in evidence.

The hardware, the computers themselves, have dropped in price substantially over the last few years. It was estimated that the average monetary requirement for a system with all the basic programs needed to allow a researcher to use computer-aided investigations skills, was about $10,000 three years ago. It's now completely available with a loose $1,500 to $3,000. Even that is not a necessary outlay if one is willing to use a Rent-a-Computer Center and pay an hourly rate for equipment access.

Any personal computer will work on any database due to the fact that it's going over a modem which standardizes information transfer. The most popular computer for researching is no doubt the IBM PC or clone thereof. It does work quite efficiently. My personal pick is the Mac because of both the ease of use and the fact that it just seems to have more flat out personality than the IBM.

The computer must have sufficient memory (RAM) to process the software and incoming data. I would suggest a minimum of one meg, preferably three or four and a clock speed of sufficient rate to process the on-line data. Remember the more time spent on the service crunching numbers, the higher the bills will be.

The microprocessor itself should be the most advanced your budget can handle—8088 chips still used in many IBM clones are slow and cumbersome. The 8086 is about 50% faster and at least gets you in the ballpark. The 8286 is about twice as fast as the 8088 and is the primary chip in the IBM AT. The 8386 which is again, you guessed it, twice as fast as the 8286 is the primary chip in the Model 70 in the Compact 386.

The fastest chip available right now is the 8486, which actually gives processing power heretofore enjoyed only by mainframes.

A hard disk drive is almost a necessity in order to capture incoming data and a Hayes based modem is also mandatory. Most databases operate at either 1200 or 2400 baud although we can expect to see some of the better ones moving up into the 9600 range in the near future.

In addition to the hardware a variety of software is necessary that will run somewhere between $0 to $600 per, depending on your contacts and feeling about copyright laws in general. This will include the operating system the computer runs on and a standard word processing program to handle text files. Your WP program should be one of the major ones such as: MacWrite, WordStar, MicroSoft, or comparable. You'll want a database program to sort, index, and store your records, plus a communications program to operate your modem. It is also possible to get a variety of utility programs that perform various speciality tasks for maximizing your database access time.

What is a database? A database is a collection of information available on-line, and in some cases in hard copy text formats. Databases can live in any computer and some large databases, in fact, live in not one but in a number of computers on a net simultaneously.

Information is normally fed into a database by hired readers who scan sources of information including most major newspapers, journals, graduate theses, books, newsletters, technical and scientific papers, popular magazines, scientific and military application papers, law abstracts, court cases, congressional records, proceedings of private organizations, names, addresses, change of addresses, school information, etc.

This information is read by the input person and then typed into the database. It is also cross indexed by title and by key word, a very important concept in our access path. Many larger databases are updated on an hourly or in the worst case scenario, daily basis while some of the more obscure bases may be only updated when new relevant information becomes available, say on a weekly basis.

What is available from databases? Damn near everything: DataTimes makes available new articles as well as recent year morgue articles from a number of papers representing every region in the United States from *The New York Times* and *Washington Post* down to *The Illinois Wheat Farmer Beater.*

This particular database is extremely important to anyone trying to locate a target or make up a dossier on a person or a company. Newspaper articles can provide valuable information on just about any subject who may have been in the news. This doesn't limit the subject to national news but even small town newspapers that report arrest records or social registers will have these files available in DataTimes.

Not only is this a convenient methodology of locating a particular article or file, it exposes an area that is mostly completely virgin to investigators simply because newspapers will, generally speaking, not let outsiders into their morgues and are reluctant to part with proprietary information. DataTimes makes this access available, convenient, and focuses a huge number of articles/morgue files in one place!

Because the articles are entered not only under their title but also under their key word, it is much easier to search for a particular subject than it would be in any form of sequential, page search pattern. After entering a database and giving it one or more key words to search on, the database will look through every single piece of information it has for any appearance of the word you want. A search of real estate fraud, Marina County, California, would produce only articles or references to reports of real estate fraud in Marina County, California, probably a very specific list with maybe 20 or 30 entries.

The same database would provide literally thousands of listings if the search was simply entered as real estate, perhaps only a few hundred with the delimiters of real estate fraud. A good investigator can narrow his search down in a matter of moments by watching the number of "hits" that the database provides on any topic. If there are too many hits to deal with, one must simply go back and re-ask the

question by coupling another delimiter word (such as Marina County, California, as in the above example) to the original search question in order to bring the amount of material down to a manageable size.

By the same token, if there are no hits or very few hits, the original questions can be quickly expanded upon by removing a delimiter or actually using the command "expand" in many databases to widen the field of search.

Once the database has listed the number of incidences of the word in question, the researcher can now ask for a look at the titles and sources of the reference material which contains the key word. Some databases will actually allow you to scan abstracts of the articles in questions and all will allow full text readouts and printouts of any paper or article in which the key word incurs.

These commercial databases can be used to track people down, find out anything that has been written about any particular subject or simply provide leads for further research. In the above example, if one was searching for information on a corporation that one suspected was involved in real estate fraud, perhaps under a variety of different names in a particular area, the articles produced could be searched for references to names of people involved with the company, reporters who researched the company, DA's or police officers who investigated the company, lawyers who represented either side of any disputes, persons who've brought claims against the company and on and on.

A specific search on a person's name will often bring up good background information on the person and often leads to his/her whereabouts. Because general databases are not oriented towards any specific research group, one must learn some creativity in searching — a good example of this was accomplished by a PI I know who needed to find some information on a fairly well respected businessman. He suspected the man would belong to the local branch of the Commonwealth Club, a rather prestigious organization for businessmen, and knew he could probably get information from some of the man's cohorts and competitors. He called the Commonwealth Club only to be rather less than politely rebuffed about the possible availability of any membership roster on their part. Such things were simply not done...

Under normal circumstances he might have gone to a number of meetings, staked out the parking lot, ran license tag searches, and gradually tried to sift his way through a mountain of information. Instead, he punched up a database, punched up a listing of Who's Who (on-line and available), and then did a key word search of Who's Who using the name of the Commonwealth Club as a delimiter. As might be expected, persons who write their entries in Who's Who and wish to impress their professional colleagues, often include references to prestigious organizations; for instance, the Commonwealth Club, to which they belong.

In a matter of seconds he had a list of almost the complete membership of the chapter of the Commonwealth Club that he was looking for plus contract addresses, background information and methods of social engineering access on every member at his fingertips.

It took two phone calls to find out exactly where the subject was, what the man was doing and what he had done to both the contacted members of the club and my friend's client...

Databases can be a panacea for many questions. However, as with anything, there is always a trade-off factor. In this case say these three words to yourself: good, fast, cheap.

Now pick two of the above.

This premise shows how databases work. One can get things quick. One can get things detailed. One can get things not normally accessible or which would take days and days of footwork, in a matter of moments. Or one can get them cheap, but pal, one ain't going to get all three together...

DATABASE ACCESS

How does an investigator actually get hands-on database access? As I mentioned, there are literally thousands of databases with new ones appearing all the time. Searching for the correct database can become just as important a task as accessing the database itself. As one might suspect, there are actually databases of databases.

One on-line database is called EasyNet, a directory of databases that is constantly updated.

ON-LINE SERVICES/SUPERMARKETS

Because of the huge number of databases, most are available through other providers that group databases together and offer a "value added" doorway. Small databases may not even be accessible *except* thru the auspices of a provider, and most large databases are approachable in a number of providers.

The biggest providers are "supermarkets" where one electronically browses among lists of data, choosing only those things on one's shopping list.

This is a partial list of some of the largest and most applicable on-line service providers. If no sign-up info is given, they are available through one or more of the "majors."

AMA/NET

MEDICAL: Database with info. from CDC

OFFICE OF THE SURGEON GENERAL

NATIONAL LIBRARY OF MEDICINE

NATIONAL INSTITUTES OF HEALTH: Includes access to CDC MMWR and the AIDS, SURVEILLANCE REPORT

AMERICAN POLITICAL DAILY ABSTRACTS: News election coverage

BASELINE: An entertainment database which includes information on cast and crew of virtually every feature, foreign and domestic film, as well as TV mini-series and American stage productions. Baseline identifies 10,000+ industry-related companies and organizations, lists box office receipts, academy award nominations and industry news.

BRS NEWS SERVICE: BRS Information Technologies Maxwell Online, 8000 Westpark Drive, McLean, VA 22102, 800/456–7248, 703/442–0900 (VA). A competitor to Dialog they offer low cost searching on a wide range of databases in a special after hours service.

BUREAU OF LABOR STATISTICS: Complete text of BLS news releases, U.S. Import and Export price indexes, earnings, employment news, cost indexes and consumer price indexes.

BUTEXT: Provides full text of many regional newspapers including the Miami Herald, Philadelphia Inquirer and the Annapolis Capital.

COMMERCE DEPARTMENT BULLETIN BOARD: A bulletin board which provides economic news information produced by the Department of Commerce and other federal government agencies.

COMPUSERVE: A consumer-oriented database provider which offers shopping services, special interest groups (SIGS), forums, daily news reports, information on weather, sports, travel, computers, stock quotes and general information on specific companies. CompuServe is inexpensive, at this time a $10.00 a month flat rate plus an hourly charge of $6.00–$12.00 depending on time of usage. Also offers access to a number of more specific databases for which it is a vendor. This means that CompuServe will get the searcher into specific databases as well as suggesting databases for a particular search based on the key word. It does access several good databases including military and scientific information from separate colleges. On the whole, however, CompuServe is a bit chatty and low-end in access.

CQ/WASHINGTON ALERT: Information on federal legislation, bills, resolutions, abstracts, text of the congressional record, committee and floor schedules, floor votes, member and district profiles and other reports.

DATACALL: The complete text of all stories wired in the past 24 hours from the L. A. Times and Washington Post news service, the German news agency and French news agency. Provides up-to-the minute coverage of breaking news on an international basis.

DATATIMES: DataTimes Corporation, 14000 Quail Springs Parkway, Suite 450, Oklahoma City, OK 73134, 405/751–6400, 800/642–2525. DataTimes provides a complete text of more than 30 regional newspapers including the Orange County Register, St. Petersburg Times, Minneapolis Star and Tribune, Dallas Morning News, San Francisco Chronicle, on and on... They offer a number of exclusives of a number of newspapers and are the No. 2 supplier of regional newspapers after VU/TEXT. They formerly were accessed through EASYNET but now they required access through individual memberships or through DOW JONES NEWS RETRIEVAL.

DIALOG: Dialog is the largest commercial database provider in the world and gives access to more than 600 on-line sources. It contains abstracts and complete texts of national journals, newspapers and industry newsletters and information sources from politics, government, business, finance, science, technology, law and a host of other things that boggles the mind. Dialog is the first and probably the most practical database provider for an investigator to join.

DOW JONES: Dow Jones/News Retrieval, Information Services Group, Dow Jones and Company, Inc., P. O. Box 300, Princeton, NJ 08543, 609/520–4000. Besides being the leading business news service, they offer access to Data Times Regional Newspaper selection.

DJ stocks current business and financial news worldwide from the Wall Street Journal, Barons Business Date Line, the Business Library and the Washington Post.

EASYNET/TELEBASE SYSTEMS, INC.: Well supported access to about 1,000 data bases from 12 leading search services. The EASYNET service is accessible through more than 15 different electronic mail and bulletin board services including CompuServe where it's known as IQ Quest. If you purchase access time directly from the parent company with a credit card, you'll reach all the EASYNET access interfaces. EASYNET supports its service with round-the-clock line searchers available through view searches and suggests improvements. They will also hard copy deliver articles.

FEC: Federal Election Commission provides campaign finance data on congressional and presidential candidates and the names of individuals who contribute $1,000 or more to any candidate.

HUD PUBLIC AFFAIRS: The complete text of official HUD news releases, biographies of HUD candidates, directory actions announced by the secretary of HUD since 1989, and a national list of HUD information contacts.

INFO GLOBE: On-line access to text of Canadian newspapers and directory information including selected federal and provincial budget speeches and public papers. INSTANT YELLOW PAGES SERVICE, P. O. Box 27347, Omaha, NB 68127, 402/331–7169. Access to Yellow Pages of most phone books in the United States.

INVESTEXT/PLUS: Financial and market information on more than 10,000 foreign and domestic companies and 50 industries written by industry specialists from over 48 major financial research firms and investment houses world wide.

LEGISLATE: Status and text of congressional bills and legislation, voting records, committee schedules, a look at the congressional record and profiles of members.

LUSKNET: A regional database for the District of Columbia and surrounding counties that includes real estate sales, loan transactions, ownership of properties, assessments, property sales in the covered counties. Should be expanding in the near future.

NEXTUS/LEXIS: MEAD DATA CENTRAL, 9393 Springboro Pike, P.O. Box 933, Dayton, OH 45401, 800/227–4908. Complete text of numerous national magazines and newspapers such as New York Times and L.A. Times, regional business publications, science, technology, and medical databases. Lexus provides the full text of decisions from federal and state courts as well as lien information from most states. NEXTUS produces their own search aid software which facilitates searching through their newspaper and wire service data banks.

ORBIT SEARCH SERVICE: Maxwell Online, 8000 Westpark Drive, McLean, VA 22102, 703/442–0900, 800/456–7248. A supermarket of over 100 databases with a bent towards science and technology. A number of these databases are not available elsewhere including foreign patent searches and lists of accountants. PACER. A database for the docket histories of District of Columbia's court records.

PROFILE: Full text, Financial Times, London Times, The Independent and The Guardian. Also provides access to the Associated Press, BBC news services, The Economist, Global News Analysis, New Scientist, TASS, Today and The Washington Post.

REUTERS HISTORICAL INFORMATION: 2 First Canadian Place, Suite 1900, Toronto, Ontario, M5X 1E3, Canada. Reuters is the world's largest news organization and they supply information to the world's financial and business communities, news agencies, newspapers, radios and TV shows in 137 countries. The creation of the Reuter file brings together data resources from a number of a different services. USNI Military database. Weapons systems, armed forces of various nations, defense organizations, military terms, and profiles of U.S. officers.

VU/TEXT INFORMATION SERVICES, INC.: 325 Chestnut St., Suite 1300, Philadelphia, PA 19106, 215/574–4400. Also can be reached through EASYNET. VU/TEXT is similar to DIALOG in many respects although they offer access to many more local papers than DIALOG.

WESTERN UNION INFOMASTER: 1 Lake Street, Upper Saddle River, NJ 05458, 800/779–1111. Infomaster provides access to 800 databases from many vendors including other supermarkets, think of it as sort of an electronic mall where you can access Diaglog, NewsNet, Orbit, Vu/Text, BRS, among others, making it the largest collection to quote Western Union of online databases anywhere.
Infomaster offers three levels of searching. It will recommend databases based on your topic, offers a menu based approach where the user supplies the database, and a company name mode where one simply enters the company name to find out how many times it is featured in each database. One can subscribe directly to Infomaster or it can be accessed through Western Union's E-Mail service EasyLink.

WESTLAW: West Publishing Company, 50 W. Kellogg Blvd., St. Paul, MN 55164 or 800–WESTLAW. Westlaw is the nation's oldest and largest legal publisher. They now have a database which is in itself a collection of different legal databases and will supply full text access to various topics including bankruptcy, energy, and patents. Westlaw puts over 200 legal magazines directly online and will help customers formulate search queries until the right legal points are found.

At this juncture I should point out there are a number of services that will perform database searches for you. These brokers usually consist of research librarians or other types who make a substantial living by performing database searches for customers. The three largest "document delivery" vendors are:

Information on Demand
8000 West Park Drive,
MacClean, Virginia 22102,
800–999–4463

Research on Demand
2030 Addison Street
Suite 400
Berkeley, California 94704
800–227–0750

Savage Information Services
2510 West 237th Street
Suite 200
Torrance, California 90505
213–530–4747

I should point out that these companies charge for their services and one could expect a typical report to run at least $250, but if it's on an expense account supplied a rich client...

A LOOK AT DIALOG
DIALOG is truly a database supermarket that offers direct access to hundreds of individual databases that vary greatly in scope and content. The individual databases vary greatly in format and content. Each one has "blue sheet" or database description that contains the scope of coverage, file size and update frequency for the database itself. These blue sheets can be pulled on-line from DIALOG.

DIALOG is reasonably priced. Sign up fees average around $100 which includes hard copy instructions and necessary reference materials and they usually offer the sign up fee back in search time.

The data found in most DIALOG databases falls into one or more of the following categories:

- Bibliographic records containing citations and sometimes abstracts to original documents listing authors, titles, and original source information.
- Complete text records. Full narrative text of an article or publication.
- Directories. Full listings, directories, dictionaries, handbooks, organizations, description, listings of available grants or other source materials.
- Numeric data. Records that consist primarily of numeric statistics and tables, such as financial data, etc.

Some databases fall into more than one category. As such they are classified in more than one category.

A TRICK

Some databases, including DIALOG, offer services that are both useful and not necessarily apparent in their descriptive literature.
For instance...
A quick way to ID and pull up info about many businesses, if one is armed only with a phone number, can be had by using telephone numbers as a search field. Go to TRINET on DIALOG and tell it you want to search an additional field by specifying S TE= XXX–XXX–XXXX. Where the XXX's are the phone number of the target. This command will search out each and every company in the database by the phone number entered and, when found, will pull up a fountain of information about the target company.

This trick is fast, cheap, and works on many target companies. Other databases will also search on the "additional field" syntax but may require slight adjustments in the input instructions.

Each DIALOG database has a specific rate for its services, a DIALOG access number and a descriptor sheet available. A quick look at some of the databases (they are proceeded by their DIALOG file number) that would be of interest in our profession(s) would be:

ERIC. The database that DIALOG puts each user into to begin his/her search.
211 NEWSEARCH. 545 INVEST TEXT.
635 BUSINESS DATA LINES. 648 TRADE AND INDUSTRY. 470 BOOKS IN PRINT.
421–426 REMARK BOOKS. 66 U.S.
GOVERNMENT GPO MONTHLY CATALOG.
166 GPO REFERENCE FILE. 47 MAGAZINE INDEX. 111 NATIONAL NEWSPAPER INDEX.
137 BOOK REVIEW INDEX. 603 NEWSPAPER ABSTRACTS. 90 FOREIGN TRADE AND ECON ABSTRACTS. 148 TRADE AND INDUSTRY INDEX. 583 INFOMET INTERNATIONAL BUSINESS. 95 COMMERCE BUSINESS DAILY.
636 PTS NEWSLETTER DATABASE. 150 LEGAL RESOURCE INDEX. 243, 244 LABOR LAW.
132 STANDARD AND POOR'S NEWS. 548 M & A FILINGS. 549 INSIDER TRADING MONITOR.
550 IDD M&A TRANSACTIONS. 556 MOODY'S CORPORATE NEWS. 610 BUSINESS WIRE.
649 NEWSWIRE ASAP. 196 FINE DEX.
646 CONSUMER REPORTS. 675 COMPUTER ASAP. 535 THOMAS REGISTER ON-LINE.
111 NATIONAL NEWSPAPER INDEX.
146 WASHINGTON POST ON-LINE.
633 CHICAGO TRIBUNE. 635 BUSINESS DATE LINE. 375 COMPUTER DATABASE. 17 PTS ANNUAL REPORTS, ABSTRACTS. 518 D&B INTERNATIONAL MARKET IDENTIFIERS.
560 FINANCIAL TIMES COMPANY ABSTRACTS.
561 ICC BRITISH COMPANY DIRECTORY.
600 McGRAW HILL NEWS. 100 DISCLOSURE DATABASE. 133 STANDARD & POOR'S CORPORATE DESCRIPTIONS.
540 DISCLOSURES/SPECTRUM OWNERSHIP.
546 MEDIA GENERAL PLUS. 555 MOODY'S CORPORATE PROFILES. 513 CORPORATE AFFILIATIONS. 515 D&B ELECTRONIC YELLOW PAGES. 517 D&B MILLION DOLLAR DIRECTORY. 519 D&B FINANCIAL RECORDS PLUS. 238 SUPERTECH. 635 BUSINESS DATE LINE. 232 MENU (THE International Software Database). 570 PTS MARKETING AND

ADVERTISING REFERENCE SERVICE.
135 CONGRESSIONAL REGISTER ABSTRACTS.
136 FEDERAL REGISTER ABSTRACTS.
171 CRIMINAL JUSTICE PERIODICAL INDEX.
258 AP NEWS. 259 AP NEWS BACKFILE.
261 UPI NEWS. 260 UPI NEWS BACKFILE.
264 FACTS ON FILE. 644 USA TODAY DECISION
LINE. 645 CURRENT DIGEST OF THE SOVIET
PRESS. 649 NEWSWIRE ASAP. 611 REUTERS.
123 CLAIMS (PATENTS). 125 U.S. PATENTS
ABSTRACTS WEEKLY. 351 WORLD PATENTS
INDEX. 180 ACADEMIC AMERICAN
ENCYCLOPEDIA. 162 CAREER PLACEMEN.
REGISTRY. 183 EXPERNET. 234 WHO'S WHO.
236 AMERICAN MEN AND WOMEN OF
SCIENCE. 526 STANDARD & POOR'S
BIOGRAPHICAL REGISTER. 214 PETERSON'S
COLLEGE DATABASE. 273 GRAD LINE.
511D&B ELECTRONIC DIRECTORY OF
EDUCATION. 6 NTIS. 8 COMDEX PLUS.
13 INSPECTS. 7761LEASE OPT. 170 ON-LINE
CHRONICLE. 202 INFORMATION SCIENCE
ABSTRACTS. 7 SOCIAL SCISEARCH. 121 BRITISH
EDUCATION ANNEX. 35 DISSERTATION
ABSTRACTS ON-LINE and for those really tough
days...

297 THE KING JAMES VERSION OF THE HOLY
BIBLE, ON-LINE...

This is by no means a complete list of DIALOG
databases. It is simply some that are of interest.

Let's expand that a bit and look at some of
the more useful ones.

603 NEWSPAPER ABSTRACTS: An on-line
newspaper indexing and abstracting service of
University Microfilms International. Provides
comprehensive indexing for 19 major regional
and international newspapers from the New
York Times to the Wall Street Journal. Provides
article abstracts and indexes, information
included in special series and supplements.
Search options include abstract, company name,
descriptor, person, title. It is possible to limit the
search in this particular category by pub. year.

647 MAGAZINE ASAP: Provides complete text
and indexing of more than 100 frequent sited
American magazines. Articles, news reports,
editorials, product evaluations, biographical
pieces, recipes and reviews are included. It will
search all words within the text, thus enabling
searches for quotes, figures, names, company
names, or subject coverage.

Inclusive dates are 1983 to the present and
they update approximately 1,000 records per
month.

636 PTS NEWSLETTER DATABASE: Lets subscribers retrieve any available issue of a newsletter, displays table of contents, listing articles
contained in selected issues, and print the text
of the newsletter article selected by title. Subject coverage is wide from biotechnology to
telecommunications.

600 McGRAW HILL NEWS: Provides complete
text of current news stories covering top business
events around the world and when appropriate,
utilizes McGraw Hill news editors to add to the
original news item by putting more detailed
research including names of sources. This
includes the work of 800 McGraw Hill specialist
editors at 88 different publications.

624 McGRAW HILL PUBLICATIONS ON-LINE:
This is the complete text of over 30 magazines
and newsletters published by McGraw Hill, Inc.
All text of articles from these publications are
included in this database along with some
ancillary information.

479 COMPANY INTELLIGENCE: This is a combined directory and company news file from
Information Access Company which contains
the current address, financial and marketing
information on 100,000 U.S. private and public
companies. This database also has up to 10
of the most recent news references on each
company in the database. Compiled through
public information and questionaires/tele-
phone interviews with private company
personnel.

The public information is obtained primarily from annual reports and 10K's but much of the private company information including names of the officers, citations, street addresses, access code and telephone numbers, parents and wards, along with special features which can not be found anywhere else.

531 TRINET U.S. BUSINESSES: A directory file produced by Trinet Inc. Contains the addresses, telephone numbers, financial, employment data and corporate linkages to about 7.5 *MILLION* U.S. business establishments. Trinet covers public and private U.S. companies in all sectors of industry and is classified into SIC codes. Information available is similar to the last file with some additional marketing features such as market shares and statistical information.

139 ECONOMIC LITERATURE INDEX: Provides world-wide coverage of the literature in economics from more than over 300 major economic journals and collective volumes. This is a great database for business intelligence.

648 TRADE AND INDUSTRY ASAP: This provides complete text and indexing for major articles for more than 90 trade specific and general business publications as well as wire stories from worldwide news wires and is an excellent source of names, leads and background information useful before any interviews or telephone calls take place.

540 DISCLOSURE/SPECTRUM OWNERSHIP: This database has detailed ownership information for 5,000 public companies. It is probably the most widely used set of public corporate ownership information available. Names of insiders who hold shares along with information about their holdings as well as institution and corporate insider ownership information is included.

DATABASE DIRECTORIES AND TECHNIQUES

DATABASE DIRECTORIES: Directory of Online Databases: Cuadra-Elsevier, 11835 W. Olympic Boulevard, Suite 855, Los Angeles, CA 90064, 213/478-0066. This covers all commercially available files worldwide and some controlled access files. It is online with a number of specialized services, the most successful one being EasyNet. Otherwise it is available (updated twice a year) basis for $150 (at this writing) in a choice of media.

COMPUTER-READABLE DATABASES; A DIRECTORY AND DATA SOURCEBOOK: Gale Research Inc., Book Tower, Detroit, MI 48226, 800/521-0707, 313/961-2242. For $160 it does just what it says. If you don't plan on using this service extensively, access it online by going through Dialog and asking for File 230. It can also be reached through EasyNet.

DATABASE DIRECTORY SERVICE: Knowledge Industry Publications, Inc., 701 Westchester Avenue, White Plains, NY 10604, 914/328-9157, 800/248-5474. Semi-annual release with monthly updates available for $400 through EasyNet.

FULLTEXT SOURCES ONLINE: Bibliodata, P. O. Box 61, Needham Heights, MA 02194, 617/444-1154. Published semi-annually for $45 (full text). Is primarily concerned with individual journals, newspapers, and books that are available in full text version.

NATIONAL DIRECTORY OF BULLETIN BOARD SYSTEMS: Ric Manning, Meckler Corp., 11 Ferry Lane West, Westport, CT 06880. Does what it says it does...

THE ULTIMATE DATABASE

DB technology is moving so rapidly one could not help but hope, maybe even assume, that the federal government would jump into the fray. Worry not, the largest artificial intelligence program ever created is busy correlating data on you.

And more than likely, on me...

FinCEN (Financial Crimes Enforcement Network), is sponsored by the various government officials who are, in general, opposed to any form of privacy, is designed to circumvent the laws that deny different agencies (FBI, IRS, etc.) from sharing financial data among themselves.

FinCEN allows each agency to feed in packets of data that can be withdrawn by any other agency.

Share data? Hell no...

FinCEN simply inputs bank deposit info, Fed bank reports, FDIC info, Controller info and currency receipts and compares them with census income figures, customs monetary receipts, secret service credit receipts and FBI/ DEA data and then searches on ANY field for any agency.

With 200 employees from the IRS, FBI, BATF, CIA and Defense Intelligence Agency, the system is capable of learning from its own mistakes and reporting virtually any monetary transaction to any agency.

For those of you who missed out on living in Soviet Bloc countries during the Stalin years, here's...FinCEN!!!

DETECTIVE DATABASES

Detective databases are specialized information resources that are designed to help detectives, attorneys, skip tracers locate people, find assets, dig out motor vehicle records, college transcripts credit histories, phone numbers, forwarding addresses, references, and so on. Because of a some changes in the law these databases can now can be accessed by anyone with a little knowledge and a few bucks.

In the past few years two major changes have occurred that are of great interest to detectives, researchers and generally nosy people. The first landmark was when some unnamed judge passed down a decision that will forever change the fields of investigation, research and surveillance. Our hero, the judge, decided that not all the information contained in a credit report fell under the auspices of The Fair Credit Reporting Act; that is to say information that did not actually report on the condition of the subject's credit, so called header information, did not come under The Fair Credit Reporting Act.

The Fair Credit Reporting Act, or as we fondly think of it, Public Law 91-508, deals with the legitimacy of credit report requests and specifically lists the reasons under which a consumer report may be obtained. Basically the law reads that this information will be turned over to the order of a court having jurisdiction to issue such an order, or in accordance with the written instructions of the consumer (target) to whom it relates, or to a person which it has reason to believe intends to use the information in connection with a credit transaction involving the consumer on whom the information is to be furnished and involving the extension of credit to or review of collection of account of the customer, or intends to use the information for employment purposes, or intends to use the information in connection with underwriting of insurance, or intends to use the information in connection with determining the target's eligibility for a license or other benefit granted by a government agency, or otherwise has a legitimate business need for

the information in connection with a business transaction *involving the consumer.*

I'd also like to point out that the law has teeth in it and anyone who "knowingly and willfully obtains information from a consumer reporting agency under false pretenses shall be fined not more than $5,000 or imprisoned more than one year or both."

This has limited the availability of credit reports to investigators. In fact, any time you are having a bad day and need a good laugh, call up a credit agency and tell them you are a private investigator and want a credit report.

You'll all share a moment of humor.

As you probably realize, the FCR Act limits the accessibility to credit reports; it would not be a terrible over simplification to say it helps direct credit reports only to people who have legitimate requests from the consumer to run a credit check. It is designed to control or eliminate credit checks from unscrupulous aluminum siding dealers as well as from those who would spy upon their neighbors.

For our purposes, the credit data on a credit report is by far the least important portion of the report. The rest of the data, the header data if you will, is packed with golden information that can be a similar computer bank, cross-referenced and then searched in many different approaches.

The decision to make this data available opened the doors for a flood of investigation-by telephone as third party companies formed to correlate and make available this header data from companies like TRW.

What kind of information does this data reveal to a skillful keyboard investigator? Social security numbers, skip trace information, employment information, address verification...

And searches are just the tip of the iceberg. We'll take a look at how an innovative telephone manipulator can draw upon these various banks for information that was completely unavailable until a few years ago. Now it's just a few seconds away.

The other Big Decision was that most information collected by public funds—i.e., taxpayers monies—did in fact belong to the public. Some of the juiciest background and crystal intelligence information was immediately set loose by this decision as government data banks began to take private inquiries.

What sort of information has this particular decision set loose upon the world? License tag address searches, social security number searches, postal forwarding files, just to name some of the "new age" information that may have been previously unavailable, or at least difficult to access, that is now just a dial tone away.

The only down side to this scenario is going to be its impact on our favorite television shows. No more will Spencer, Rockford, or Magnum dash through asphalt jungles chasing their unwary quarry avoiding certain death and dismemberment at every turn, protected only by their large, black, weight-lifting, philosophied degreed partners to keep them afloat in a maelstrom of scum bags packing their trusty Smith and Wesson model 29's Glaser 44 mag slugs to fend off hostile kidnapping crack dealers.

No, tomorrow's TV detectives, in keeping with the realistic nature of television, will be men of slight stature dressed in pin striped Van Husen dress shirts, tie knots slightly askew as sweat pours into their plastic pocket protectors, from grasping a telephone handset too tightly while they keep hitting the redial button. The only tension in the scene will come from our hero worrying about whether his wife may or may not believe he was late for dinner because the computer was down...

But even at the risk of losing an entire genre of television shows, the new on-line search methods are worth their weight in gold. Anybody, private detective or private person, can access these services on one level or another and track, trace, or find out information on nearly anyone who has ever gotten a driver's license, purchased anything on credit, has a listed address or phone number, or, frankly, anybody who's not gone to great extremes to make sure they do not appear in some node on a commercial or government data bank.

There are data banks on people and there are data banks on businesses. There are data banks on data. With a little practice, whole fields of information are available to the skillful interrogator.

Shortly after the above two decisions were entered into the public record, both government agencies and credit reporting agencies realized there was money to be made by franchising out their information to interested parties, and both began to do so.

By law these agencies had to make the data available to anyone. Yet they didn't want to be bothered with setting up accounts for people who are curious about the girl next door or are desperately trying to find Susan.

The qualifying factor became one of money. Most of the large agencies will allow access on a minimum billing status. This fee is usually quite high (averages about $2,000 a month) so even though the per record cost is slight, any investigator wishing direct access to a major data bank had better plan on filling his idle hours with requests for information or he'll be paying for unused time.

By no means does this mean that single record or single report access is impossible. Rather it simply brings us back to our parable of the supermarkets—a number of vendors have packaged database access, in essence putting themselves in the supermarket information business.

Each of these vendors have put together one or more packages which makes them unique in the data procurement industry. Most have also set up there own front-end software to help guide the uninitiated through the path of informational nodes.

Access to the supermarkets varies; some vendors charge a one-time set-up fee of several hundred dollars for their software, a password, and a phone number for the on-line searcher, plus of course, a per record or per search charge.

These are "added value" vendors. The investigator will be paying a surcharge for the system's availability and gateway to more expensive databases. For a private investigator or serious surveillance buff, the supermarket approach is the way to go. By joining one or two of these programs it is possible to provide your clients with an amazing array of data, for which, of course, the investigator adds his surcharge in turn.

Suppose you're not a private investigator or suppose you're a bad private investigator with just a couple of clients or let me take that back, you're a *great* private investigator with one big client. At any rate, what if you don't need multiple access but simply want to check on a certain person's habits. I don't know, say you were getting married or getting a business partner or even buying a used car and wanted to trace the previous owners, operators, and acquaintances of any of the above?

In this case, one doesn't even have to go to the supermarkets, one can go to the 7-11's.

Specific investigators and information brokers exist who will deal with you as a client, adding the obligatory value-added surcharge onto each record retrieval but still keeping the cost far, far under what it would run the average Joe off the street to walk into an investigator's office, "I want everything you can find out about this guy."

Let's take a look at a couple of the supermarkets who will sell you anything you want from cereal to steak, informationally speaking of course...

U.S. DATALINK
800–527–7930, 671 Bayway Drive, Baytown, TX 77520. U.S. Datalink represents over 250 information brokers with the idea that its customers can have one-call access to public documents in 50 states, including some records that do not exist in a machine readable form. USDL has four different in-house data bank

nodes and access programs. Each one costs approximately $380 for a setup fee or all three can be installed for a one-time charge of $975. After that each individual search will cost somewhere between $4.50 and $55.00 depending on how difficult the search is and how much human intervention it requires to complete.

USDL charges its customers only for hits, a feature which becomes a favorite of anybody who searches public databases and pays for $10–$25 records that really have nothing to do with their search.

Once you have your password, you call up USDL or access them via Telenet but, the real key to their successful access is the ability of USDL's front-end software programs to provide the user to set up a macro search strategy offline using his personal computer before coming on-line to access USDL's facilities. This brings the average time of a inquiry transmission including report retrieval to less than one minute per search, saving on those all too prevalent phone charges.

USDL's databases include PC LOCATOR which processes credit header information. One enters a name, social security number, or an address or phone number and is able to scan over 600 million public records to verify identities or find anyone anywhere. Unlisted or unpublished phone numbers are not included in the database that any of these organizations will search. However, many of them drift into the records because people will respond when an operator asks for the phone number when ordering something with a credit card or they will fill out the phone number space on an order slip. These records are carefully entered by highly paid, $5.00 an hour or so, college dropouts who spend their productive hours matching information.

PC PROFILE
Provides links to employment data, criminal histories, driving records, licenses, professional certifications, verification of degrees from over

5,000 colleges and trade schools. One of the USDL sub-contractors will even get on the phone and call past employers to verify references and previous employment for a mere $15.00. A bargain when you consider what it would cost you in time and effort and callbacks to trace down this information.

PC CORPORATE
Deals with business records including Uniform Commercial Credit Reports on businesses, corporation and DBA records, office reports, bankruptcies, federal filings, etc. This file is ideal for anyone who is checking out a company before ordering a product, buying stock or even for people who have a job offer and want to check out their perspective employer's history of dealing with people.

PC AUTO
The final and by no means least interesting segment of USDL. As one might suspect from the name, this provides access to motor vehicles, pleasure boats, FAA, pilot licenses and driver's license records on a nationwide basis. Anyone can trace either a vehicle or a driver from a tag number, serial number, date of birth or name and develop cross connected relationships between a person, his vehicle, and his life.

At the present time 47 out of the 50 states release DMV information to anyone with the necessary credentials (in this case about $8.00 in cash), but it should be noted that there is a trend to go the other way on this particular search and if not deny access entirely, at least limit access to law enforcement or insurance oriented requests. An example of this information being misapplied was in California where recently an actress was tracked down by a "fan" who saw her get into a car and traced her address through the DMV. He showed up on her doorstep to proclaim his life-long admiration for her and the fact that no one else would be permitted the same privileges.

He shot her dead.

Due to public pressure after the above event, California stopped releasing home addresses

from DMV files for a couple of years, but has just recently approved a new bill by the Senate Judiciary Committee which modifies the bill stopping home addresses from being released. Home addresses will be kept secret only in cases where motorists specifically request confidentiality. In all other cases California will release the address.

Who uses U.S. Datalink? PI's! Their second largest customer base is attorneys or researchers working for attorneys (gosh, I wonder why an attorney would want to run down someone's assets?), and they process over 100,000 report searches a year. U.S. Datalink is one of the grandfather gateways in the information broker business.

NCI
(National Credit Information Network) NCI was one of the first vendors of header information. They have broken that original information down into a number of different access paths and cross indexees to provide skip trace and credit data. NCI is sold by a number of different brokers including the main man, Jeff Kirkpatrick, P. O. Box 1021, Jackson, Michigan, 49204, (517) 783–4545.

NCI is an investigator-oriented database service that accesses all five major credit agencies, pulling their header information off and selling it to anyone who cares enough to ask. Their software and information package is a one time investment of about $500, this is offset by the fact they charge no annual fees or monthly access costs and sport a minimum monthly usage charge of only $10.00.

NCI scans 250 million credit bureau files and consumer profiles along with 9 million profiles on businesses. They also tap into the forwarding address card data bank held by the U. S. Post office and subscribe to every crisscross (reverse) directory in the country. The average cost of an NCI report after subscribing is somewhere between $4.00 and $17.00.

One of their claims to fame is that they are the best source to instantaneously trace a social security number or name and last known address to obtain the most current address and identifying information. They also offer an immediate (60 seconds being immediate in this case) on-line response on most records.

NCI will perform a social security locate, as we mentioned above, from either the number or the name and address and provide you with the facets you don't have.

There are actually three different data banks within NCI for social security number sweeps and each one should be consulted for each sweep. The banks will not only provide current or last known address information, but indications of who else may be using the number or other numbers the subject may be using as well as, if it is a valid ss number.

The National Identifier Address Update allows the operator to enter a name and a social security number, or a name and last known address, and will kick out identifying information, such as names, aliases, date of birth, employer, and all known addresses in a few seconds.

NCI's national telephone crisscross is a telephone number database which allows you to input a number and obtain the current address as well as (9) of the nearest neighbors with their names, addresses, and telephone numbers. This is a national crisscross directory that has been compiled from nationwide telephone books and voter registration files. (You might bear the sources in mind if you don't care to be listed in these kinds of directories.) It does not give 100% hit rate nor is it up-to-the-second accurate but it is a very useful step.

NCI now offers a toll-free number for access and they are open 24 hours a day every day of the year. They are adding new searches all the time, the newest probably being the Nationalwide Surname Search which provides people with the same last name and their telephone listings on a nationwide state, city, or zip code basis. NCI will provide full credit

reports as long as you comply with the guidelines set up in the Fair Credit Reporting Act and offers such niceities as your own electronic mailbox so you can get electronic mail from NCI as soon as it's ready for delivery.

Probably the most popular of all the search services, NCI offers accesses to all five major credit bureaus, access to all credit bureau header information files, a 90–1,000,000 name national crisscross directory that will work miracles with names, addresses, phone numbers as well as produce the obligatory 9 neighbors, commercial credit reports, and access to the post office forwarding files a wonderful service called eviction alert that is a database used by apartment complexes and real estate firms that to check on past history of renters as well as all available DMV searches.

NCI taps into the last postal forwarding address bank. (One could tap into this bank without going through NCI as long as one wanted to do $2,000 a month worth of business, but generally it's easier to pay NCI a few bucks to do it for you.) This database is nationwide in scope and is compiled from those lovely little green change-of-address cards that people, even most-wanted fugitives, fill out innocently and hand back to the post office assuming it's a confidential transaction because they don't want to lose that ever so vital issue of *Police Gazette* when they move to a new address.

Driver records are obtained from all the states that will provide them, giving the investigator license violations, traffic tickets, accidents, etc. These particular records take at least a day to return because most states simply do not have instant turn around at this time. License plate and VIN searches are accomplished in the same manner.

NCI also offers commercial credit reports that are done through the major commercial agencies including TRW, Standard and Poor's and a few others. They will poll some public findings and can be considered a source for business intelligence.

CDB INFOTEK

CDB is a database provider with several important advantages including retrieval of stored records in 2 hours and most public records available instantly, on demand. CDB offers nationwide access to motor vehicle records, general public record filings including court records, fictitious name statements, marriage-divorce proceedings, voter registration, and death certificate information.

They provide business and consumer credit information (the subscriber signs an agreement not to violate the credit act) social security tracks, postal address update info, moving index, neighborhood search index and a telephone reverse directory search among others.

CDB is designed for attorneys, insurance investigators, and detectives. The sign up fee is a reasonable $275.00 and searches run from $4.45 for a driver's record to $35.00 for business credit reports with most averaging about $6.00.

CDB draws together a very powerful selection of data banks and would be a nice choice for a primary information provider. Subscription includes a free "get started" class and information kit. They are accessed directly via a modem and personal computer.

CDB can be reached at 800–992–7889, or in California at 800–427–3747. I recommend a very nice marketing representative by the name of Janelle Bright...

TRACERS WORLDWIDE

A nice combination of gateway data bank access proprietary collections is offered by George Theodore who runs Tracers Worldwide. George will deal with anyone, and although he's not cheap, he is one of the best sources for literally any recorded information anywhere. To paraphrase George, "If it's legal, I'll get it for you."

The following interview was conducted with the founder of TI and generally considered to be about the best in the biz:

George: Tracers is an information company. It specializes in being an information resource for the private investigative industry.
Lee: What services do you offer precisely?
George: Information.
Lee: Specifically. I'm a PI. I want to know...
George: Can I be really frank with you?
Lee Sure.
George: Lee, you can ask me anything legal and I can get it for you.
Lee: George, say I'm trying to run somebody down, get a credit report on them and I don't have their social security number. I can give you a name and date of birth, something like that, can you do an SSI?
Lee: This interview is for people who want to use your service basically and want to know why to go to you instead of...somebody else.
George: For instance I can provide better access to driiver's records than NCI along with a whole slew of things like employment history.
Lee: Credit type searches?
George: I provide credit type searches provided they are within the Fair Credit Reporting Act, as long as they are within the guidelines.
Lee: Fine. Sounds good. You had mentioned to me at one point that you have a death data bank.
George: I have a death records data bank with over 40 million records that is exclusively Tracer's.
Lee: Who uses that? What kind of customers?
George: Heir chasers...insurance companies...
Lee: How did you compile it?
George: Through a confederation of several

hundred thousand death notices and other public information.

Lee: Other data banks…that you would have…

George: I have everybody. If you give me a person's name, I can run the whole USA to see if they have a telephone, just by name. I get everybody who has a telephone in that name.

Lee: And we're speaking listed here?

George: Yeah. I can run telephone numbers. I can get some unlisted telephone numbers.

Lee: Great. O.k., let's say I have a legit reason, I'm a PI, I fall within the guidelines, I need the unlisted telephone number, what kind of time am I talking about?

George: Usually within a couple of days. Sometimes I can get it to you in five to ten minutes. Depends on how busy we are. I can also do real estate. I'm in the process of adding two new data bases. One is I want to have everybody who is a registered voter on my system. The other one will have everybody who has a driver's license on my system.

Lee: How do I get on your system? Is there a join-up fee up front?

George: No, not at this point.

Lee: So it's strictly…

George: You will have to make out a credit application.

Lee: And then it's a per search fee basis.

George: Yes.

Lee: Give me just some price ranges because the thing with us is this book will sit around for 10 years and I won't say $43 for this because you may change, but give me some price range for searches.

George: You can pay as little as $10 to several hundred. I have an asset search that is bar none the best in the United States. If you have an asset, I can find it. If it's a liquid asset, I can find it. Let's leave it at that.

George: Tracers does a lot of do criminal record searches and pre employment checks. We can do a complete scan. Lots of states, searches of judgements…corporate—I do all of that stuff.

Lee: Let's say I'm hiring some guy and spend 150 a year on his salary, I want to do a pre-

employment search. I've got his resume in hand. What can I expect to be charged…?

George: It depends on how deep you want to go. Provided you give me enough volume, I have a tiny little search on which I check their credit, I check their driving history, I check their criminal record and verify the fact that their social security number belongs to them for $59. That's a pretty good deal.

Lee: What's the bulk of your customers, PI's?

George: Yes.

Lee: How did you get into this? Are you a PI?

George: No, I'm not. I got started quite by accident. I was an heir chaser essentially for many years. I developed resources for locating these people, establishing their identity and things like that. The result was that I developed a whole string of techniques, methods and expert knowledge in locating and ascertaining information about individuals.

One of my friends was a private investigator and did extensive searches, always needed something and he would ask me. I invariably said sure and would get it. He said, George, how much of this could you use yourself in terms of your capacity. I said maybe 1%. Did you ever think of selling the other 99? I said no and he said, why don't you do it? That's how I got started.

Now I can do all the good stuff—forwarding addresses from the post office, reverse directories, anything that's legal with the telephone. What I'm trying to do is turn Tracers into the most complete information resource available. The supermarket of information…"

A final note—George became so involved with PI's he recently married one—his wife runs PI Unlimited in Texas one of the first female agencies in the U.S. As she put it, "I had to marry him, I was running up too much of a bill with Tracers…"

7-11's

A number of private investigators and research administrators offer access to one or more of the above services for a no setup but value added charge basis. The biggest and probably best of these would be:

DATAFAX

National Association and Investigative Specialists, Inc., P.O. Box 33244, Austin, TX, 78764.

Datafax is operated by Ralph Thomas, a name that should be familiar to anyone who has done any reading in the fields of surveillance and investigation. Ralph is a licensed private detective who publishes a newsletter, writes articles for magazines, and puts out what appears to be approximately a book a week, generally on finding people, finding things, or on-line investigations. If I was as prolific as Ralph Thomas, you wouldn't be reading this book but rather seeing me on Saturday night being interviewed by Robin Leach (boy, there's an apt name, huh?) on *Life Styles of the Rich and Famous.*

At any rate, Ralph, through Datafax, offers what he calls, "The information source for private investigators and investigative news reporters." The advantage to Datafax is availability to NCI data banks without any setup charges or even necessarily a computer. Ralph also adds some other source information services into Datafax which will lead the investigator to the prime source rather than doing a strict value added search.

Datafax requires only a $60 user deposit which is charged against upcoming reports and requires no minimums on either a monthly or per search basis, no setup fees, and to quote Ralph, "No expensive equipment."

Datafax can be accessed by telephone or through the investigator's on-line network and offers lower search and research prices for NAIS members. (I guess you can figure out now who runs NAIS?) At any rate, all that is required to get started with Ralph is a $60 use deposit or a valid Visa or Master Card number.

Datafax offers all the NCI personal information including cross directory access, postal forwarding, data banks, information locators, social security sweep, employment checks, county records and research checks and criminal records plus he offers access to "Research Information Specialists" in every 50 state capital and will tell you how long they have been in business so you can go to them directly and not have to go through a value added source.

Ralph also has "specialized source locators who provide—you guessed it—specialized sources as well as references to investigators in different parts of the country that are in good standing with Datafax and can be expected to do a good job for you.

JOHN RUSSELL

7211 Northdale Mabry, Suite 205, Tampa, FL 33614, 800–237–2542. John is an old friend who has been around for years providing information on damn near anything anybody wants—he has been instrumental in bringing down corrupt politicians and finding lost children, to name but a couple of his areas of speciality.

SUPER BUREAU, INC.

P. O. Box 368, Campbell, CA 95008, 408–559–7603. Accesses a number of national credit bureaus and databases on a per record fee basis.

NIGHTHAWK ENTERPRISES

5311 Miller Ave, Klamath Falls, OR 97603, 503–884–7400. Business, consumer credit, DMV, asset searches plus lots of Oregon stuff not available elsewhere. Fifty buck sign up or add fifteen bucks onto their regular prices as a non-subscriber.

INVESTIGATIONS UNLIMITED, INC.

200 S. Merdian, No. 320, Ind, Ill 46225. 317–639–4638. Access to NCI searches for an average of $20.00 per search, no sign up. I tested them and they performed as advertised.

RESEARCH DESK, INC.

P.O.B. 92741, San Francisco, CA 94119. 415–956–4131. A rather unusual full service agency that accesses hundreds of general data banks along with detective bases and some specialized digging that I have not seen offered anywhere else.

Who's the man behind the business card? RDI provides comprehensive individual and corporate background searches from a only a name and a phone number. Is the person in question an officer or just an employee? What other businesses (present or past) have the person or company been involved with?

Newspaper, newsletter, journal searches both in the U.S. and abroad. In the words of Mr. Warhol, everybody is famous for fifteen minutes. Has the subject ever been mentioned in any paper, no matter how regional? RDI will come up with the story...

Costs are held down because they operate on the theory that someone else may already have the answer to your question. Unlike the cut and dried-retrieve-the-record agencies RDI will also do "value added" searches that utilize other, more organic sources including human experts and investigators.

Good resources for foreign digging and specialized citations in the field of forensic science.

Quick action, some problems solved in real time over the phone, or through the auspices of Fed Ex, the FAX or the modem.

NETWORK(S)

Another investigation resource that bears mentioning is known as the ION NETWORK.

ION NETWORK

(Investigators On-line Network), 5303 S. Rural Road, Suite 1, Tempe, AZ 85283, 602–730–8082. Provides several unique services for investigators who can get their hands on a computer. They have a number of sub-group offerings including the Resource Line, which is offered nationwide to clients at no cost who need to identify and contract an appropriate investigator in an area where they don't already know one. In order for a layman to make use of this, one would talk to Resource Line personnel, indicating what criteria he requires and what sort of case has to be made.

The ION people then consult their database of over 5,000 investigators and contact them personally, passing on the best contacts to the client. ION gets paid by the investigator who is asked to pay a referral fee of 20% when they are paid. No membership is required to receive Research Line referrals and they do keep an ongoing client/investigator rating service in order to eliminate bad investigators and/or slow pay clients.

ION is increasing every year and is a good idea that is apparently filling a service for both people who want to find out stuff and for people who know stuff. The ION network is a bulletin board for investigators with a PC and a modem and for a fee of $20 per month anyone can access it and participate in conferences and trade information.

The ION COOP is a cooperating marketing program wherein members pay $500 per year of $50 per month and are given special rates on ION services and trade show participation as well as priority assignments that come in via ION's Resource Line.

ION was founded by an investigator to serve other investigators. (Leroy Cook, founder, has since dealt himself out of the deck by not taking any of the assignments that come in, rather, he acts strictly as an information and referral source for other investigators.) ION puts on conferences and provides some good guidelines for both clients and investigators.

SCRAMBLING
IGRBMSALCN
SCRAMBLING

Scrambling

Scrambling offers one of the only methods of ensuring the security of any conversation or data exchange. Scramblers can be used over phone lines, on radios, cellular phones, modems, and faxes. Good scramblers rearrange the data so that it is unintelligible to the human ear, transmit it within the confines of the medium involved, and then recreate the original input at the receiver.

Top level scramblers work quite well and true to the laws of basic economics, cheap ones work, well, sort of cheaply. The primary setback to scrambling every conversation is simply cost: since the units must always be used in pairs, (with one cute exception which we'll see in a minute), every potential called party needs to be equipped with the same type of scrambler as the caller.

If used in a radio system, every set must also be equipped and at an average of several hundred dollars per, the overall system cost soon rises beyond most budgets. Some police departments do encrypt their radio transmissions to defeat scanner users but the idea has not really had a high priority.

Federal agencies which depend on mobile conversations such as the FBI and the DEA are encrypting most of their units at this point in time.

If one plans on calling only 21 people from a cellular phone, for instance, all 21 of them must be supplied with matching scramblers so that anybody one calls at any time is ready to switch over to the encrypted signal to continue the conversation. Besides the problem of cost,

there's a weakening of security because the system has a large number of pieces of equipment, all of which are capable of intercepting any call. What if one unit disappears? The whole system is now compromised and someone has got to change everybody's keys.

The most common method of scrambling a conversation has traditionally been audio frequency band scrambling, a method which dates back to WWII.

Another technique uses some kind of a time synchronized key signal to modulate the speech in the audio end, but the newer technologies which have come into use in the last 5–6 years, fully digitize the speech and then encrypt the digital signal. This required microprocessor technology to reach a certain level of compactness and power.

The first two methods sometimes work, but in general they leave a lot to be desired.

In audio band scrambling the speech signal comes in to the unit and is put through a bank of different frequency filters. One filter eliminates the high and middle tones, leaving only the low frequencies. Another eliminates the high and low frequencies leaving only the middle frequencies and a final one does the reverse, leaving only the high frequencies, eliminating the middle and the low.

Our new signal is fed into frequency shifters that are usually hetrodynamic in nature, shifting the frequency of the signal that remains after the filtering process, either up or down the scale. The frequencies at the lowest band may be shifted up so they fall into the highest band; the two in the middle are dropped down to the low band, while the highest set is dropped in the middle.

This produces a strange Donald-Duck-On-Acid output that is difficult to understand with the naked ear.

In a static system the combinations stay that way all the time. Most real systems don't use just three bands any more, they use 5, 6, or 10. The outputs of all these frequency shifters are recombined at the receiver.

One disadvantage of this concept is that if a person normally talks with all the energy in his voice in the low and high bands with nothing in the middle, it may average out to silence.

This type of static audio scrambling offers some protection but it can be immediately recognized as speech, it's got all the changes and pauses and characteristics of speech, and if one makes a recording of it and spends a little time playing around with a limited number of choices for the permutations of the frequencies, with a simple graphic equalizer one will eventually reconstruct the speech.

Some electronic suppliers sell "descramblers" that do this reconstruction on the fly.

One way to improve on static band scrambling is to make it a little more secure by having a time switching arrangement built into the scheme of things where a switch moves the output of these filters periodically. Every half second or so a good unit will switch them all around, moving the output of one or more to a different position, only to switch it around again and again.

Time duration shifters are a better choice for speech scrambling and are approximately the state of the available art in small, cheap, handheld radio scrambling systems today, but *this is changing.* Already, rolling shifters are being replaced on telephone systems by digital units in the same price range ($300+).

If a determined person has access to a recorder and has plenty of time to rearrange the settings every second and is working with only a limited number of choices, (6 filters would give about 30 choices), he can break the signal. Agencies use computers to control the switching while tracking the frequency energy to break these scramblers pretty easily.

There are some exceptions to this generalization—the best low priced, walkie talkie orientated voice scamblers are probably those produced by MIDIAN ELECTRONICS which offers radiotelephone and two way modules that do a pretty good job of hiding simple conversations from $50 up and a reasonable cellular scrambler which uses a rolling code premise with 100 million different codes for about $400.

MIDIAN scramblers have been used for Indy car pit crews, cops, and taxi companies to name but a few applications.

A really practicable cellular protection method is offered by COMMAND COMMUNI-CATIONS. They use an extremely complicated rolling method that handshakes the two units together and then frequency hops 400 times per second with one million possible lock-on combinations. This makes eavesdropping very, very difficult.

The unique part of the COMMAND system is that it is being installed at cellular switches as we speak, and in some parts of the country any cellular user can purchase or lease a pair of scramblers, putting one on his telephone and one on the cellular company's switch so that *every* call made on the mobile unit will be scrambled during the radio portion of the call, no matter who it is directed towards.

Of course the MTSO (land line) potion of the call is still in the open, but this solution effectively blocks most types of cellular eavesdropping.

A couple of unconfirmed sources have told me the CIA and most probably the FBI use COMMAND scramblers on their cellular telephones...

Another technique is to take the input audio and put it through a modulator, mixing it with some other kind of scrambling key signal, (an audio signal that varies in some way). The result, if it's a good scrambling signal, will be that the signal won't even sound like speech. There'll be some kind of a buzz or hiss all the time due to the scrambling signal really not talking. This is quite hard to find and fairly hard to break.

The problem is if the system doesn't pick a good key signal, if it utilizes a simple sine wave, anyone can almost understand the speech without doing any descrambling because the proper characteristics aren't there. The signal has to be variable and noisy. It has to sound like frying eggs in a pan with a benchmark sentence and has to be random and unpredictable. If it's periodic and every cycle is the same as the other, it doesn't do much.

Speech is pretty rough to scramble. If the signal is pretty straightforward and periodic, somebody can figure out what it is, duplicate it, decrypt it at the other end, even though they don't have the actual key to descramble the piece at hand.

There's also a very serious practical problem in synchronization. If a system can't maintain synchronization between the transmitter and the receiver, the whole process doesn't work very well.

DIGITAL
The other option is to go digital: turn the speech into data, by audio sampling or any other workable method, and then encrypt the data. The is the way to go for several reasons:

A. Data is, by nature, both easier to encrypt and more difficult to monitor.
B. Computers, Fax, etc. are already in the form of data.
C. Cellular phones and some radio systems will be data based in the next few years.

In fact cellular phone networks are already designing built-in encrpytion systems that will be available to callers as soon as the system goes digital. When the network provides the encryption, the system will be built into the set and the base radio. This will at least protect the call during the radio portion which is the most sensitive part of the system. It doesn't do anything special on the land lines because at that point, the speech comes back in the form of clear talk, but it will take the fun right out of scanner cellular monitoring...

How do modern digital encryption systems keep from being compromised? The key is, that the key is not in the hardware but is "public," meaning it is set up and passed between the

equipment on every call, making each call a separate algorithm so no unit can be used to eavesdrop on each other unit in the system.

Once the voice has been digitized or we're dealing with a computer that generates data, the encryption process of most systems revolves around two types of ideas:

The first one is to add a digital signal key to the data at the transmitting end and then subtract it out at the receiving. A special form of adding that combines bytes, synchronizes them, and then transmits them.

At the receiving end the scrambled digital bytes come in and automatically synchronize the data screen at the receiver to subtract our key leaving the original bytes.

This process is used in a number of systems whether they are low, high, or medium security. It may be supplemented by permuting or rearranging the bytes with regard to time.

A combination of both of these is used widely. The data encryption standard called DES standard, is a combined adding plus permuting approach. It has to be done 16 times in reverse order at the receiver in order to get everything back, but it's still a much simpler process and much more reliable than any analog scrambling.

The keys will be arranged in such a way that the exact stream that is added and subtracted will be different for every call. This is done by giving out a new key for each call so the mobile encryptions are different every time while using the same technique, different incoming byte streams for scrambling purposes.

This key changing concept was encouraged by the fact that the government claimed their (prior to DES) system was unbreakable until a 17 year old kid with an Apple II computer sat down and broke it for them in public...

Another system that should be considered in this section, even though it is not scrambling or cyphering per say, is that of burst transmissions. A good burst system will do several things: A. Compress audio for maximum intelligibility. B. Compress data and digitally-encrypted audio. C. Minimize the time needed to transmit this signal.

The United States Department of Defense has accepted a standard (algorithm LPC-10) that operates at a 4:1 ratio for normal 9600 bps speech. This method actually helps improve sounds in the voice bandwidth and allows a one minute audio message to be transmitted in 20 seconds.

To an uninformed observer, or eavesdropper, this will be quite gibberish-like unless it is recorded and slowed down to the proper speed.

APPLIED SYSTEMS CORPORATION offers algorithms that compress at ratios of up to 24 times and claim the same audio quality as the DOD 4:1 method. This means 24 minutes of audio could be transmitted in one minute to minimize interception and effectively "hide" the audio.

The system also increases the effective radiated power of a radio signal by compressing the channel bandwidth, and ASC claims it is nearly impossible to decode the original message without a close approximation of the original voice statistics.

A TRICK

How does one employ a scrambler if one is calling different people from a cellular or various land line phones? Like this...

Put one scrambler on the cellular (or carry it along to apply to any phone in question), put the matching half of the scrambler on a "buried" telephone that has a cheesebox, call forwarding, or a simple slave-like box which will connect the incoming call to another outgoing line. An audio (Radio Shack) dialer can then place the second half of the call on landline but the primary link will be scrambled, no matter who the call is aimed at.

Move the buried, or forwarded line often...

EAVESDROPPING ON SCRAMBLED CONVERSATIONS

How does a serious agent crack *any* scrambled conversation? Simple—one bypasses it. Plant a bug *before* the scrambler—in the room, in the car, by the phone—so at least one side of any encrypted conversation will be broadcast in the clear.

STU PHONES

True digital scrambling—the taking of the human voice, converting it to a series of on-off electronic signals by sampling the audio at X times a second—has long been the only method relied on by governments to protect their real secrets, but has been unobtainable in civilian applications. A sequence of events has now changed that, for the better.

In 1977 an encryption algorithm known as DES (Digital Encryption Standard), a modified IBM algorithm was adopted by the federal government, after the last "completely secure" standard was broken by a teenager with an Apple II computer, in front of a rather startled audience of NSA people and spooks.

The Achilles heel of most DES systems is that they are a "private key" system—the confidentiality of any message depends on keeping the key a secret shared only between the sender and the receiver.

DES is still pretty secure, i.e., home hackers are unlikely to break it. The NSA? The Russians? Real pro's?

It's long gone. Too inviting of a target to hack, even though NSA claims there are "no known security risks involved with using DES."

One must also remember that the NSA monitors *every* overseas phone call, telex transmissions, and many microwave phone transmissions within friendly borders and they might, just might, have some interest in seeing encrypted transmissions that *they can break.*

Just a thought, mind you...

Because the DES algorithm is known, the privacy of any conversation depends only on the "key" owned by the sender/receiver of any transmission. If the encryption key is compromised, third parties can read the conversation.

A more secure method is to use public keys wherein an asymmetric cipher uses a pair of keys: one to encrypt, one to decrypt. Party A can announce the cypher he is using so anyone can communicate with him, but keep his decrycpting key a secret so someone who has access to the public section can not decrypt the message.

Motorola, along with a couple of other companies, has long set the standards for reliable encrypted telephones. Traditionally it's been a standard that has not been made available to the general public, but times they are a' changing and the technology is now available.

One of the problems with past units has been user friendliness. If a secure phone is difficult for people to use one can't expect to have it widely deployed. Versatility is another factor—does it shift from one environment to another easily? Will it go from an office environment into a field environment if so required?

The idea of a true secure phone was first birthed in the early 1970's. The STU I was bulky, big, expensive, and didn't work too well. Other than that it was a bargain.

In the late 70's the STU II appeared and was required for all top secret government calls. It was deployed in the field until just a short time ago. The main problem with both these systems, from a security standpoint, was that each unit contained a "key." If one was stolen it could be reverse engineered in order to break other STU II calls.

In fact, the FBI complained, some years back, that the Russians had stolen so many of them they were using them for their own calls.

When STU II's were still in use a few bright folks realized an entirely different system had to be designed to be more secure and not dependent on the phone itself. What's the solution? How to design a device that is low cost, easy to use, and meets all the necessary security qualifications?

The solution was to appoint the largest government agency in the world, the NSA, to solve it.

The NSA did just that by putting out a directive, known as National Security Directive 145 that told private contractors to make it happen.

The next question was how to pay for something that would cost about a half billion dollars in research? The government answer to this problem is a study in perfect bureaucratic mapping.

First you require any private contractor who is going to do business with the feds to purchase one.

Why? Because security is a vital part of doing business with the U.S. Department of Defense and private agencies who work on classified projects are simply going to have to obtain this equipment.

Then you allow the contractors to charge the government—in the cost of the contract—to obtain this equipment so it becomes a lot easier for defense contractors to comply with the directive.

A lot of policies contributed to this whole program called Future Secure Voice Systems and the objectives were simple: button up telecommunications by the early 1990's was the number one priority, how to talk about classified material over open telephone lines. The second half was to provide a low cost solution.

Enter the STU III, a package that uses a DOD standard voice processing algorithm that's totally intelligible. Encryption is not yet classified even though the unit is keyed so a III can sit on a desk at night without the owner worrying about locking it up in a vault, and it offers full duplex operation over normal telephone lines.

The STU algorythym, called CCP 10, actually produces a model of the speaker's vocal track, digitizes it, and then recreates it at the receiver's end. An EPROM chip card stores the variable key which is mixed with the traded (public) key to produce a unique mix for each conversation.

STU's also work for FAX transmission and have the added security of looking for any third party on the line before beginning the exchange of data.

Today almost 200,000 STU III's from all three vendors have been purchased by the National Security Agency or Department of Defense contractors set up for Type One Encryption.

It does this by employing a public or semi-public keying system. The electronics, the unit itself, is not a military secret, in fact it is considered to be only a controlled cryptographic Item. If a STU III is stolen, a few measures are put into gear and there is no need to worry about system security.

The original target goal was to make a $2,000 secure telephone. The STU III sells for about $2100 so it has been pretty close.

A number of STU III type choices are available, but the most popular is the Motorola terminal known as a Sectel or Secure Telephone Model 1000. It's a universal type of telephone that will work in the U.S. or in any NATO nation. The STU III is also a feature phone. It works just like an ordinary telephone with last number redial, hook flash keys, volume controls—all the goodies expected with a modern telephone unit.

STU III type technology is limited to U.S. personnel, or U.S. allies with U.S. supervision.

Keys

Keys are the codes, the hardware and the algorithims that govern the encryption of the data itself. The STU III has a key management scenario that is totally different from the normal "enclosed key." Every STU III is uniquely keyed at a certain classification level. When the handshake process is going on, the two terminals trade encryption information including what the various levels of security are involved.

In this type of system the "key" is not loaded into the phone by the user, turning it into a potentially dangerous piece of classified gear; it's "traded" between the two phones establishing a new, horrendously random key for each call.

One part of the key is still loaded into the phone mechanically, but the other part is decided and loaded electronically, making it impossible (or as much so as anything is) to eavesdrop and pick up enough data to replicate the key. This system is known as a public key system with each key being a variable used to encrypt the data on that call only. This concept represents the highest level of security available today.

Once the call is over, the key is thrown away. Because there is no "net" using a same-same key, it cannot be remotely distributed and compromised.

STU III's require about 12 seconds for the units to handshake and secure and synchronize before data can be exchanged. A liquid crystal display lets the operator know what's going on, including the level of security involved.

This level will be the lower of the two parties involved—if I'm classified top secret and you are secret, the phones will establish a secret security level.

In the private sector, the term "proprietary" is substituted for "secret." It is possible to have different levels of keys for different levels of executives within an organization if required.

All the necessary information for each call is loaded into the STU III from a device called a crypto emission key. It's a memory chip that looks like a real key and the upshot is that it initiates and pulls this information into a RAM inside the phone. When the "mechanical" key is removed it locks and hides the variable away so the phone, even though it's keyed, can sit around at night and the crypto ignition key can be taken away from the premises without compromising security. This is an important ability that was not possible before the STU III type phones.

If the "solid" key is lost, the operator can tell the system to ignore it in future transactions. No system compromise exists. As a rule, each key will only work on one terminal. It is impossible to plug it in to anybody's terminal and use it.

How secure is this public key system? With the best Cray computers paralleled together, crunching away, the NSA estimates it would take a month long, continuous call, to even give them a chance to break in on it.

A single call. A month long. Each call is a new algorithm.

More traditional communications security systems use a key for a certain period of time called a crypto period. Not only is it a less secure algorithm, the same key is in use for a specified period of time. With STU III technology, each time a call is made a new key is established.

The microphone on a STU III handset has to meet a guideline set called TSG5, or Technical Security Guideline No. 5 which governs parameters for on-hook audio security. In the STU II and in many other "secure" phones, audio could be pulled out from the wires leading from the handset. No matter how secure a phone is, catch it before it's encrypted and the rest of the system is useless.

STU III is also out in a cellular version that is compatible with American and some foreign cellular services.

STU III technology should be available in all digital telephones within the next 3–5 years. It's actually cheaper to manufacture digital than it is to make analog phones. It takes a simple Kodak chip to convert any voice to 64 kilobits and then encrypt it. Motorola plans on entering this into the civilian market at about $500 a phone, significantly lowering the price of this level of security.

Type 2 STU III's are being made for "sponsored" clients. This will not put them in hands of the general public, but it will let police and other agencies who have a federal sponsor (like the FBI) purchase them. These 2's operate on line with the type 1's STU III. The key techniques used, the public key part of it, is the same. It affords public key protection which in itself is really substantial. There's another level of encryption after that that's not quite as severe as the type 1 phone, but it's still better than anything out there.

Type 3 is what was originally scheduled to be 2, but one thing led to another and now type 3 is on the market as a true commercial device. It will handshake and operate upwards with the type 2 units.

The main difference is that if a system has a type 3 on either end it will use DES (Digital Encryption Standard) or a proprietary algorithm such as Motorola's Digital Voice Protection, which is available to the masses. Since this algorithm is passed between the phones on each call it is possible to configure it with various levels of security. The III is sold in the U.S. and Canada only, but it truly brings secure eycryption within everyone's reach.

STU III type telephones are becoming a part of doing business for any government contractor and this idea will soon filter into the private section. If one is an engineer and one has to discuss some classified information with a customer, it costs a lot of money to jump on a plane, pay hotel and car rental bills for a week.

If the same engineer can pick up the telephone and go secure, and do all that in 45 minutes, the only charge is for the call. As Motorola says, "A good secure phone replaces a normal phone. It's not an additional phone."

How is the quality of a STU III? Good, almost great. At 9600 baud the human voice is very clear and distinct. There is virtually no chance for any loss due to comprehension problems, although it may not be possible to immediately recognize the speaker's voice because there is some harmonic loss when switching to digital and back again to analog.

There is a slight feeling of talking into a well, and complete duplex conversations have just a moment of hesitation between sentence breaks, but it is as good as was open wire phone connections a few years ago, and almost as good as cellular is today.

2400 baud (used on some other systems) leaves a bit more to be desired. There is a very noticeable pause while the equipment does its thing and one has to be careful not to step on the other person's sentence endings. Also, there is a bit of Donald Duck in every call. At 1200 baud, (not used in modern systems), you'd better say "over" at the end of each transaction and don't plan on talking to anything that sounds even vaguely human...

Company proprietary data, software, bids on a big contract, hiring and firing, stock buys, are just as important to companies as stealth technology is to the government and should be treated that way.

There have been numerous cases of insider trading, leaks and fraud that have been attributed to clear speak on a cellular telephone.

You think newspapers don't know how to use a scanner? You think PI's don't, you think maybe that thing your wife tried to tell you was just a big calculator might have been something else?

Nah...

A good, secure level scrambler is the only way to effectively protect any information.

STUIII — A secure phone.

COUNTERMEASURES SURVEYS

The most important element of any counter-measures survey is a physical search. It's the number one most important thing in any technical counter-surveillance measures group. All sort of fancy electronic equipment is great, It's going to help you find stuff, but what if the bug isn't in use any more? What if the battery's run down? What if the bug is equipped with a switch so when the bad guys hear you searching they turn it off? This is not outrageous. This technique is used by the FBI, used by a lot of other people as well. They hear signs of a search, they turn the transmitter off. Few electronic devices are going to find that.

When one is planning out a countermea-sures survey, one needs to decide an important factor, i.e., is it a problem if the people who are listening know there is a search in progress? In most cases, this should be a yes. You do mind because if they hear the search, if they hear certain telltale sounds that show the target has found the bug, it's useless to them and they will get in their car and drive away.

If the bug is exposed without the bad guys knowing, one has an opportunity to plant all sorts of false information, things to be passed on that may or may not be true. The other option is to simply try and catch them by planting seeds and seeing who harvests...

Let's consider an office environment search. Start with everything available. Begin from the top and work down. Particular attention should be paid to anything that has a battery in it or that plugs into the wall as well as things that may have been gifts.

What's the best way to plant a bug without committing a burglary?—give it to the target. Here's a calculator from XYZ printing where the company has all its printing done. Con-gratulations. The calculator has a battery in it and could easily have a transmitter in it.

The telephone has its own power and is often, I say, often, used as a bugging device.

Turn over anything on the desk, any funny looking things. Where did this come from?

Does it have a transmitter in it? Very possibly. Find out where it came from and do whatever you can. In some cases, counter searchers actually X-ray stuff or fluoroscope stuff, but usually a physical search will find bad things that are there.

Use a typewriter? If so it's plugged into the wall and it's an ideal hidey hole. Open it up. Look around. There may be computers, a local area network. Who uses these items? The target and his secretary...

A physical search means examining every-thing: looking in books, under books, behind books, behind wall pictures, curtains (an ideal place for a bug), lamps, behind calendars—any place. There may be a bug. Take the time, go through, and look for something that doesn't belong there. Take apart the base of the lamp to see if there is a little black box in there. See if there's some circuitry that shouldn't be there. This is how a lot of bugs are found.

Pictures on the wall or plants are a real special favorite for people to plant bugs—no pun intended. Put the device in a plant that and it sits on the executive's desk. I've even found clever folks who place a bug in an envelope, often a special delivery or express mail envelope, address it to somebody who they know is on vacation for a couple weeks, with "personal and confidential" written on it.

Today's bugging units can be so flat—especially if one uses a flat Poloroid camera battery, with surface technology components—it feels like a letter. Mail it to the guy and the secretary lays it on his desk. It sits there in a very hot area for who knows how long and broadcasts until the battery runs down.

Something else to remember when we're talking about bugs is that most bugs, especially those that work on a battery, have a limited life span. How long? Well, it depends on the bug, it depends on the power output, and it depends on the batteries involved. It's generally safe to say that a bug will last anywhere from one to three days. This means that most people will not just go in, take a risk, plant a bug on a random basis, a fishing trip. *Most bugs are targeted for specific time.*

Is there a big conference meeting? Do we have a budget meeting. Are the design engineers getting together? That's when the bug should be in use and that's when a countermeasures person want to look for the bug, not two days before because it may not be there and not two days afterwards because it may not be there. Right before the meeting.

The other common option is for the unit to be hooked up to the mains, the power lines that come into the office where it can run forever. Unlike the battery-powered unit that has a limited life span nobody has to come in a change the batteries, eliminating a major point of exposure.

The easiest, most practical way to bug some place is simply to hide a miniature microphone in the room or in a small hole in the wall near the room, run some wires out. This doesn't radiate RF—very difficult to find except by physical search. If any wire is found running out of the area—alarm wires, wires in a telephone cable, or just little wires that seem to be running some place, a sweeper must trace them down to their source and make sure it's not a hardwire bug.

If the bad guys had minimal access to a room, say for 30 seconds or 60 seconds, and wanted to plant a bug, how would they do it? One of the bests ways is to slip it underneath a cabinet, or a shelf, and with a little bit of double sided tape and it's planted.

A physical search for bugs has to include any telephones in the area. The first thing to do is disassemble the phone and look for things that shouldn't be there. This is known as the strip search or the sneak and peak. Check out the microphone button, make sure it looks and feels o.k., look behind it in the handset, and make sure nothing is clipped on the wires or stuffed up inside the handset itself.

The correct way to completely disassemble a phone is to get two identical (or at least similar) phones. Take both apart, and make sure the questionable instrument has no extraneous materials or little things clipped to it.

Look for small taps that might be hidden underneath the circuit board. Look at the "good" phone and compare the circuits. In one of our demo phones (see the photo) there is extra circuitry that the clean phone doesn't have.

This is an infinity transmitter. This particular unit is a LISTEN ELECTRONICS version, is built professionally into the unit and looks *very much* like phone company equipment.

Notice how difficult it is to find the extraneous circuity. Remember, bugs can be underneath the circuit board, attached to the board itself, or anywhere in the wiring in order to look like they're part of the original electronics.

Listen Electronics modern infinity transmitter.

Tracing all wires, phone, electric, alarm, or non-identified is a must in any search. Phone wires will often disappear into cable that holds many wires of similar shape and size, like a phone cable, what's the most effective method to trace them?

The easiest way to do it is to use a tone generator (the Fox) made by Triplet Corporation and sold by various suppliers including JENSEN TOOLS. It injects electronic signals into any wire and lets the operator hear a low tone or a high tone or a warble.

Along with the injector comes a device called the Hound. The Hound is an inductive amplifier that does not have to be connected up to the cable. If one places the Fox, onto the wires, injects a tone into the wire, one can, low and behold, follow the tone.

What happens when the wire merges into a cable? The tone can still be traced all the way down the cable for a number of miles. One can follow the tone down a phone cable or cable like a phone cable for miles even if the cable disappears in the wall. As long as the amplifier is coupled inductively to the cable (a few inches or maybe a foot), it will work.

Fox-Hound combos are about $85 from JENSEN TOOL CORPORATION, made for telephone linemen, telephone installers. They are several hundred dollars if bought from commercial countermeasure's suppliers.

Buy them from Jensen.

An even hipper idea is to use a device that injects *an RF* signal into the wires. This device will follow wires or cables through thick walls or under four feet of earth…

FIRST STEPS

The simplest, easiest, not to mention the cheapest, step in bug hunting is to take an all-band radio, turn the volume up high, and tune through the bands. In order to use the all-band radio as a device to locate bugs, turn the volume up and put it in the room where a suspect bug might be, (if the possibility of alerting the people who might be listening poses no hazard). Now tune through all the frequencies.

When radio is tuned across an active frequency, feedback will immediately occur. Back off slightly and local audio will come through.

The reason this works on many small transmitters is that bugs don't have coils to suppress harmonics. Harmonics are signals that are doubles and triples of the original frequency.

This phenomenon reproduces the bug's signal in several portions of the spectrum, giving a good chance of feedback squeal even if the frequency of the unit itself is outside the bandwidth of the receiver in use.

Once feedback is encountered one can use a frequency counter such as one of those made by OPTO ELECTRONICS to pinpoint the location of the transmitter.

These units sell for a couple hundred bucks with a range of 1 MHz to 550 MHz+ with fair sensitivity. Newer units lock on faster and have a greater range factor.

For a $75 outlay one can increase the sensitivity of any counter (or scanner) with the addition of a pre-amplifier, often called an active antenna, which increases the gain a bit.

When one activates the frequency counter it begins ranging through random numbers on it's LED display. It's self-oscillating, trying to be very sensitive to all frequencies in the vicinity.

Frequency counters are not nearly as sensitive as radio receivers or scanners. Inherently a counter has a broadband response, it's sensitive to all frequencies at the same time without having to be tuned. A radio receiver can only be tuned to one frequency at a time. The radio must be retuned to receive a different frequency. The tuning, however, makes the radio very sensitive at the frequency it's tuned to. Receiver sensitivities can be well below one microvolt.

The counter, on the other hand, must be close enough to the source of the radio frequency transmission to pick up enough signal to let it count. In the old days, lab counters which worked on benches, were not nearly sensitive enough to pick up the type of units we're looking for, but these new devices are just that. The counter is so sensitive that it can't help but self-oscillate. The only way to stop that is to make it less sensitive.

The counter can be used in the presence of major radio signals because it will only pick up within a certain radius. It also has a separate detection circuit that can be adjusted to trigger at a certain threshold that triggers an LED when the ambient RF exceeds the pre set level.

When the unit is first activated is will self-oscillate, the frequency readout will randomly drift. When a signal comes within range, the counter will grab the frequency and hold it.

This accomplishes a number of things. It alerts the operator to the fact that there is a transmitter present, it is in the area and the exact frequency of it so one can then verify that it is a bug by dialing the frequency on a scanner or a receiver and listening to it.

To use a counter, sweep around the room, rubbing the antenna over everything suspicious, until it locks on a frequency. The counter will only read one frequency. If another, more powerful unit turns on, the counter will immediately will go to the more powerful signal.

A 30 milliwatt transmitter will read about 4–4-$^1/_2$' away from the unit. At this range it will lock up and the RF light will come on. This unit will allow one to sweep and find most RF transmitters.

Using a portable frequency counter and a scanner together is a powerful, first level search strategy. The two units together cost far less than the price of a normal countermeasure scan and they can be reused over and over.

A synergistic relationship.

The next rung of the countermeasure value ladder is held down by two units, the REI CPM 700 and the OPTOELECTRONICS preselector. For information on the OPTO unit see the SCANLOCK section.

The CPM 700, from RESEARCH ELECTRON-ICS, INC. a company that has been around a long time and designed a number of useful things, is a step upward both financially as well as in sensitivity and selectivity. It is a broad-band receiver that doesn't have to be tuned. This is in the $1,500 to $2,000 range, but does a lot of things that more expensive equipment will not do and does them well.

The device can be put in one of two modes. In the search mode, a scale, a bar graph, tells us the relative RF intensity in any particular area. If one walks around a room, holding the antenna vertical, one can study the display and see what the RF intensity level is.

Two modes of search are available for one's enjoyment. In the search mode one walks around until a high reading appears on the graph.

These features allow one to pinpoint the location of an RF source. In the search mode, a gain control can be adjusted to track the signal source and it can then be outputted through a speaker to give feedback if there is a device in the area or one can plug in headphones so the audio can be listened to without alerting the bad guys of the search.

Besides the search mode, one can push a button and put the 700 into a monitor mode and just let it run. Adjust the threshold control for the average RF level in a room and the machine will simply monitor the ambient RF.

If the level suddenly goes up—somebody walks in a meeting with a body wire on or someone turns on an RF transmitter in the area, the threshold control will go overboard, and indicate, by a beeping tone, and/or a light that there's a new RF source in the area.

The 700 can then be put back in the search mode and track the new source down or one can simply listen with the headphones and verify that indeed the transmitter is a bug.

In my tests the CPM 700 readily detected a SHEFFIELD ELECTRONICS mini transmitter to a distance of about 6' on low gain. By switching the unit to "high" gain the same bug appeared at a range of almost 20 feet. This is a very sensitive unit and gives a good indication of what's going on in any area.

CPM 700 from Research Electronics.

One other inexpensive unit is available for in place RF monitoring. Sold by KAISER electronics it's a wide band receiver-detector that produces a strong feedback squeal when a transmitter is activated in the area. Cops are not big on these devices because it makes it very difficult to wear a body wire into a room...

There are some units out now that use their own noise source. It's their noise source that they will recognize. What they're doing is actually putting a noise source in a room itself and then it's a scanner. It's demodulating and then if it hears or sees that noise on the frequency that's being demodulated, it will lock into that. The reason they do that is for voice activation of a transmitter in case it's not transmitting, it puts a noise source in it and works without the telltale sound of a feedback detector.

An ancillary, but very useful piece of gear is the RANGELOK sold by TSA which simplifies the process of bug location after a suspicious signal is isolated.

The unit will unalertingly show exactly where the bug is located using triangulation. It accepts audio from any receiver, scanner, or Scan Lock and produces its own tiny "click" which is recognized as it comes back through the receiver and then the Rangelok tells the operator how many feet away and in what direction the transmitter is located.

This patented device offers an accuracy rate of 95% in telling exactly how far away the bug is without alerting any listeners as to its presence.

RangeLock pin-points hidden transmitters.

Another room attack, a great one for bugging, is to take a transmitter that effectively transmits over the wires in the wall. Radio Shack is the main source of these units known as Carrier Current Transmitters. Once plugged into an electrical socket, it blocks out the AC from the socket, picks up room audio through a small microphone, transmits extremely low frequency RF through the wiring in the house.

The matching receiver can be plugged in another outlet as long as it's on the same wiring pattern as the transmitter.

How does one test for a carrier current transmitter? The frequency counter won't lock up on a CC signal. The unit doesn't go low enough to detect the very low frequency of a carrier current transmitter.

The first thing we can use is the REI unit. The 700 has a special low frequency probe that will detect VLF RF on building wiring.

A spectrum analyzer will also pick up and display CC bugs as will specialized devices such as SHERWOOD's CCR3, an advanced carrier current receiver that can use an RF input, meaning RF input via either the plug-in AC cord or alligator clips attached to other wires, an audio input for use as an amplifier. It locks on a signal to display the frequency up to 500 KHz; it will operate from its internal battery;

it has a speaker on and off switch; you can adjust the tone or attenuate it 20–30 decibels. It has audio output for a recorder and it can be left in an alarming mode where it won't turn on the recorder unless somebody activates the carrier current receiver.

Is there a cheap alternative for detecting CC bugs? Only one.

Most of these units come from Radio Shack and can be picked up by other RS "wireless intercoms" BUT note these units operate on several different frequencies and the sweeper will have to try each separate unit to cover all the shots.

This solution will not find everything. A unit that is custom made is on a different frequency then this won't find it. However, 90% of all units out there are Radio Shack room monitors.

RECEIVERS AND SPECTRUM ANALYZERS

Basically there are two types of receivers—manual and automatic. Most people are familiar with a manual receiver. The automatic receiver is more commonly called a spectrum analyzer. They basically do the same thing with only a few differences between the two.

Let's start with a typical manual receiver like an ICOM receiver which is representative of a good but not great VHF receiver. My sample tunes from 30 MHz to about 1 GHz and covers the bands one would commonly search for small transmitters. Like most receivers it has a knob for tuning, and my particular model has a digital display of the actual frequency being looked at, and the capability of entering a frequency from a digital keypad.

A receiver, by its inherent design only receives one frequency at a time. If one wants to listen to something else, one can tune across and stop at anything that might be interesting, however it does take a long time to cover the band in this fashion.

If one were to manually tune across the band and every time a signal was received one noted the S meter reading and the frequency, one would end up with a chart of frequency vs. amplitude.

Several software programs are on the market which operate with IBM PC's to control, to work in conjunction with the ICOM receiver. So equipped, the receiver will automatically scan and give a printout of all occupied frequencies.

Hewlett Packard sells similar programs for much more that actually take out the signal frequency, break it out, demodulate it, print it and go back in the scanning mode. It still requires a human to operate it or one could record it and then come back later and listen to the recording. These software programs are available and getting more sophisticated to the point where they will spot new additions to the local RF spectrum making them ideal for repeat sweeps or as an in place monitoring system.

Special receivers designed just for countersurveillance work made by MASON among others are also good receivers but are rapidly being overtaken by more sophisticated general purpose receivers and cheaper spectrum analyzers.

The main difference between a manually tuned receiver and a spectrum analyzer is that the spectrum analyzer does all the work for the operator. Otherwise it's exactly the same thing.

One of the things about any receiver is that it requires an antenna. The easiest solution for sweep work is to use a whip antenna, which is readily available at any radio supply house.

If a directional antenna cut for the band in question is used it should be directional enough to provide an indication of where the signal comes from.

The automatic receiver is called a spectrum analyzer. There's a wide range of spectrum analyzers ranging in quality and price, some designed for normal electronic work, some for surveillance work but they all do the same thing; isolate and display electronic signals.

As one might expect, the more expensive the analyzer the more features in quality and resolutions it will have available. Spectrum analyzers have been relatively widely produced now for over 20 years and a lot of them are available used. Prices on new units are dropping from $7,000 into the $1500 (or less) range.

For this section I am using a top line Tektronix 2710 that has digital storage and digital displays of everything. It's easy to use but it's not unique.

The lower cost analyzers are equally useable but they're a little bit less precise. If one is looking for specific frequencies, it's a little harder to find them. The cheapest SA's do not have a digital display, they're only precise enough to tell if something's there or not.

All spectrum analyzers have a display. On the 7210's display, and on most spectrum analyzers, the horizontal scale is frequency. The vertical scale is amplitude, the actual strength of the signal. The display is graduated in ranges that are variable.

The unit has a noise floor where the display flattens out. It can't receive anything that has less power than that. The 7210 because it's digitally controlled, uses a lot of buttons to do things. In the older analyzers everything was done with rotary knobs and selectors. All of them have a frequency marker knob which will dial up whatever frequency one wants to put in the exact center of the display.

One can change the frequency manually or enter it directly from the keyboard which is a lot faster. Frequency scan per division is also variable, as is the horizontal scale of the display.

One can change the display by increasing or decreasing the scan for each division. As it goes into more of a narrow scan per division, the displayed signal spreads apart.

On a 7210 a row of buttons control how broad of a band is being swept any one time. There is a distinct trade-off between accuracy and resolution. The more accurate the display, the more resolution power available, the slower the display has to be to keep the accuracy.

More expensive analyzers have a built in detector that will allow the operator to demodulate and listen to the signals being displayed. This is a good addition for any SA that is to be used for countermeasure use.

One of the neat things one can do is to put this unit in a very slow sweep mode allowing one to hear a little bit of each signal it goes by. Even at a slow scan it is hard to make out what is going on but any indication of feedback from a local transmitter is immediately evident. There is also a mode called zero scan, that, when selected, makes the unit into a fixed frequency receiver just like a manually tuned receiver.

The other thing that is important to watch is the bandwidth of the receiver, if it is too narrow to demodulate a wide band FM station one has to increase the bandwidth in order to make it intelligible.

One of the strongest and most numerous type of signals one will encounter are TV stations. They are easy to identify using just the visual component of the signal—first comes the powerful carrier spike and then, 4-$\frac{1}{2}$ MHz directly above that, the aural sub-carrier. In the United States every visual carrier will have an aural 4.5 MHz above it's main frequency. If one is looking at the whole TV band, there will be a carrier every 6 MHz.

There is a technique which some spectrum analyzers have as an additional add-on option, called raster analysis, which will actually allow one to demodulate the TV picture and watch it on the display screen, if for some reason that escapes me, one would want to watch TV on a $20,000 custom analyzer...

For the FM band set the divisions to 800 kilohertz per division because most FM stations are spaced by 800.

What's important when one tries to look for things is to have a good idea of what's going on in whatever band that under observation because there's lots of stuff out there, most of which it is perfectly legitimate transmitters and some may be spurious noise caused by computers or other electronic devices in the neighborhood. Some of it may be bugging transmitters...

A very useful piece of advice—particularly for those who have never used an analyzer before—is to get one's hands on one, take it home and learn how to use the instrument and learn what is actually out there in the RF band. There are hundreds, sometimes thousands of legitimate transmissions going on in any given area. One needs to know which ones are legit, which ones are noise and something caused maybe by computer and which ones just might be a transmitter...

In a real life situation in which carriers come and go it's hard to pick out what's there and what isn't. The safest approach is to dial through and listen to each type and learn what they sound like.

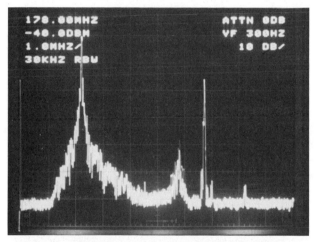

A TV station (above) and a commercial FM station (below) as seen on a spectrum analyzer.

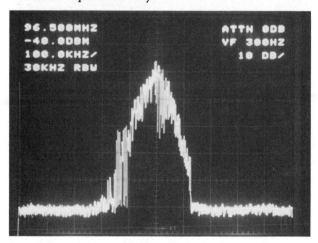

Learn what paging sounds like, what a commerical and two way radio sounds like, and what various tones of digital transmissions sound like, what a TV signal looks and sounds like, what FM broadcast sounds and looks like, and so on, because each one can be buried all over the band and once the operator can ID them in a slow scan mode it allows a more efficient use of the spectrum analyzer.

The first step in using a SA for countermeasure work is to select the widest sweep option available in the analyzer. This will provide a picture of the entire spectrum between 0 and 120 GHz. Assuming the operator knows where the FM band and the TV band and the miscellaneous radio people live, unusual stuff will jump out of the display.

One of the first things that's obvious when we reduce the sensitivity is that most of the transmitters are relatively far away, so if one is operating in an area that might be close to a very low power transmitter it will not only show up, but it will say hello with a flourish.

If the operator has a good idea of what the target signal should look like, he can find it.

If I turn on a Sheffield bug and then go back to max span on the spec an, all of a sudden, at about 180 MHz, there's a carrier spike that's actually off the top of the screen. It is this obvious because this example is a very strong little transmitter operating just a few feet away from the receiver.

Even at a very low sensitivity setting I still see something there and several harmonics also show up. If the carrier is at 180 there will be a harmonic at about 360 plus a third and fourth harmonic above that. Each harmonic is lower in power than the main signal but mathematically related to the original carrier.

Any time something very strong appears with other spikes inter-related to it, nine times out of ten the signal is emanating from a very simple inexpensive low power transmitter that doesn't have the harmonic attenuation that more sophisticated transmitters have. They tend to be pretty easy to see.

Next dial up the main frequency exactly. By using the 7210's internal detector, I can hear the signal (with headphones) or get feedback with the speaker as the display slow scans through the carrier. Set the unit on zero span and it becomes a manual receiver.

If I look at another portion of the spectrum, there's a number of carriers present all about in the same ampitude, none of them particularly strong. This is when it gets hard to find things because bugs that are well buried or "snuggled" against a strong carrier by a pro do not stand out of the general display.

When I watch the display for a few moments, I notice that many of the signals turn on and off. Carriers that come and go can be discounted because that behavior indicates a two-way radio kind of application.

By putting the 7210 in a slow scan mode and listening to the detector I can get a quick sample of the audio on each signal. Carriers that have continuous tone on them, or have digital paging beeps or telemetery noise can be noted and eliminated. If the analyzer involved does not have an internal detector a continuous tuning receiver or scanner should be used to verify the signals.

By slow scanning or using the tune knob to manually tune through the spectrum is it possible to find many off the shelf bugs on the first try.

The harder to find small transmitters are the ones that will test an operator's knowledge, skills and patience because they invariably will be buried with a bunch of other things that will tend to obscure their existence.

Spectrum analyzers are like any other tools. At the trained and experienced end, they are very useful. They're not hard to use. Don't be intimidated by them. It's just about impossible to hurt a spec an by playing around with it.

Spectrum analyzers are great at locating devices operating in unusual areas of the spectrum, in ranges where one wouldn't expect a signal like VLF carrier current transmitters.

An oddity here is that most of the very expensive digital systems are still too slow to catch hoppers. IFR units and other top digital analyzers, stand more of a chance of missing them than do old time systems.

Spectrum analyzers come in moderately simple versions that are usually good enough for countermeasure work in the $2,000–$3,500 range, while the HP and other engineering units can set a budget back $7,500 plus.

SA's can also be rented from some electronic supply houses on a short term basis, be sure the unit will go up to at least one gig in range and has an audio detector or can have one added on. It should also be portable, preferably battery powered and rugged.

Like the CPM 700, the Scanlock, software driven receivers and the feedback detectors good SA's can be used as an in-place monitoring device by storing and comparing the signals in the RF spectrum.

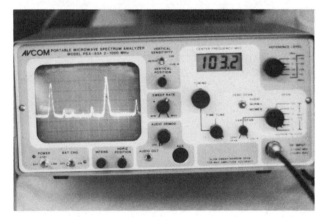

Spectrum analyzer from AVCOM.

There's one other countermeasures item that's in vogue, the non-linear junction detector. What does a non-linear junction detector do? It detects non-linear junctions! It's nice to find things with straighforward names isn't it?

Two dissimilar metals make up a non-linear junction. What is a diode or a transistor? Two dissimilar materials pressing together that react in a certain manner when signals are put through them. That's what non-linear detectors look for, because, in theory at least, all transmitting devices and all bugs have to have a non-linear junction within them, be it a diode or transistor.

The way they operate is to send out a microwave signal (around 900 megs) that excites non-linear junctions. Said excitation can be picked up on the unit's antenna and made to alert the operator.

In other words, the junction oscillates and transmits and gives a signal back to the detector. The signal is powerful enough to look within walls for buried devices. Note the transmitter does NOT have to be operating in order for the detector to find it. It may be voice activated, switched off by the operator or the batteries may even be dead, it makes no difference to a non-linear detector.

This sounds great but one or two little problems arise in operation—most of them give all kinds of false readings if the operator is not careful. Chairs have metal in them, and the walls have nails, and the ceiling has reinforcements and aluminum conduit meeting steel wall boxes...which will all register on the detector.

And nothing ruins a good party like tearing down a wall only to find a bent nail touching a screw somewhere...

The units also cost in the neighborhood of $15,000.

Two examples are manufactured in the United States. One is the Boomerang, made by ISA and the other is the Super Scout which is made by Mitel. A couple more are made in Europe which are not FCC type approved and are not supposed to be brought into this country, although they appear on used markets from time to time.

Any serious countermeasures effort should be ongoing; always do random follow-up sweeps based on various considerations whether or not a bug is found. Do more sweeps. Don't let people know when they are to be conducted and even if a bug is located, don't stop there. A good eavesdropper will often plant more than one bug.

TELEPHONE COUNTERMEASURES

Telephone tapping is the most often employed type of electronic eavesdropping. It's done more often than room bugging be it a wired microphone, an RF transmitter or a modification of a phone instrument to pick-up room conversation.

Why is that so? Everything one needs is in place and many times you don't have to trespass to reach it. By nature, telephone conversations tend to be more concentrated than in person conversations (my ex-wife being an obvious exception to this rule) and convey important data.

Telephone lines tend to be soft targets that may be accessed without dealing with security guards, ID badges, building and elevator physical security systems and so on.

There is a lovely little device from a popular mail order (about $45) company called a Tap Detector. For $45 bucks you hook it up to a phone and a little red light comes on and it shows if there is tap on the wire. It solves the problem, right? No, not really. They are a little bit better than useless. They will sometimes, on a good day if one's Karma's right, show if an extension phone is picked up off the hook or if you're in a hotel they will sometimes show if the PBX operator, if it's the old-fashioned type of PBX, plugs in and listens to your phone calls, and that's about it. Don't ever depend on something like this. At $45 nothing is not going to tell you if you phone's tapped.

In fact, to be real honest, there's nothing on the market today that will tell you electronically if you're phone's tapped by a professional. There is nothing that will give 100% security.

Telephone taps can be hardwired, consisting of nothing more complicated than a VOX recorder and a capacitor across the lines or a Radio Shack recorder starter, or they can be RF transmitters, radio starter switches. There are many, many items that can be run across the phone lines. How do we detect a phone tap?

Automatic telephone analyzers are available from a number of companies—most based on the mid-sixties MASON ENGINEERING design.

Do they detect taps?

Some. Not many. They are designed to find audio on the phone lines by cross checking all the possible combinations. In itself this is a good test, although it can be preformed with a stand alone amplifier and some patience, the only exception being large offices which might have hundreds of combinations to check.

What kind of tests do the stock analyzers do? Some send a high voltage pulse down wire, most run a tone sweep. Those are not outstandingly helpful tests. They are simply designed to turn on old fashioned infinity transmitters (which no longer work on most systems) or cue any hookswitch defeat device like a zener diode.

Hookswitch defeats are a rare form of bug in the phone, designed to turn it on to make it hot, make it into a room bug. Most of your telephone analyzers have a set of meters to do what they call "on-line testing" for telephone tapping devices.

Telephone analyzers are really not designed to detect telephone taps, they are designed specifically to look inside the phone and see if it has been modified in any way to turn it into a room bug.

Most telephone analyzers, check for a tap, say to take your phone off hook, and then they put a variable resistor across it and log in the voltage. The telephone analyzer will say that voltage is going to be anywhere from four–eight volts. Then it's going to say hang up the phone and it should read somewhere between 48–52 volts, and that's what they're doing for telephone tap-testing on their telephone analyzers. On hook and off hook testing.

This is rather basic and anyone can perform a series of much more sophisticated tests with a $40 ohm meter and some wire.

The best shot for finding most units is a device called a TDR, or Time Domain Reflectometer but traditionally they have been both expensive and hard to use. What any TRD does is send a little pulse down the wire and then look at the returning reflection just like radar. This will show every junction, every solder joint, anything that's clipped on the wire, every appearance, will appear on the TDR screen.

Does this mean you can just hook it up, look at the central office and see if anything's on your wire? No, it does not. It means one has to hook it on one's phone wire, learn how to use it, go to the first junction, look at that junction, short it out, hook the TDR up there, and go to the next junction. One may have to go to three frames offices before you hit your central office. One also has to know somebody and get them to connect across the frames.

Otherwise it will give one a shot at only those stretches of wire that can be physically accessed. Each connection that does show up must then be tracked down and identified. The lines should be "shot" every so often in order to compare the returns to see if anything has been added to the phone system.

It takes practice to use a TDR. Exactly what it will display is dependent on how sensitive the unit is and the frequency and duration of the pulse employed. If the pulse is too long it will miss some connections.

At best it will find things if you're able to go isolate every appearance and look at the TDR. A commercial TDR will run $8,000–$10,000 however BIDDLE (long time electronics manufacturer) now has a miniature, handheld TDR designed to be used on phone lines. For a more reasonable $1500 it will radar phone systems.

No TDR will tell if somebody decides to tap the phone five minutes after the TDR is taken off the line, nor can one leave it on the line and watch it. However a TDR is a good investment if serious sweeps are to occur, and if a paid sweeper is brought in I would damn sure want him to be TDR literate...

They're a number of other tests that will find most bugs. Not the top, not the professional, not the stuff the FBI is going to put on at the central office. That's just not going to be found.

Life's tough all over. Bear that in mind when you talk on the phone. However, if your threat assessment level is lower than government agencies; if it's a business partner, a spouse, or a private detective, you've got a good shot at finding the offensive unit.

As with bug searches, physical inspection is very important. Take any phone in the target area apart and look for discrepancies.

It's important to locate the place where your phone line makes it's first appearance (the first B box) for many of the tests we want to run on the system. This is usually pretty easy to locate, especially if it's above ground, SEE THE SECTION ON TELEPHONE TAPPING FOR EXACT DETAILS ON WIRE LOCATION AND CABLING. Once the box is located and opened the next step is to locate the line to be tested from the rest of the connections. How?

Two ways. The easiest is to find a friendly phone guy and have him look it up in his book and tell you exactly where your line terminates in the contacts before going on to the CO.

Second easiest way is to install a little oscillator at the other end of the wire (Fox and Hound, for instance). This puts a tone on the wires which can then be traced by running our inductive amplifier along the wires looking for the tone. One can test all the contacts just by running the amp near them. Once we've identified the correct contacts, for the first set of tests, we jump them with a little jumper cable across the contacts. All this is doing is shorting the wire out to itself. This allows the tester to go back to the house and take resistance measurements on the wire.

So go down to the first appearance and short the wires out, if this seems too extreme, at least short the wires out where they drop from the main cable and enter the house or office in question.

Why do this? Take an ohm meter and measure the resistance between the telephone jack (by adding a little breakout jack from Radio Shack) and the first appearance.

The 22 gauge phone line runs about 40 ohms per thousand feet so read the meter and calculate the distance to the box and back. If nothing there's adding any more resistance than it should it is a good sign. It doesn't prove anything positively, but it's a first step.

Record the numbers and check the line from time to time. If the resistance jumps suddenly, especially an increment of 80, or 90 ohms, it's a problem. Follow the line down and find what the problem is. Good chance it's a series bug drawing power and adding resistance to the line.

Look for two types of phone devices—parallel devices and series devices. The easiest way to tell the difference is all parallel (or almost all), use a battery. Even though a parallel device clips across the phone wires, it draws its current from the battery which limits its life span, but makes it much harder to detect. Series devices draw current making them easier to find.

Some parallel devices have a battery and trickle charge off the phone wires so they actually charge the battery when the phone is not in use. This is the best of two worlds—long range, long power and very hard to detect.

Series devices that do not have a battery but have clips or wires to be hooked up to a phone (purchased through SHEFFIELD, SHERWOOD, DECO and thru consumer magazines) have to be brake one side of the ring or tip wire, usually the red wire, and hooked in series so they can draw their power from the phone line and are a little bit easier to find.

An important measurement is on-hook and off-hook voltage. It used to be that the voltage was very exact and any deviation meant a problem. In those halcyon days of yore phone companies ran on a backup system that consisted of car batteries. Today they run on electronic systems with generators so voltage will vary around the country. The important thing is that every time it's measured, the voltage should be the same. Any two any lines coming from the same exchange, (first three digits are the same), should read the exact same voltage. If one has two lines in the same house or office, check them both. If not, go next door and check it. Should be almost identical. Any deviation, say a volt or more, means there's something drawing power. Could be a bug, could be a short or worn wiring, but it's something to check out.

The on-hook voltage should be between 48 and 54 volts. Plug in a little parallel connect that opens into spades, get the multimeter set up, and check between the tip and the ring, and see what the voltage is. Take the phone off the hook then and measure the off-hook voltage in the same fashion you measured the on-hook voltage. 5–8 volts is very legitimate. Record those voltages in a little log and check often.

The next thing we have to do is run a wire to earth-ground. Take a piece of wire and run it outside and hook it around a cold water pipe that goes into the ground. This is a real ground, the same ground that the phone company uses some where down the line but we can access it at a more convenient location than the CO—the back yard...

With the phone on-hook measure both the tip and the ring (red and the green) voltages to the ground wire and write them down.

The negative, or green should be just about what we had before when we measured full battery. In other words, about 51 volts. Move the multimeter dial so it will read millivolts and take the red wire to ground measurement. It should be just a few millivolts. Record this also.

Once you have those readings, the next step is to solder two identical 2700 ohm resistors together and attach a clip lead to the center of the two resistors. Wire across the red and the green wires with the resistors.

Measure the voltage from the center tap of these resistors—right between them—and use very good tolerance resistors here, very close, 1% preferably, measure the voltage from the center to ground and write that down.

Because we have, in effect, terminated the phone line the voltage is going to be negative and should be one-half the "battery voltage" we originally recorded. If the line is unbalanced, one side has an addition that is altering the characteristics, it should show up here.

The next measurement to do here is to unhook the ring side and measure current flowing through here, the same way. Measure current from the center tap of the line. If you're not familiar with current you always have to do it in series, actually clip the wire or unhook the wire, hook this in series and measure current flowing through.

Next take the voltage measurement from the real ground to the center tap of the two resistors and double it. Now add the voltage measured from our true ground to the ring wire to the voltage measured from the true ground to the tip wire. These need to be added algebraically so we keep the signs correct.

Now we need to find out the difference in these two steps. This will be a small figure which we will take and divide by the current we measure flowing through out resistors in miliampheres. The result will be the true difference in both sides of our balanced loop. This difference should be quite small. If it's greater than 90–100 ohms, our line is very unbalanced and there's a strong possibility of a series tap in the line.

Any RF tap, i.e., a tap that transmits the signal instead of just recording it, can be searched with the same methods used for ferreting out RF bugs including the use of counters, receivers, and spectrum analyzers.

Check out the phone, the drop wire, the line, B boxes for the presence of a radiating device. Some of these units utilize the phone wire for an antenna making the job of finding the signal a bit easier as the RF tends to travel down the wire for some distance.

There are a number of hook switch defeats popular with eavesdroppers. What these do is basically short out across the hook switch so even though a telephone is sitting on-hook, its very sensitive microphone is picking up all the conversation in the room and sending it down the wire. As an eavesdropper, all I have to do is go out someplace along the line, tap into the wire, amplify it and I'll hear all the conversation in the room. There's a lot of ways to do this. The infinity transmitter's a good one. Also, one can set up high voltage devices so if a pulse is sent down the wire, it turns on automatically and lets the audio come down the wire. A relay, some transistors, diodes, are some of the ways to do this.

Go to the wall, leave the phone on-hook and search the wires for room audio. If one can hear audio coming down these wires, there's a problem. It doesn't necessarily indicate a tap, because a number of modern electronic PBX phones *carry room audio even though they're on-hook.*

An infamous example of accidental audio was the duck phone sold through a number of Sharper Image type catalogs. Made from a wooden duck decoy the phone "quacked" when a call came in. It turned out that the transducer that produced the "quack" was an ideal microphone and was on-line all the time, eavesdroppers figured it out pretty fast.

Take a powerful little amplifier and using head phones, a source of room audio and check every combination in the cable. It's important not to just check the red and the green because if I was going to send conversation down this wire I wouldn't send it down those two. They're too obvious. I'd pick another pair, maybe the yellow and the black or the green and the yellow, that wouldn't normally be suspect.

If the phone is a multi-wire going into a cable, I'd use any two I could find. Most cable phones don't use all the wires. They usually have spare wires sitting free wires for me to send conversation down the hook.

Most electronic phones use a six wire cable with at least two of the wires doing absolutely nothing but offering opportunity.

Check them all out.

USER FRIENDLY TDR

Time Domain Reflectometery is gradually falling before the forces of high(er) technology as well as the laws of supply and demand.

Top level (read Tektronix here) instruments are still extremely expensive, quite difficult to utilize in a fashion that will actually allow one to qualitively state that a line is free of electronic surveillance and getting better all the time.

However, several manufacturers are offering lower priced TDR's with different features than the top of the line models. Some are still scope based, offering a visualization of the line condition as their main method of communication with the operator. Biddle would be a good example of this type, with models checking in at about $1500, while others are combining computer CPU's and liquid crystal readouts for human interface.

The Biddle is designed, or at least marketed, with TSCM applications in mind and seems to work fairly well in that it does mark faults and "found" several units we had placed on our test line.

It should be noted that one of our operators felt the produced pulse was too long in duration. If the energy expelled by the unit exceeds the length of the fault it will miss the fault and reflect back that the line is ok.

Biddle handheld TDR.

An example of the other type of TDR is represented by the Microtest Pair Scanner. This handheld, keyboard based unit is actually designed to find problems in computer LAN lines but will also work quite effectively on twisted pair as well as on other types of telephone cabling schemes.

The Microtest unit does not have an oscilloscope built into the unit (although the output can be routed to a stand alone scope) but rather tells the operator what is going on by the use of an LCD display that speaks the King's English.

The device performs a number of tests, the most important two, at least to our kind of people, is the length and scan tests. The length measures the time required for the speed of light pulse to travel the length of the pair and reads the distance out in feet. The length function looks for the largest impedence mismatch on the line and presumes it to be the end of the cable where the wires are either open or shorted together.

The scan function looks for the first mismatch, regardless of size, and then signals the distance to the fault, indicates whether it is an open or a short and shows the strength of the returned signal by way of a bar graph.

The scanner is preset with the necessary numbers to test one of ten types of cables at the touch of a button (including shielded and unshielded twisted pair and coax) but it can also calculate the efficiency of any pair (officially known as the Nominal Velocity of Propagation) if the operator feeds in the exact length of a sample of the cable. It will store this factor in a memory and then recall it upon demand.

The scanner will also automatically perform several other tests of interest: exact resistance readouts, cross talk and noise (including data and audio leaks), and dB of level lost down any stretch of cable.

This last figure is calculated when the unit listens to it's own noise source and subtracts the result from the known level of the source. The noise used is a fairly innocuous "click" that would probably not alert a tapper to the presence of a sweep in progress.

I tested the Microtest unit and was fairly happy with it in a TSCM application even though it was not designed directly for this task. The unit seems to be quite sensitive and in fact will find most any splice or telephone company connection block and often considers this to be the end of the cable.

Microtest user-friendly TDR.

The unit reports problems as opens, shorts, or faults, and with some practice, it is possible to hazard a good guess as to what the indication will be before you actually find it. This is good from the standpoint of forcing the track-down and physical verification of appearances or connections which could, in fact be something that does not belong on the circuit, but not so good if you are trying to "shoot through" a certain stretch of line that includes some telco connects.

It should be pointed out, however, that it is a lot easier to track down a fault when the exact distance to it is displayed in real numbers than it is to read a display.

The unit does allow the operator to decrease its sensitivity so as to avoid known connections.

Series taps, parallel bugs, and splices all showed up quite faithfully on the unit when it was used correctly. We had a bit more of a problem finding a parallel recorder starter but it did vary the readings some, also indicating a drop in line level when measured on a "before and after" basis.

An RS 232 port will dump the onboard buffer (2,000 characters) or active scan results into a printer or computer for later comparison.

The unit can actually be programmed to dial a phone number and report an alarm when preset parameters are exceeded. Conceivably, this feature could allow the unit to serve as an in-place line checker, alerting the operator to any change in the line's condition as soon as it took place, making life quite difficult for a would-be tamperer.

The ease of operation of this unit is great for anyone who is not an experienced radar operator, but also carries with it the dreaded veil of respectability.

It's all to easy to forget that this is not a $10,000 unit, and that an understanding of the principles and limitations involved is still required for effective use.

Because it is now pretty mandatory for a TSCM technician to utilize a TDR in the phone portion of any search, ("mostly due to your damn books," to quote one expert), a less experienced operator could use this unit to demonstrate, quite convincingly, that he is taking every possible avenue of detection.

Maybe yes, maybe no...

The Microtest unit has a range limitation of 2,000 feet (compared to 10,000 in a Tektronix) and does not like to work at distances of under 20 feet, a feature which can force the operator to do a bit of cable connecting or move to a new test point.

This particular scanner sells for about $2,500 at this writing from Microtest and from Jensen Tools, but a couple of similar units are making their market debuts in the fifteen hundred range.

If at all possible, arrange for a demonstration and test of any TDR before purchasing it to see if it will actually find taps.

IN PLACE COUNTERMEASURES

Certain countermeasures can be utilized in an on going fashion to prevent or detect various electronic eavesdropping attacks. Most notable would be wideband receivers and feed back detectors such as the Scanlock, CPM 700 and Kaiser detectors.

These units will can be adjusted for the ambient RF level in a room and will alert the operator when any new signal, such as that from a body wire or bug, enters the picture.

Another option would be to use PC software packages that drive general purpose (ICOM type) receivers to establish each and every signal in the local spectrum and then run periodic scans to establish the presence of any new signals.

At one time or another people have come up with interesting alternatives to the standard countermeasures such as RF and audio jammers.

The former idea will work, however it has a few drawbacks including the unintentional disruption of local television and radio reception and the fact that it is seriously, seriously frowned upon by the FCC.

In order for an RF jammer to work it must be powerful enough to blanket all other incoming signals for some distance as there is no way of knowing where the listening post is actually located. It must also flood the entire RF spectrum with noise as there is no way of knowing on what frequency any transmitter might be operating.

The only thing that fits this criteria is a powerful RF noise generator that simply disrupts the entire electronic spectrum with several watts of power.

The second approach is to use audio jamming to overwhelm the microphone on any type of bug. This approach does, at least in theory, prevent most types of surreptitious monitoring as all units, hardwired, transmitters, infinity transmitters, etc. use a microphone to pick up the target audio.

Masking sound generators in the room, and even music, offers some protection if it is louder than the conversation which is the target of the attack. This concept should not be considered a given because modern filtering techniques can often "bring out" buried audio, especially if the masking sound is not specifically engineered to mingle with and cover human speech.

Several firms have marketed plans and in a couple of cases, actual devices which employ ultrasonic energy to cancel out microphones. The units beam ultrasonic energy at two different frequencies into the target room. The above-audible sound "beats" or hetrodynes causing a whole slew of plus and minus frequencies that overwhelm the diaphragm in any nearby microphone destroying its ability to pick up audio.

The idea is sound, no pun intended, the application is a bit less so. Tests have shown that in order to actually disrupt the microphone the power level of the ultrasonic sound must be so great that it becomes extremely uncomfortable to any humans and most animals in the vicinity.

I have an 8 transducer ultrasound generator that will, in fact, screw up surveillance attempts. It will also cause anybody I don't feel like sharing time with to leave the area, usually screaming and/or cursing.

A mixed blessing at best...

Protection from telephone taps is a bit more tangible—there are several devices on the market that do in fact provide some degree of protection. A rather unusual device from a Canadian firm prevents the use of the telephone instrument itself from being used as a bug (as in infinity transmitters or hookswitch defeats) by electronically disconnecting the handset from the rest of the instrument until it is picked up by someone placing or receiving a call.

Not a bad idea, but I must add that, ah, you could save about five hundred bucks by unplugging the handset from the phone when it's not in use, or installing a little mercury switch to do the same thing for a few bucks...

Other in place tap defeat systems, such as SHERWOOD's "Telephone Line Bug De-Activator" or a similar unit from EXECUTIVE PROTECTION PRODUCTS, operate by raising the off hook line voltage of the system.

The telco central office switch will actually work on a higher off hook voltage than most systems use. By balancing the line, raising the off hook voltage, recorder starters (drop out relays), by far the number one most popular form of telephone tapping will not sense the off hook condition and will not start their associated recorders.

The same thing holds true with some series transmitters that depend on the off hook voltage drop to begin transmitting.

If a voltage adjuster is to be employed it is wise to only use it on calls that are to be kept confidential, because the elusive eavesdropper may realize something is wrong when *no* calls are monitored by his fine system and switch tactics.

Some of these units also flood the line with white noise when the phone is on hook. They sell in the $200 range and do offer two hundred bucks worth of protection.

A TRICK

> One method that has been used to trap eavesdroppers is to have a voice activated recorder on the line that is suspect. There is a good chance that anyone tapping the line will call in after hours to test out his unit.
>
> Play the tapes back every day and look for unusual calls.
>
> A more expensive type of counter-tapping is offered by several devices which flood the phone line with white or pink noise WHILE THE PHONE IS IN OPERATION. The level of the noise is adjustable, and when cranked up they really will mask any and all audio that's going down the wire.
>
> So how come the called party can understand the conversation if it is masked by static? The central office's equipment will automatically remove this noise and pass unaltered audio from the CO to the callee.
>
> If a tap or drop out is installed on the caller's line it will pick up only harsh white noise.

Voltage compensators offer some protection from recorders and series transmitters.

A TRICK

> *Someone you know and love using a noise masker to protect a conversation that God meant for you to overhear? Go to your friendly Radio Shack store and purchase two RF chokes and two small capacitors and connect them across the line in question.*
>
> *This $2.00 filter will remove the masking noise quite effectively.*
>
> *By the way, phone companies are not real fond of people who feed noise down their lines...*

TEMPEST COUNTERMEASURES

How does one stop Tempest-type attacks? Dr. Van Eck suggests two approaches: A. screen and shield all CRT's internally. While this is possible, there are very few on the market and the expected price increase would be at least 300% on any manufactured pre-shielded VDU; B. change the internal electronics to provide random beam displays (normal CRT's use a predicable top to bottom interlace pattern) to confuse the synchronization of electronic eavesdroppers.

Possible, but I'm personally unaware of anybody who employs this technique.

The "normal" way to guard against Tempest activities is simple—it's in use in most military fighter planes and helicopters, in important government installations, and in high security computer rooms already. The concept is simple: shield the entire room with a close grid of copper wire and then ground the entire mess so no electronic signal can possibly escape.

Besides this all—*all*—openings to the room, doors, windows, air ducts, wires, electrical conduits, etc. must also be protected in a similar fashion. The UHF broad banded radiation emitted by CRT's loves to cling to metal and will use ducts or conduits as wave guides.

I have personally seen a gentleman use this type of electronic penetration on a room that was thought to be shielded by simply pointing the receiving antenna at the end of an air duct some 100' away. The signal came thru loud and clear...

This is not a new concept. The problem is to meet Tempest guidelines you simply have to build a cage, that is, a special room that's lined with double steel walls and copper aluminum foil or copper screening. Before you start tearing down the drywall in your house, let me point out this is not cheap.

In the last couple of years a new product has been put on the market called Saf'n'Shielded from International Paper Company. This is a non-woven fiber that's made by laying down randomly arranged metal fibers and pressing them together in a binding agent. The product itself is a paper thin fabric composed of nickel coated graphite and can attenuate electromagnet signals from 0–40 gigahertz by over 100 decibels, effectively cutting them off.

This paper is simply applied like wallpaper and, in fact, has sort of a art deco look about it not unpleasant to the eye. The paper catches the electromagnetic waves in its random pattern and prevents them from leaving the area. As a byproduct, much of the sound will also be trapped by this product providing not only electromagnetic espionage protection but a degree of audio protection at the same time. Safe'n'Shielded will meet Tempest security standards but at a far, far cheaper price than building a shielded room.

The paper must be overlapped at the edges and have virtually no holes, or rips to effectively block stray signal release. This paper, as with a shielded room, will also make the transmission of RF signals (room bugs, body wires) difficult if not impossible.

AUDIO TEMPEST

The same principles involved in securing an area from electromagnetic emissions can be transferred into audio terms. If one is to control or virtually stop transmission of any audio from a target area, many types of eavesdropping become impossible including spike mikes, contact mikes, infrared, lasers, and some types of electronic transmitters. On the theory that any reduction is a good one, conventional soundproofing or the Saf'n'Shielded wall coverings can be utilized to cut down on transmitted sound. However, once again, all openings or "thin" areas such as windows, air ducts, doors and conduits must also be protected by the addition of mufflers, vibration devices, or masking devices in order to make this type of protection a reality.

If noise attenuation is coupled with noise flooding, that is the addition of white or pink noise transmitters or even background music in the target area, it becomes difficult to intercept the audio.

At best, this solution is spotty in nature and if one is serious about constructing acoustically secure environment, there's one other technique that does work.

Remember on the market anyone can commercially purchase tools which include subminiature microphones, highly directional microphones, laser microphones, fiber optic microphones, and phased array microphones, all backed by signal processing equipment to recover conversations buried in noise.

Since walls cover the largest part of the surface perimeter to a room, securing the room from audio surveillance requires adequate protection of them.

The current technique for designing walls for audio security is to make them as sound attenuating as possible, which implies making them thicker, more massive, and much more expensive. Such an approach does not necessarily solve the problem for several fundamental reasons.

The first reason is that the sound attenuation path through the wall is only one of many; thus knowing the walls' characteristics is not sufficient to guarantee knowing the sound attenuation of the entire room. Secondly, the sound attenuation of the room is only one of three factors that determine the intelligibility of speech transmitted. The other two factors are the loudness of the speech inside the room and the loudness of the background sound at the listening point. Thirdly, sound attenuation

characteristics are only specified for airborne sound transmission from room-to-room, and tell us nothing about what occurs within, or on, the wall.

There's one company on the market, DYNASOUND, 6439 Atlantic Blvd., Norcross, GA 30071, that has developed an intriguing solution to the problem of stray audio. Their idea is to recognize the existence of, and control, the three important factors, and then balance their application in order to minimize costs.

The method employed is called MASKING SOUND. It is a carefully tailored random sound that is added to cover (mask) all conversations or machine noise transmitted from a secure area. This technique achieves audio security by burying the conversation in the masking sound at potential listening locations. The masking is created with an electronic generator and then is converted into sound through a variety of loudspeakers and transducers. A nonstationary generator is available that reduces the effectiveness of any technique that attempts to recover the speech from the masking. Services are available to guarantee successful applications, and avoid mistakes that were made in applying this technique in the past.

Masking sound has been used in the office environment continuously for over 20 years so the technology is well advanced. There are a number of significant benefits to be gained in applying this technique to audio security.

Dynasound's methods of sound masking utilizes a number of proprietary devices that basically define a perimeter and then secures the enclosed area by placing their special transducers inside the walls themselves allowing for a low degree of interference in the room where the speech is being conducted, but effectively blocking the transmission of audio from the target room. They also have devices to mask doors, windows, and ducts to further secure the area.

Although the sound of masking seems like air conditioning noise to the ear, it is not. The nature of the masking signal that drives the maskers is crucial. Dynasound makes four types of generators just to make and adjust the spectrum of the masking signal. Depending on the threat analysis, one of these generators should be chosen. The two important features of masking generators are: (1) the nature (statistics) of the random signal, and (2) the equalization network that permits a given sound spectrum to be created.

Once a masking sound is recorded by an eavesdropper, he may do several things electronically to recover the speech buried in the masking. In direct listening, the brain is only able to process information up to a certain limit of masking, but with signal processing techniques that ability can be greatly enhanced. The type of masking signal is very important in rendering these techniques less effective. There are several types that can be created in Dynasound's units:

DIGITAL PSEUDO-RANDOM NOISE
This is a signal that sounds random to the ear, but is in fact a signal that is repeated continuously. The repeat times can be as short as one minute, too long for the brain to recognize the pattern, but perfect for a recording/analysis system to identify.

Listening devices can use these properties to artificially reduce the noise, thus making speech that was buried in the noise intelligible once again. A generator with this type of noise is primarily intended to defeat direct human listening.

ANALOG STATIONARY NOISE
This is a signal that is truly random; it never repeats. The statistics of the noise, such as mean and variance, and the spectrum shape (balance of high and low freq.) are both constant with time.

There are adaptive filter algorithms that use this constancy to predict the noise, and thus leave open a path to reversing the noise signal and adding it to the recorded signal to reduce the noise. As a result, the speech is partially uncovered. A generator with this type of noise is intended for listening devices used by all but the most sophisticated eavesdroppers.

ANALOG NON-STATIONARY NOISE
This is a signal that is not only truly random but the statistics and spectrum of the noise varies randomly with time. If the masking is properly designed, adaptive filters have difficulty tracking it, which reduces their ability to artificially reduce it and thus limits their effectiveness in recovering speech sounds buried in the masking.

The amount of sound energy at any frequency relative to that at other frequencies determines the frequency spectrum. This is important because the ability to understand speech is much greater in the band of frequencies from 1000 to 3000 Hz than at other frequencies; it is imperative that they be adequately covered.

The other bands must also be covered in order to make the sound as acceptable as possible. Adjustment of the frequency spectrum is called equalization and is done with an equalization network. The most effective is called 1/3rd octave band equalization, and the least effective is a low pass filter. The accuracy of the results and the acceptability of the sound is determined by this network.

MUSIC OVERLAY
Music by itself is not an adequate masking signal. It does not have the proper temporal or spectrum characteristics to mask conversations. Most often, the music signal is reproduced so it is available to the sophisticated listener for complete cancellation. As an overlay to masking, music can be made into an additional complicating factor to signal recovery as well as provide a more pleasant atmosphere.

Dynasound also features a unique computer program that, when coupled with a sound meter, allows an independent party to rate a specific room or other target area and plan effective sound masking techniques.

OTHER NEAT IDEAS

If you remember the first episodes of the TV show Get Smart (one of the most realistic shows ever recorded for my money) you remember that when Maxwell Smart needed to talk to his Chief or Agent 99 in complete privacy, a large, double-domed plastic canopy descended from the ceiling, fitting over both their heads as securely as the cockpit of an F16, or more accurately the cockpit of a '56 Cadillac...

This idea is not all that bad. In fact, it was taken one step further a few years ago by Sheffield Electronics with a rather comical looking but none-the-less effective device that will provide secure two-way voice transmission for any two people in almost any location regardless of the type of attack method invoked.

As for instruction, I believe the picture speaks pretty much for itself...

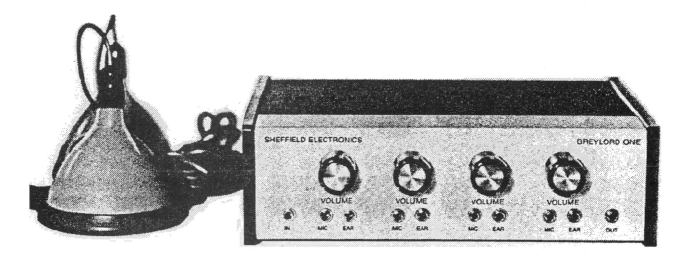

Best countermeasures gear

Is there one ultimate piece of counter surveillance gear? Yeah, it's called the Scanlock and is made by an English company called Audiotel International. (See photo page 196.)

As a friend of mine on the law enforcement side of things said to me, "be sure and tell all those readers of yours who are perps that there is one way to tell if they're under surveillance: carry a Scanlock."

In the region of ten grand apiece ($4–5,000 used ones are available) they ain't for everyone, but if you can afford it, don't leave home without it.

Scanlocks are basically a broadbanded receiver that will lock in on any sort of local signal, automatically. In most environments they will automatically ignore commercial signals and lock on to any signal emanating in the area of the unit.

This means a Scanlock will instantly pick up just about any bug as soon as it starts transmitting, regardless of frequency. It will also home in on portable two-ways, such as those routinely used by law enforcement types when they come within a certain radius of the unit.

They're portable and versatile, and they demodulate and lock on to anything be it wide band, narrow band, sub carriers, even carrier current transmitters. With some practice they will even grab, or at least show noise, if a frequency hopper is activated in the vicinity of the unit.

Very inconspicuous and it's just a killer receiver.

Cellular phones? 300–400' away and the unit grabs right on. Even if someone is using scrambling, the scrambled transmissions going in concert with one's movements will indicate surveillance.

More than one person I know of simply keeps their Scanlock on at all times, in the office, in the car, at home as a continuous surveillance checker.

In one instance, one of the gentlemen discovered he was the target of a fairly complex moving stakeout by the competition, involving cars and airplanes.

As he said, "It gets the adrenalin flowing to be cruising down the road and hear the guys in the next car talking to a plane *about you.*"

Only two problems I know of: You cannot program frequencies into the unit to be ignored or concentrated on, but TSA makes an option that will computerize the Scanlock to do just this, it will load up every frequency in an area and memorize them.

The TSA unit loads frequencies and manipulates the memory. It locks onto good things and locks out the boring things. It's possible to auto record everything in an area and then step through the memory.

The other problem is that in some very hot RF environments, like downtown NY, the unit may have to be manually tuned if you are working in a highrise office building although there are a couple of filters available that will knock out the commercial AM/FM bands to help with this problem.

It's a patented device developed by one of the true masters of the industry, Glen Whidden. He's with Technical Services Agency in Ft. Washington, Maryland. Prior to that he had 28 years as a technical services agent with the Central Intelligence Agency and knows his business; he's reportedly one of the top 10 most knowledgeable guys in the industry.

The only other thing around that will compare with a Scanlock is called the Eagle and is also made by TSA. In the same price ballpark it has several features the Scanlock lacks and I have heard very good reports on the unit, I'm just not personally familiar with it. (See photo page 196.)

Frequency counters need to be within 12" to find a cordless phone—this unit 100'. When we start talking about UHF/VHF transmitters, with a couple watts of power, we're talking 1/4 m.–1/2 m. range rather than 75 or 100'.

It will also find several milliwatt surveillance transmitters from a fair distance, giving the option to sweep a room from one point, or in ideal conditions sweep a small *building* from outside its walls.

A handheld directional antenna, using a nearfield or yagi approach will dramatically boost the performance of the OPTO preselector although they are a bit hard to come by.

The OPTO preselector needs to couple with one of their counters although it works best with the UTC 3000, and the 2600H. They have the 16 segment input level so as one is sweeping with this unit, the minute a signal comes within the filter's bandwidth, it produces a deflection on the bar graph.

Add a programmable scanner or ICOM type receiver to this in order to listen to the suspect surreptitious signal and you have a $500 to $1,000 system that offers many of the advantages of the Scanlock.

As I write this, the OPTOELECTRONIC's Preselector is priced in the $1,000 range which is considerably cheaper than anything that will do this and a year from now they're looking to bring it in for under $300.

For an encore OPTO is putting the whole thing in a card for a PC personal computer. Working in Windows 3, one pulls down the menu and selects an ICOM receiver allowing the unit to actually direct tune the receiver. If a transmitter is present it will actually tune the receiver, no searching, no scanning involved.

Future plans are to front end that with several active pre-selectors to run can a pair of 4 MHz filters, moving them around or overlap them to further increase the sensitivity and do some automatic logging.

This is pretty much the cutting edge of the technology, it gives something that's reasonably priced that gives more power to a counter-measure's person than does a spectrum analyzer because it still has the basic advantage of not showing every RF frequency in the world.

As mentioned in the cellular section, one can also use this unit to follow a cellular phone and instantly switch frequencies as it hands off. The computer model (which will eventually be out of the computer) will do this automatically without losing any of the conversation.

Law enforcement folks who wish to follow a suspect, especially if he may be using an altered-number phone, should find this device quite useful.

I know I do…

A TRICK

A brand new unit, the APS 104, from OPTOELECTRONICS will do many of the same things the SCANLOCK will do at less than 1/10th of the price.

OPTO's unit mixes new technology, (patent pending), along with a basic frequency counter. Although the counter responds instantly and doesn't require any tuning, it has a disadvantage in that it is sensitive to all signals at once. The new unit solves this little problem while increasing the distance or range, not by tuning, but by narrowing the RF spectrum it is looking at, at any given time.

The engineers at OPTOELECTONICS have come up with an extremely innovative system to do that by using an active pre-selector that hetrodynes signals in order to move a 4 MHz-wide filter from 10 MHz up through at least one gigahertz.

Sensitivity? It will lock onto an active cellular phone from about 200' using an omni-directional antenna. Better with a directional model.

Scanlock countermeasures receiver.

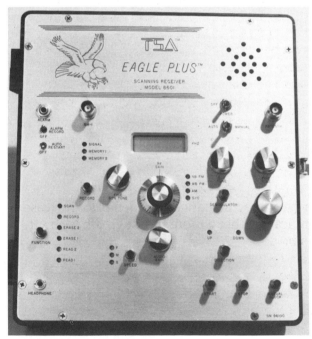

Eagle Plus TSCM receiver.

TSCM SOURCES

If a person feels he, or his business, may be subject to electronic surveillance the choices are two: get out the gear and look for it yourself, or hire someone to do it for you.

And, to paraphrase Kipling, best beloved, it's a jungle out there...

Due to the paranoia inherent in the concept of surveillance, some folk are a bit too slick with the pitch and practice of countermeasures. It's a field that requires both expertise as well as morals—some operators both overcharge and underlook.

Technical Surveillance Countermeasures people should be experienced in both electronics and surveillance, have the proper gear, not make false promises and not take advantage of people who "think someone is watching them."

It's a down and dirty, hands-on business that lends itself to falsehood(s). One infamous company offers searches from "experts" who have impeccable credentials: A. They have put up a huge fee for training and bought some useless equipment and B. Have attended four days of classes. Hot damn.

Some "experts" flash boxes with nice meters and displays and then explain how they have to work alone, while others offer some sort of ironclad guarantee that they will find something.

Which, of course, they will...

One countermeasures group (AIC in Las Vegas) offers to actually place a bug and let other teams search for it with the idea that if the debugging contractor fails to find the test bug, or if he demands a sudden price increase indicating that a more thorough job is about to be done, AIC would "appreciate being considered as a replacement."

What makes a good countermeasure guy? What qualities put the fear of God into vicious eavesdroppers? What separates the Joe Montana's from the college level quarterbacks of countermeasures?

Maybe that simile is stretched a bit, but I'm working on Sunday and the game is on in the background...

A good countermeasures person with a grasp of basic electronics and telephony can get 85% of what they need to know by reading or going to a school. The next 10% comes from doing. The next 3% have got to have an "in" because the real tricks are traded around among the master countermeasures guys the way magicians guard their secrets.

A magician might do his special trick for 20 years before he gives it up to his apprentice. The trainee has got to be somebody in the field and have a track record.

The last 2% simply cannot be passed on simply because it's a constantly changing field and if one doesn't have an open mind and actively work to stay on top of the subject, he'll blink and it's gone. It's very easy to rest on one's laurels and fall behind the times. The cutting edge is very real in this field and must be maintained.

There *are* good people out there, the problem is only in separating the wheat from the chaff...

In order for an electronics countermeasure person to be worth hiring, he must fulfill several requirements:

1. Be good. Know what bugs and taps exist and how to find them. Be willing and able to run down phone lines and appearances even if it requires physical effort and/or a bit of creative trespass.

2. Be trustworthy. Be true to your client; don't hide bugs so they can be "found" during the search; don't lie about exactly how secure any room or line is, and DO tell the client if something suspicious is found.

   This last sentence may seem unnecessary but consider the fact that many counter measures people worked on the other side of the fence at one time. Will an ex-cop tell you if he finds evidence of a law enforcement type bug? He should.

3. Have the correct equipment. This should include a TDR, good wide band receiver (SCANLOCK, EAGLE, ICOM), possibly a spectrum analyzer, carrier current detection equipment, and so on.

4. Charge a reasonable price and account for the time.

5. Provide an analysis of the subject's vulnerability level and suggest appropriate measures to counter possible threats.

The following is a list of some individuals who I personally know or who have been recommended to me by sources I trust. If you feel you need a sweep and don't find a person in your immediate area, bear in mind that a poor sweep is worse than no sweep.

Tim Johnson, International Logistics 602.786.0909

Dave Fox, Fox Consulting 201.652.0165

Kevin Murray 800.635.0811

Ray Jarvis, ex-government, also a top TSCM instructor, Jarvis International Intelligence 918.835.3130

Thomas Canastar (ex New York cop) 315.823.1345

John Hart, Counterforce 513.891.2144

Mike Russell 215.357.9065

Ed Bradley 800 YES TSCM

The Hanratty Group 212.733.0944

PolyTronics 800.345.5730

Rainer A. Melucci (ex NY Police Detective) 212.991.1210

Glenn Mortimer 216.749.2150

The Orion Group 800.451.4404 (in Kansas 913.451.5657)

Thomas Ciacciarelli 201.887.7764

Hilton And Associates 713.370.6591

Tom Larsen, CSC Counter Surveillance 303.252.0811

This is by no means a complete list, use the above guidelines and don't be afraid to ask "How are you going to find this?"

Schools

There are no "schools" available to the general public that teach the fine art of surveillance, per se. Jarvis International Intelligence offers courses in TSCM measures that include a detailed look at how the bad guys operate as well as really interesting seminars and courses in lock bypass and active surveillance to law enforcement personnel.

I can personally attest to the quality of Mr. Jarvis' efforts—well worth it. PolyTronics also offers TSCM seminars that come recommended.

Charles Taylor teaches, or at least has taught, hands-on counter surveillance courses at the University of Texas which also come very highly recommended.

James Ross of Ross Engineering (address under suppliers) gives seminars in various parts of the country on TSCM measures. He also puts out a newsletter entitled *SURVEILLANCE* and stages an annual convention where one can mix with some real pros in the surveillance business as well as a lot of folks in black shoes and white socks...

A number of equipment suppliers show their goodies at the Surveillance Expo and a number of knowledgeable people give hour long speeches on all aspects of surveillance.

Hey, dentists have conventions, why not spies?

A more law enforcement oriented show is the COPEX (Covert & Operational Procurement Exhibition). It shows weapons, surveillance, riot control, counter insurgency, and other neat stuff each year but it takes a badge, warrant card, or special invitation to be admitted. Sponsored by Osprey USA in Naples, Florida.

And then there's the National Technical Investigators Association which puts on annual conferences full of feds and fed suppliers that pretty much decides the future of surveillance.

From what I hear, it's really fun. Ah, see, they really don't want anyone like me, actually there...

William C. Dear, a licensed private investigator runs a 7 week course in private detective stuff, including surveillance, at the William C. Dear Academy in Desoto Texas.

Hart Investigations runs a school in Casselberry, Florida called ISTM which is a non-profit organization licensed by the state to teach investigative methodology which utilizes 14 different PI's as course leaders.

AID (the largest manufacturer of *Law Enforcement Only* surveillance equipment in the U.S.) runs a technical training facility committed exclusively to the specialized instruction of federal, state, and local law enforcement officers. It graduates about 800 personnel per year.

The school, known as the National Intelligence Academy, lives in Fort Lauderdale, Florida and teaches technical intercepts, countermeasures, telephone systems and "instant entry" techniques. They also offer instructional video tapes in the same subjects.

Intelligence Support Group in Little Falls, NJ puts on seminars in tech surveillance, phone systems, and locking devices and alarms that are restricted to law enforcement officers.

The U.S. Treasury operates the Customs Technical Surveillance School to teach feds how to spy, but it's so secret I'm not even going to tell you where it's located...

SPY SHOPS

Over the last few years the surveillance business has taken an unusual turn—toward the retail end of things. A number of stores offering everything from dropout recorders and night vision devices, to fairly sophisticated audio intelligence gathering devices and transmitters, have opened in various parts of the U.S. Many of these shops sell walk-in, cash-down, walk-out equipment that is difficult if not impossible to purchase anywhere else without lengthy and possibly overseas mail order delays. Some of the shops also offer ancillary services such as PCSM searches and countermeasure sweeps, and a few provide a mail order catalog for those impatient customers who don't want to fly from Muskogee, Oklahoma to New York City in order to purchase a parallel telephone tap.

Most spy stores offer a variety of counter-measure's gear, stun guns, fancy microphones, useless hidden safes, auto alarms, "bug detectors," recording devices, tear gas, bulletproof vests, batons, metal detectors, voice changers, handcuffs, camcorders and other examples of low end consumer-oriented surveillance gear. However, each store or chain of stores differs in its personality, some bring in gear from other countries to resell and a few even manufacture a number of their own proprietary and often interesting devices.

The first spy stores were probably in Florida. For some unknown reason, Florida seems to be full of people who want to spy on each other or are afraid that someone, very likely a member of a Federal Agency, is spying on them.

Spy Tech, 1460 Brickell, Miami, Florida.
The usual electronics plus some imported mini transmitters.

Counter Intelligence, 1950 N. W. 94th Ave., Miami, Florida.

Miami Spy Equipment, 2695 Biscayne Road, Miami, Florida.

From Florida we jump to New York which offers a pair of spy shops. The first one is **Spy Tech, Inc.**, 350 Fifth Avenue (Empire State Building), Suite 8024, New York, N. Y. 10118.

S.T.I. is run by Bernie Sklar, a fairly knowledgeable gentleman who has been in this field for a number of years. Bernie's shop carries the usual low-end specialized microphones, recorders, starters and countermeasure's gear coupled with some nice high-end night vision equipment and a dynamite selection of video gear that the shop has put together for their customers including a complete VCR built into a normal television set with a pinhole lens and a motion detector that switches on when someone enters a room, records for a preset duration and then switches off, a variety of unusual "video traps" built into computers, fire extinguishers, plants, file cabinets, and devices that are definitely meant to go in a bedroom as well as (see the video section) some very cute, cuddly stuffed animals that are equipped with their own cameras.

S.T.I. sells mail order and has been featured on a number of television shows and in print articles. Pretty neat stuff and OK prices.

Second New York offering is:
Spy Shop, 164 Christopher Street, N.Y., NY
Spy Shop is owned and run by one Frank Jones. Offers a selection of items including high-end countermeasure gear and sweep services. The Spy Shop has been *allegedly* involved in some deals that may have fallen through at the last moment.

It would not be my personal recommendation of a place to shop for goods.

The largest group of spy shops owned by a single party would have to be the **Spy Factories**, which sell the usual low-end parabolic microphones, voice changes, etc., as well as a very nice selection of Kony and Ruby telephone transmitters and wireless microphones imported directly from Japan and England. As one would expect there's a slight surcharge for this availability, say in the neighborhood of *1,000 percent;* my $30 Cony wireless mikes are tagged at $300+. In fact, the Spy Factory offers so many phone transmitters that it appears to me that there are at least 11 or 12 felonies-to-go sitting on their shelf at any one time. Spy Factory, at this writing, has 13 locations across the country.

Spy Factory locations:

Corporate Headquarters,
4836 Whirlwind, San Antonio, TX 78217

San Antonio,
6991 Blanco Rd., San Antonio, TX 78216

El Paso,
4224 N. Mesa, Suite A, El Paso, TX 79912

Dallas,
3701 W. Northwest Hwy., #164, Dallas, TX 75220

Houston,
5358 Westheimer, Houston, Tx 77056

San Diego,
3555 Rosecrans, #104 B, San Diego, CA 92110

Las Vegas,
2228 Paradise Rd., Las Vegas, NV 89104

Tucson,
4702 E. Broadway, #106, Tucson, AZ 85711

Costa Mesa,
1914 Harbor Blvd., Costa Mesa, CA 92627

Hollywood,
8521 Sunset Blvd., W. Hollywood, CA 90069

Sacramento,
3110 Arden Way, Sacramento, CA 95825

San Francisco,
500 Beach St., #119, San Francisco, CA 94133

The most interesting retail spy shop in the country to my way of thinking would be the **Intelligence Group**, 1620 Lombard Street, San Francisco, California 94123. Intelligence Group is owned by one John Hancock, I swear that's his real name, who I have known for a number of years. Many of you will remember John as the inventor of Cobra Electronic Pick, the device that opened many locks like magic and enjoyed a few years of popularity before John phased it out. The Intelligence Group offers retail items selected by John for their uniqueness and the fact that they flat out do what they are supposed to do.

He offers camera lens, ID's, some very nice lock picks including a new version of the Cobra, and some very nice electronics. In addition to the over-the-counter items, John is employing a top electronics engineer to design and manufacture his own goodies including some very unique "shooting" stun guns, digital tape recorders, parabolic mikes, wireless remote turn-on video briefcases, and on-body wireless or tape-based video recording systems.

At the time of this writing the Intelligence Group does not have a catalog but one should probably give them a call if shopping for any particular piece of surveillance or counter-surveillance equipment as the markup seems to be reasonable and their equipment good.

The Intelligence Group, like many spy shops, seems to be drifting away from the concept of audio surveillance (which falls under a number of rather nasty laws) to legitimate video surveillance units, but unlike many of the other shops the Intelligence Group offers some very unique devices.

A

AARON SECURITY, POB 420929, San Francisco, CA 94142. A source for nearly anything in the fields of surveillance or locksmithing. AARON's prices are reasonable for unusual equipment and they shred all transaction records to guarantee the privacy of their clients.

Abcor Security Products, Inc., The Smith Building, 16 S. Washington, Suite 208, Cookeville, TN 38501. Abcore stocks a number of other people's goods including Research Electronics countersurveillance equipment, fax scramblers from TRW, through wall microphones from Research Electronics and long-play tape recorders. They have a nice brochure and the prices seem within reason.

ACE COMMUNICATIONS, 10707 E. 106th St., Indianapolis, IN 46256. Ace is one of the largest AOR scanner suppliers in the United States. Excellent prices.

ACIS, 7910 Frost Street, Suite 209, San Diego, CA 92123. Custom video still camera surveillance pictures that can be shot in complete darkness by the use of remote cameras and infrared flash setups.

AEROMARITIME, Hanauer Strasse 105, 8000 Munchen 50. Manufacturers of a proprietary fax intercept system that utilizes a modem custom software and an IBM PC or a compatible. The system can be configured to use a laptop or to utilize the customer's own computer by the addition of plug-in cards and software. Designed for law enforcement. This is a very comprehensive system that is not cheap.

ATET V. G. Da Verrazzano, 42, 1012, Torino, Italy. World's smallest crystal controlled surveillance transmitters. Operate in the 700–900MhZ bands. Quite stable, slightly larger than your thumb nail.

AUDIO INTELLIGENCE DEVICES, 1400 N.W. 62nd Street, Fort Lauderdale, FL 33309. AID is the largest, bar none, surveillance supplier in the United States. They are law enforcement only and offer a diverse line of gear from complete intelligence systems such as their UNITEL series that offer scrambled or clear voice, high band operation, rechargeable batteries, complete unattended recorder, performance to scramblers, body mikes, hard wires, through wall devices, processors, acoustic sensors, transmitters that come packaged in envelopes, pagers, baseball caps, cigarette packs, wall outlets, eye glass cases, and even, one of my all time favorites, transmitters packaged in semi-automatic pistols. AID develops and manufactures their own equipment. Their stuff works, as could be attested to by probably 10% of all federal prison inmates, and they are priced accordingly with small transmitters starting at about $800 and going up into the $20,000 range for some of their high-end gear.

It's a fun catalog full of fun things, it's too bad they probably won't send it to you.

ALTERNATIVE INPHORMATION, P. O. Box #4, Carthage, TX 75633. AI has been around for many years selling really good information on hacking, tapping, compromising, and protecting one's self. I highly recommend you subscribe to their catalog.

AMERICAN FIBERTEK INC., 370 W. 35th Street, New York, N.Y. 10001. Manufacturers of "Sentry Vision" fiber optic transmission system with sound channels that provide near broadcast quality pictures from any location.

AMC SALES INC., Dept. A, 9335 Lubec St., Box 928, Downey, CA 90241. AMC is one of the grandfathers of low-cost surveillance equipment. They specialize in dropout recorders (excuse me, I mean phone recording adapters), vox control switches and modified LP cassette recorders.

ANACAPA SCIENCES, INC., P. O. Drawer Q, Santa Barbara, CA 93102. For 20 years ANACAPA has been offering courses in analytical investigation methods and computer aid intelligence analysis. A rather interesting group.

ANTENNA SPECIALISTS CO., 30500 Bruce Industrial Parkway, Cleveland, OH 44139. Microchokes that offer pinpoint resonance in the cellular telephone bands plus a number of general purpose antennas designed to provide the optimum site geometry for both receivers and transmitters.

APPLIED SYSTEMS CORPORATION, 212 Dominion Road, Vienna, VA 22180. Rather high-end burst communication devices, night vision goggles and ultra miniature video transmitters.

AUDIOTEL INTERNATIONAL LTD., Cavendish Courtyard, Sallow Road, Weldon, Corby, Northants NN17 1DZ ENGLAND. Interesting diversity of both countersurveillance and surveillance equipment, many of which can not be legally purchased or brought into this country, but it still makes for interesting reading.

AVCOM OF VIRGINIA, INC., 500 Southlake Blvd., Richmond, VA 23236. Probably the best under $2,000 spectrum analyzer (RSA-35AA) available anywhere on the market plus other test equipment and a broadcast quality microwave transmitting system.

B

BARTLETT TECHNOLOGIES CORP., 6858 N.W. 75th Street, Bldg. 3, Miami, FL. 33166. Data intercept technology, loop extenders, slaves, and dialled number recorders for the law enforcement community. Priced as expected.

BH&A, 266 San Lorenzo St., Pomona, CA 91766. General consumer supplier of transcribers and portable cassette recorders at discount prices.

C

CANCOM, 103-20651 56th Ave., Langley, B.C. Canada, V3A 3Y9. Canadian supplier of exotic surveillance equipment including IR beacons built into baseball caps, pulsed tracking transmitters, self contained voice transmitters that operate at extremely high frequencies, modified recorders, a great night video surveillance system known as the KS-V Knight Stalker for mobile or fixed surveillance that uses two 750,000 candle power IR lights coupled to a fully controllable CCD video camera and lens, a couple of super miniature covert surveillance transmitters, quick plant transmitters hidden inside 6 outlet electrical plugs, microwave video links, and body wires hidden inside Motorola pagers.

My favorite all time CanCom product is, of course, their CST 385 V solid state micro electronic VHF voice transmitters that are hidden inside a working butane lighter. Having had a chance to see this unit in operation, I can assure you the frequency stability is excellent (plus or minus .0025% of a signed channel), has very little harmonics or spurious outputs, and is the kind of thing that makes agents not want to have sex at home with their wives because they don't have anything left after reading this catalog...

Canadian Countermeasures Electronics., P. O. Box L50, Station A, Longueuil, Quebec, Canada, J4H 3W6. Their primary product is known as the Stopper which is a unique product that mechanically and electronically disconnects any telephone unit from the line physically prohibiting infinity transmitters, jumped hook switches, and telephone microphone shorting devices.

CAPRI ELECTRONICS CORP., P. O. Box 589, Bayfield, CO 81122. Capri is a OEM manufacturer of some very low price and very effective countermeasures and "privacy assurance" devices including microwave detectors, video camera detectors, bug detectors, countermeasures sets, and an extremely useful item known as the ScanRecord which will automatically turn on a tape recorder when a scanner is receiving a message. An ideal device for remote listening posts.

Carol Products Co., Inc., 1750 Brielle Avenue, Ocean, New Jersey 07712. Carol Products is a video surveillance supplier who cleverly secretes miniature cameras in things such as smoke alarms, thermal detectors, notebooks, speakers, thermostats, *plants* (?), deodorizers, sirens, exit signs, and fire boxes. They also stock wide angle and a couple of pin hole lenses, complete hidden self-contained recording systems built in attache cases, and super 8mm camcorders modified to fit in household objects.

Carol offers the "video dispatcher" one of the first FCC approved 900 MHz extremely low priced wireless video transmitters. Carol's costs are extremely reasonable ($100–$175 for the wireless system plus $22 for high gain antenna) and their stuff is *neat*.

C.A.Z., 39 Star Street, London, England W2 10B. A rather unique organization who manufactures their own products which they export to about 50 countries and who stocks various other people's products that they think would be of interest to their clientele.

C.A.Z. offers night vision, x-ray systems, recording briefcases, Scanlock receivers, dialled number pen registers, "mains," transmitters, cigarette lighters, UHF (up to 1100 MHz), sub-miniature transmitters, wafer transmitters, parallel phone taps, car bomb protection systems, and a number of things so secret they won't even put them in their catalog. One might feel that the computer cracker would fall into this latter category.

C.A.Z. is priced within reason and has some nifty, nifty little things.

CCTV Corp., 315 Hudson St., New York, NY 10013. A discount surveillance video house including very cheap monitors, miniature cameras, and connecting systems.

Cellular Security Group., 4 Gerring Rd., Gloucester, MA 01930. Antennas designed to maximize cellular and/or cordless telephone reception on scanners.

Chinon America Inc., P. O. Box 1248, 1065 Bristol Rd., Mountainside, NJ 07092. The world's largest manufacturer of lenses for video camcorders and the OEM supplier for many miniature and sub-miniature video cameras which are resold by other suppliers for several times their original price.

If you're into video, you should be into Chinon.

Chugai Boyeki America Corp., 55 Mall Drive, Commack, NY 11725. An OEM manufacturer of fixed focal length, manual iris c-mount, auto iris, cs-mount, motorized zoom, manual zoom, and just about every pinhole lens one could possibly covet.

As with many other manufacturers, Chugai Boyeki products are shuffled around to various surveillance manufacturers where they are resold for many times their original price. This company is so large they have offices in London, Dusseldorf, Tokyo, Osaka, Nagoya, Hong Kong, Taipei, Manila, Bangkok, Jakarta, and Los Angeles.

R. B. Clifton Co., 11500 NW 7th Ave., Miami, FL 33168. Clifton has been around for years and years selling low-end countermeasures equipment and an occasional recorder starter or vox relay.

CMI/MPH., 316 East Ninth Street, Owensboro, KY 42301. Offers the Dark Invader Night Vision System in all its various permutations including handheld, enhanced camcorder, 35mm still illumination systems, and equipped to mount on your favorite rifle.

Dark Invader Night Vision devices offer a 70,000+ light gain coupled with an IR laser for spot illumination that allows legible license plate photography at about 1/2 a mile in complete darkness.

Cohu Inc., 5755 Kearny Villa Road, P. O. Box 85623, San Diego, CA 92138. Manufacturer of miniature and sub-miniature CCD cameras and their associated systems.

CommTronics, Inc., 120 Roesler Rd., Glen Burnie, MD 21061. Custom built portable two-way radio systems as well as body wires and covert video recording systems.

Communications Devices Ltd., 6 Riverside Park, Dogflud Way, Farnham Surrey, England GU9 7UG. High level facsimile monitoring systems, loop extenders that read pulse voltages as well as on and off hook current and then regenerate same to hide activated tape recorders and complete telephone monitoring systems that will monitor from 10 to several hundred lines in one fell swoop.

Complete Security, 14 Hollywood Rd., London, England SW10 9HT. Anti-terrorist equipment, surveillance and countersurveillance equipment that cannot normally be found inside the U.S.

Computer Handyman, P. O. Box 503, Carmel, IN 46032. A rather interesting communications and intelligence gathering and analysis program that has been developed to log transmissions on various receivers and scanners and includes such data as date, time, frequency, and emission type.

Consumertronics, 2011 Crescent Dr., P. O. Drawer 537, Alamogordo, NM 88310. John Williams, chief engineer and owner of Consumertronics, has provided unique equipment and services which are always a bargain for the past 15 or 20 years. They offer super sophisticated devices such as the Tempest Computer Tapper, covered under that section, information, plans, custom engineering and repair or maintenance of any electronic product. Consumertronics is a real bargain in any sense of the word.

Cony Mfg. Co., No. 27, 2-Chome, Kangetsu-Cho Chikusa-Ku, Nagoya 464 Japan. If you've been in the field for any length of time, you know Cony.

One of the pioneers in miniature telephone taps and room transmitters, Cony is probably the last great bargain left on the earth. If you buy Cony equipment from the factory, such devices as FM wireless microphones and telephone transmitters which can "pick up mutual telephone conversation, no battery needed" or one of my favorites, "giant power in small body"—average $30.

If writing to Japan and paying $30 doesn't interest you, for God's sake go to any number of retail suppliers including the SPY FACTORY and pay $300 for the same thing. Cony has moved around some over the years but they're still there and still healthy.

Cony transmitters.

Counter Technology Inc., 4733 Bethseda Ave., Suite 200, Bethesda, MD 20814.

Primarily a consultation firm; offers security surveys, vulnerability studies, executive protection, market and product evaluation, and equipment development in sales. CTI is one of the infamous "beltway bandits" that seem to spring up around the Washington, D. C. area and make their primary living from a number of federal agencies headquartered in the same general area. CTI has a good reputation for management studies and research projects as well as training and tech writing, having done the latter for the FBI, DEA, and LEAA, among other multi-initialed agencies.

Covert Operations International, Ltd., 276 Fifth Avenue, Suite 1106, New York, NY 10001. COI is the primary supplier of the CAN-TRAC 360 electronic tracking system as well as several other electronic trackers, pen registers, telephone decoders, and other items of interest to agents, detectives and curious folk.

COI sells what can be sold to the general public, to the general public and what is law enforcement only to law enforcement. The gentleman who runs COI has been in the business for damn near as long as I've been writing books (depressing isn't it?), and has a good reputation in the field. I highly recommend COI for advice or equipment.

CRB RESEARCH, P. O. Box 56, Commack, NY 11725. CRB is the undisputed leader in books and materials on the fine art of scanning and radio listening.

Crownbridge Industries Inc., 2 Thorncliffe Park Drive, Unit 29, Toronto, Ontario, Canada M4H 1H2. Another Canadian company, Crownbridge manufactures the infamous TRACK FINDER SYSTEM which consists of an extremely small transmitter which can be hidden in works of art, "bait money," briefcases or other personal property and tracked with the receiver from a distance of 3–5 miles on land or 20 miles in the air. Track Finder Receivers come in several levels of signal strength and size, not to mention price. They have found numerous applications in the U.S. as well as around the world within the last few years.

D

Daniel Technology, Inc., 94 East Ave., Norwalk, CT 06851. Electret microphones, expander and compressor circuits as well as sub-miniature microphones designed for surveillance use and a nicely modified Marantz recorder with low power

drain remote control, quiet shut off and direct phone line hook up jack.

DTI's equipment is designed to extend the usefulness of Nagra as well as other miniature tape recorders.

They also offer some modification and direct repair services of Nagra SNS or SNST recorders.

Datametrics, Inc., 2575 South Bayshore Dr., Suite 8A, Coconut Grove, FL 33133. Computer controlled menu-driven software that will drive an Icom receiver for autolog and autoscanning applications.

Datong Electronics Limited, Clayton Wood Close, West Park, Leeds, England, LS16 6QE. Upper level countersurveillance gear including Scanlock type receivers, direction finders, and their RANGER which introduces its own sonic footprint into the room, listens for an audio return and then calculates the exact distance to the bug, helping the operator do an immediate locate.

Their wideband direction finder includes a doppler direction finding array that will lead the operator to any transmitter in question.

DBA Systems, Inc., 1200 Woody Burke Rd., P. O. Drawer 550, Melbourne, FL 32902. Probably the best and most expensive tracking system available, DBA's video tracker processes video synchronization and timing signals to provide spacial coordinates on a moving target.

Deco Industries, Box 607, Bedford Hills, NY 10507. Complete kits for miniature room transmitters and phone taps in the under $30 range.

DELL-Star Corporation/TRON-Tek, Inc., 5401 South Sheridan, Suite 304, Tulsa, OK 74145. DELL-Star is a representative of TRON-Tek, manufacturers of some of the most exciting 900 MHz and 450 MHz transmitters available. The units themselves are actually manufactured in Italy and sold through DELL-Star and they offer an extremely compact package that fulfills most audio surveillance needs. DELL-Star materials are an example of hot surveillance applications.

Detection Systems, 2515 E. Thomas Rd., #16-B64, Phoenix, AZ 85016. Resellers of Capri Electronics, what appears to be Listen Electronics, and several other lines of recording and countermeasures devices. They do offer a fairly good selection and mix in some nice army surplus intrusion detection and radar equipment along with the mandatory tear gas and handcuff selection. Oddly enough the prices aren't too terrible on some things but they are on others.

Detection Systems and Engineering Company, 1450 Temple City Dr., P. O. Box 627, Troy, MI 48099. DSE offers color or black and white high gain intensified video cameras for remote area observation. By providing a dual channel design, the intensifier is used only at night, which extends the life of the intensifier tube and produces sharper day pictures because the camera does not look through the intensifier except when it is in use. Their system comes complete with a 25-150mm motorized zoom lens and all weather housing. This is a top unit that provides clear pictures in extremely dark environments.

I have seen this camera work in an area that sported approximately .0000001 footcandles of illumination and provided a 600 line picture. Very nice.

Digital Audio Corporation, 6512 Six Forks Rd., Suite 203B, Raleigh NC 27615. Digital filter systems and amplifiers. DAC's materials are designed for laboratory use and the enhancement of recorded tapes. One of their products, the MicroDac, is a portable automatic noise filter that combines rumble filters, hiss filters, and a tracking adaptive digital filter for limiting room noises, acoustic resonances, spectral distortion, channel interference, telephone line effects, as well as music and general background noises from voices. The MicroDac is inserted into the circuitry, ad-

justed for best effect, and then simply left alone. If new noises appear or the available noises change, the unit will automatically adapt itself to maximize intelligible conversation. DAC stuff is not cheap but it's probably the best around.

Digital Security Concepts, P. O. Box 17310, Anaheim, CA 92817. Features a battery-powered portable monitor that will record the time and date that any entry into a desk drawer, file cabinet, home, garage, warehouse, container, or restricted area occurs. The unit consists of a portable monitoring unit, 10' of cable, a light sensor, magnetic contacts, mounting hardware, and an instruction manual, and is designed to help fight thefts by showing when something was opened. It can also be used to track when a person under surveillance leaves or enters an area, moves his car, etc. This is a dynamite unit that sells for under $100...

Dirijo and Bond Electronics, 2505 Woodbridge Dr., Gastonia, NC 28054. Owned and operated by an electronics engineer, Dirijo sells kits and plans for some of the most effective and cost efficient surveillance gear on the market. See the photo of their transmitter in the surveillance section for an idea of what I'm talking about. They also feature a very nice light wave receiver that can be used for communication purposes or more nefarious, passive surveillance uses.

Diversified Wholesale Products, P. O. Box 1275, Redondo Beach, CA 90278. Resellers of Capri and Grove Electronics countermeasures gear, a few slowed-down recorders and handheld transceivers with ear microphones. Prices don't seem too bad. Their telephone activity monitor (sort of a duplicate of Radio Shack's) is $200 and I've seen the same thing for $300 in a couple of local spy stores. Their recorders seem to run about the same as in any upper level retail shop.

D. K. Video Inc., P. O. Box 63/6025, Margate, FL 33063. Low-end kits for unscrambling video signals as well as a dropout recorder or two and a cheap transmitter.

Doppler Systems, P. O. Box 31819, Phoenix, AZ 85046. Doppler is the manufacturer of the original Doppler Direction Finding System. This is a reasonably priced system which does a good job of locating a stationary transmitter. Some resellers sell the Doppler as a low to medium-priced vehicle tracking device but this is not recommended.

Dynasound, 6439 Atlantic Blvd., Norcross, GA 30071. The leaders in the field of serious audio security. See the article on Dynasound in the Tempest section.

Dynatech Tactical Communications, Inc., 6A Lyberty Way, Westford, MA 01886. A very complete line of two-way communication accessories including in ear and throat microphones.

E

Eckert Instrument Company, 109 Pinecrest Dr., Anapolis, MD 21403. A technical video resource facility that provides everything from speciality optics to miniature cameras, infrared cameras in complete systems design.

Edmund Scientific Company, 101 E Gloucester Pike, Barrington, NJ 08007. Edmund stocks a plethora of neat stuff for any techie including fiberoptic microphone kits, infrared viewers, starlight scopes, parabolic ears, and specialized microphones.

Electronic Equipment Bank, 323 Mill Street NE, Vienna, VA 22180. Good prices on Icom, Kenwood, Yaesu, and Sony receivers and scanners.

Elecktron S.A., P. O. Box 39, 84210 PERNES, FRANCE. Electron is a long-time surveillance and countermeasures supplier. They offer a number of unique items including scrambled recorders and unusual transmitters that cannot be found in the U.S.

Elestrong Corp, POB 68-291, Taipei, Taiwan, ROC. "Ten years experience in the making of FM microphone pens, FM wireless transmitters and telephone eavesdropping devices. Both OEM and ODM business."

Elmo Co., Ltd., 70 Hyde Park Road, New Hyde Park, NY 11040. Elmo is a manufacturer of subminiature color and black and white CCTV video chip cameras. Elmo stocks a large line of very good cameras which are purchased, marked up, and resold by surveillance dealers.

EI-Tec International Inc., 205 Van Buren St., Suite 220, Herndon, VA 22070. The ETI Telemonitor is one of the most intelligent monitoring devices on the market utilizing artificial intelligence and their own networks to monitor all existing fax machines and modem transmissions. It is a user friendly system that may be operated fully automatically or manually and offers such add-on abilities as the ability to decode most proprietary and some encrypted non-standard facility fax transmissions. The ability to act as a dialled number recorder, reading DTMF, pulse and multi-frequency signals and the ability to learn protocol in codes from virtually all telecommunication devices.

Executive Protection Products, Inc., 1834 First St., Napa, CA 94559. Although primarily a reseller, EPP carries one of the wider ranges of materials on the market including scramblers, night vision devices, countermeasure gear, dropout recorders, cellular telephone scanners, phone loggers, micro-cameras, pin hole lenses, communication receivers and countermeasures kits. EPP also modifies some devices giving features not found in the original models. One thing that comes to mind is their ability to install remote start/stop capability on transmitters.

F

F & P Enterprises, P. O. Box 51272, Palo Alto, CA 94303. Value-added reseller of dropout recorders, parabolic microphones, and what looks like most of Information Unlimited's entire catalog.

Felix Security Devices, P. O. Box 446, Oregon City, OR 97045. For the last 15 years Felix has been selling unusual video surveillance devices including completely equipped periscope vans (in fact, Felix owns the patent on the first van periscope ever built.) They also stock motion detectors, WatchCam video monitors, automobile video power supplies, date/time generators and modified surveillance camcorders.

G

General Technology Corporation, 6816 Washington NE, Albuquerque, NM 87109. Builds things around other things; most notably around Nagra recorders. Things like pen and pencil holders and briefcases, not to mention the camera's built into cigarette packs...Fancier briefcase holds a built in video system.

Grove Enterprises, Inc., P. O. Box 98, Brasstown, NC 28902. One-stop shopping for scanner enthusiasts, shortwave listeners, and anyone else who likes to eavesdrop on the radio spectrum.

GYYR, 1515 South Manchester Ave., Anaheim, CA 92802. GYYR manufactures the best time lapse programmable video tape recorders money can buy. Many surveillance dealers resell GYYR equipment marked up substantially.

H

H & H Technologies Inc., 1293 Denman St., Victoria, B.C. V8T 1L7. Canadian countermeasures gear manufacturer. As of this writing they feature only one product, a small apparently quite sensitive receiver designed to find unwanted transmitters. The price of the unit appears to be just under $1,500 but single lot "evaluation units" are available to resellers at a mere $450. You might want to become a reseller.

HDS, 12310 Pinecrest Rd, Reston, VA 22091.- say your firm makes some of the most sophisticated surveillance items known to mankind and yet you really don't want to advertise that fact.

What do you call it?

How about HOUSEHOLD DATA SERVICES? ("Technological Excellence Through Innovation")

HDS (law enforcement only) sells such off the shelf items as miniature and sub-miniature video transmitters in two different bands (8-10.5 GHz, and 1700-1900 MHz), microwave video links, 1" square video transmitters, body wires, dialed number recorders, FAX interception systems ($28,500), modem interceptors, pager interceptors ($12,500), scramblers, mini-audio transmitters, unique antennas and so on.

Not for the budget minded individual.

Karl Heitz, P. O. Box 427, 34-11 62nd St., Woodside, NY 11377. For approximately 40 years, Karl Heitz has sold ROBOT candid observation cameras in a variety of configurations including with radio remote release units, low light lenses and/or camouflaged in briefcases or other inert objects. Heitz is the best, if not the only, supplier of these fine German cameras in the United States.

Hekimian Laboratories, Inc., 9298 Gaither Rd., Gaithersburg, MD 20877. Expensive transmission test sets for cellular phone sites among other applications.

I

ICOM America, Inc., 116th Ave. N.E., Bellevue, WA 98004. Manufacturers of the largest line of general communication receivers and scanners. ICOM will sell you their latest products or direct you to a retailer in your area.

IFR Systems, Inc., 10200 West York St., Wichita, KS 67215. IFR manufactures several portable digital spectrum analyzers which, although not designed for surveillance use, lend themselves ideally to this application. Options include a 2 microvolt FM/AM receiver with selectable band pass filters for audible monitoring of any display signals that can be mounted internally. IFR is a respected name and is a bit cheaper than TekTronics.

INCO, P. O. Box 3111, Burbank, CA 91508. Suppliers of the amazing disappearing paper. They also stock a variety of fake ID's, badges, books, knives, hidden safes, and T-shirts.

Intelligence Support Group, Ltd., 239 Longhill Rd., Little Falls, NJ 07424. Top-end intelligence kits (receiver/recorder systems) that are modular in design in order to be easily upgraded along with a couple of small transmitters with synthesized frequency capability and a very interesting path loss calculator which purports to solve R. F. path loss in order to aid an agent in transmitter and listening post placement. Probably law enforcement only...

InPhoto, Toll free: 800-822-8220, Fax Toll free: 800-752-0720. InPhoto is technically not a supplier, they provide photographic surveillance for attorneys, private detectives, or interested parties across most of the U.S.A. by using their own personnel or contracted individuals, thereby saving travel expenses for the investigator.

ISA—Information Security Associates, Inc., 350 Fairfield Ave., Stamford, CT 06902. ISA has been around for quite a few years offering top-end countermeasures equipment including special receivers, telephone analyzers, (based on the original Mason concept), and non-linear junction detectors. ISA manufactures much of their equipment all the way from tool kits and audio amplifiers through complex analyzers. They also provide sweep services.

J

Jarvis International Intelligence, Inc., P. O. Box 690563, Tulsa, OK 74169. Ray Jarvis, having worked for the government for 20 some odd years, now teaches the fine art of countersurveillance and, to the appropriate personnel, technical intercepts. He also stocks and sells some very nice countermeasures equipment including a great many amplifiers and a line of spectrum analyzers.

Jensen Tools Inc., 7815 South 46th St., Phoenix, AZ 85044. Jensen is an electronics equipment supplier who specializes in test equipment, cases, and repair kits. Jensen stocks a wide variety of telephone company equipment including correctly coded cross connect wire strippers, push down tools, linemen's handsets, and telephone test equipment. They also stock a nice selection of tone generators and inductive amplifiers, line probes, small TDR's and the mini-tracker cable locater system that injects RF into telephone cable.

JSI Telecom, 600-294 Albert St., Ottawa, Ontario K1P 6E6 Canada. Located in Canada, this manufacturer deals primarily with the Canadian government selling a variety of dial-up slave systems, loop extenders, dialled number recorders, and other interesting hardware.

K

Martin L. Kaiser, Inc., P. O. Box 171, Cockeysville, MD 21030. Marty Kaiser is a legend in the business. For many years he was one of the primary suppliers to the FBI as well as other government agencies, of surveillance equipment and as such designed a number of pieces of gear that are now commonplace. A number of years back Mr. Kaiser allegedly discovered the FBI was stiffing the American public by reselling his gear to the government at a substantial markup and pocketing the money. He blew the whistle and was later arrested by some FBI agents for using his own equipment to supposedly spy on the spies. A number of lawsuits followed with the outcome being that there seems to be no love lost between Mr. Kaiser and the FBI any more, although he reportedly does still produce goodies for the CIA, among others.

He also sells tracking systems, stethoscopes, a very nice feedback detector and a number of other interesting pieces of countermeasures equipment to the general public.

Kant Corporation, Shiba, P. O. Box 145, Tokyo, Japan. Kant is one of those Japanese companies that everybody wants to find the address to because they produce miraculous little surveillance devices, in this case primarily transmitters and receivers, that are quartz controlled and operate outside conventional bands. Kant's equipment is purchased by many spy shops and surveillance resellers, marked up several hundred percent and resold in this country. If you want to be clever, go directly to the source. They are one of the few places you can buy a crystal-controlled series telephone tap and matching receiver, good little dropout recorders, and a vibration detector that I've not yet had a chance to check out. Kant's products have to be good because the English in their catalog, like any good Chinese restaurant, is just bad enough to insure authenticity.

Kato International, 19-18 Jingumae, 2-Chome Shibuya-Ku, Tokyo 150, Japan. Another manufacturer of cheap, yet effective surveillance equipment from Japan.

Kigre, Inc., 100 Marshland Road, Hilton Head Island, S.C. 29926. Night vision devices including some rather unusual goggles that incorporate a folded optical path, making them extremely compact and light in weight with a depth of about 1/2 that of normal night vision goggles. This reduces strain on the neck muscles and makes the goggles easier to use.

Knox Security, 335 Greenwich Rd, Greenwich, CT 06830. US distributor of the ATET bugs, a FAX interception system and other law enforcement only electronics.

L

L. M. Smith & Company, P. O. Box 286, Phoenix, AZ 85001. A reseller—the usual stuff. Stun guns, bumper peepers, a few starlight scopes and Capri's line of countermeasures equipment.

LACUE Communications Co., 132 Village Street, Johnstown, PA 15902. Good prices on handheld and mobile programmable two-way radios.

Laser Communications, Inc., 1848 Charter Lane, Suite F, Lancaster, PA 17605. A very nice handheld infrared viewer with a response from the visible spectrum to 1200nm with C-mount removable lens and adjustable focus, weather proof video cameras, cabling, and even video laser transmission setups.

Listen Electronics, 603 Elgin, Muskogee, OK 74401. I love these people. I don't know them but I love them. Slaves—oops, excuse me—"modular telephone taps," infinity transmitters by themselves or built into a telephone (makes a great gift idea at Christmas), dial-out taps, and combinations of all the above in various packages.

Very reasonably priced, well designed, and well manufactured.

Litton Electronics, 288 Littleton Rd., Suite 32, Westford, MA 01886. Third-generation aviator goggles, weapon sites, single tube night vision goggles, pocket scopes, separate intensifier tubes, and starlight binoculars, test equipment, and damn near anything else you can imagine in night vision devices. Litton is the leader and manufactures many entire items if not the tubes for "other manufacturers."

Lorraine Electronics Surveillance, 716 Lea Bridge Rd., Leyton, London E10 6AW. Just like the name says, if it's in surveillance there's a good chance Lorraine makes it. Their countermeasures gear includes spectrum analyzers, telephone and wiring analyzers, other sweeping equipment, telephone monitoring and scrambling equipment, body worn detectors, and handheld detectors. Lorraine has a good reputation. Their countermeasures gear is used by professionals the world over. Lorraine is also one of the first manufacturers of the infamous recording briefcase and they've taken that concept to a point of perfection by allowing one the choice of interior or exterior components to make sure the briefcase is not only in style but works well.

Now we get to the good stuff—Lorraine is also the manufacturer of Ruby Electronics, same address.

Ruby manufactures a range of quartz-controlled transmitters and receivers available in VHF and UHF frequencies built into little plastic boxes, hand calculators, fountain pens, wall switch plates, and other paraphernalia to be used in the appropriate circumstances. Ruby offers "mains" transmitters, parallel end series telephone taps, infinity transmitters, remote switches, and even a contact mike. Their prices are reasonable. Next to our Japanese friends they are probably as reasonable as possible with their transmitters beginning at about $90 and wandering on up into the several hundred dollar range depending on how spiffy one wants to get. Lorraine's goodies are often resold by other companies at severalfold the original price.

Louroe Electronics, 6158 Lemona Ave., Van Nuys, CA 91411. In-place audio surveillance system designed for stores, retail areas, warehouses and jails.

M

Martel Electronics, 920 A E. Orangethrope, Anaheim, CA 92801. One of the largest retail suppliers of tape recorders, drop out relays and phone products. Very good prices on sub mini recorders from most major manufacturers, some modified for long play conditions.

Mason Engineering, 35 Brentwood Ave., Fairfield, CT 06430. Mason was one of the true pioneers in countermeasures equipment having designed and manufactured some of the best telephone analyzers around. They now produce specialized wideband receivers and spectrum analyzers designed for countermeasures sweeps.

Math Associates Inc., 2200 Shames Dr., Westbury, NY 11590. Fiber optics systems, components and accessories including laser diode fiberlink transmitters.

Mega Beam, Inc., 14325 Frederick St., Suite #5, Moreno Valley, CA 92388. Handheld searchlights from 3.5 million candlepower to 6 million candlepower with power supplies, battery belt packs, and infrared filters.

Metme Corporation, 11754 Westline Industrial Dr., St. Louis, MO 63146. Producers of a public key scrambled telephone and fax scrambler.

Micro-Electronics, 1 Kada Bldg., 1-3-16, Shintomi Shou-Ku Tokyo, Japan. Manufactures and sells miniature transmitters and other surveillance gear.

Micro and Security, GmbH, Efftingestr. 19, D-2000 Hamburg 70, Germany. Why are half the good surveillance companies named Micro? I don't know. At any rate, Micro and Security are one of the original German goodie manufacturers and they stock everything from underwater metal detectors to portable satellite communication centers (assuming one has a satellite with which one needs to communicate).

Surveillance equipment includes sub-miniature crystal-controlled transmitters, transmitters built into belts, ashtrays, calculators, scrambled transmitters with their own specialized receivers, IR transmitters, stethoscope transmitters that are designed to be taped to the outside of buildings and pick up the inside sound and re-transmit it either by RF or IR, complete intelligence kits with built in transmitters, receivers, filters, etc.

In the latest catalog Micro has increased their product line with such handy things as rubber boats, armored Mercedes', mobile radio encryption units, and thermal vision systems. One could spend a year playing with everything in the Micro catalog and never be bored.

slaves and dialled number recorders that handle 1–5 lines at any given moment. Really slick, lots of bells and whistles. Law enforcement only.

Motorola, Inc., P. O. Box 1417, Scottsdale, AZ 85252. STU phones, probably the most secure telephone and data transmission systems in the world today.

N

Nagra Magnetic Recorders, Inc., 19 West 44th St., Room 715, New York, N.Y. 10036. Suppliers of the NAGRA SNS, two-speed miniature mono recorder. The NAGRA SNST mini stereo recorder and the infamous JBR stereo sub-miniature recorder, the last being sold to law enforcement only.

New York Security Systems, Inc., 20 Industrial Dr., Middletown, NY 10940. Covert audio and video systems including time lapse VCR's, wireless transmitting systems, pinhole lenses, and self contained camcorders.

And, of course, the old camera-in-a-clock.

Night Vision Equipment Co., Inc., P. O. Box 266, Emmaus, PA 18049. A wide line of Generation II and Generation III night vision devices including pocket scopes and full photographic systems. Technical support, competitive prices, and fast shipping are their claims to fame.

O

Olympus Corp., 4 Nevada Dr., Lake Success, NY 11042. Fiberscopes and borescopes for through wall and other covert viewing and film and recording applications. Unique scopes that are camouflaged to look like part of a plant, fit inside a car radio antenna, as well as 20' fiberscopes that can be lowered from a roof to view into interesting windows. Top-end equipment.

MicroTec, P. O. Box 9424, San Diego, CA 92109. The largest supplier of sub-miniature and covert camera and film systems in the world today. Authorized dealers for MINOX, ACMEL, and ROBOT camera systems. They also have a wide selection of special custom engineered or modified camera systems designed specifically for covert intelligence and document photography.

MicroTec also loads specialized film into MINOX cartridges and processes all such film.

Midian Electronics Incorporated, 2302 East 22nd St., Tucson, AZ 85713. Large selection of low-priced rolling code voice scramblers for two-way radios and telephones along with DTMF and simple inversion chips for handheld radios. Midian offers a nice cellular scrambling system for under $500 and is probably the largest manufacturer of this type of equipment in the country.

Mitel, Inc., 5400 Broken Sound Blvd., N.W., Boca Raton, FL 33487. Menu-driven programmable

Optelcom, 15930 Luanne Dr., Gaithersburg, MD 20877. Small fiber optic transmitters and receivers for video systems.

Optoelectronics, Inc., 5821 Northeast 14th Avenue, Fort Lauderdale, FL 33334. Wide line of handheld frequency counters that are extremely useful in countersurveillance applications as well as band path filters, amplifiers that extend the range of these counters, and the wondrous preselector amplifier that allows proximity monitoring of small transmitters or cellular phones...

Optical & Textile Limited, 22-26 Victoria Rd., New Barnet Herts, EN4 9PF England. Suppliers of sub-miniature (Toshiba) CCD cameras.

P

Pacific Advanced Engineering, 8755 Aero Dr, San Diego, CA 92123- Broadcast quality video receivers and encrypted receivers.

P K Electronics, Heidenkampsweg 74, 2000 Hamburg 1, Federal Republic of Germany or U.S.A. 405 Park Avenue, New York, NY 10022. Calling themselves the largest supplier of surveillance equipment in the world, P K Electronics offers a range of goodies from tool kits to complete audio and telephone surveillance sets, detection and countermeasure equipment, endoscope equipment, pin hole lens equipped cameras, special illumination equipment, video monitoring equipment, a lovely device known as the computer cracker that does just what it infers, low light surveillance equipment, telephone monitors, receivers, digital telephone analyzers, low light equipment, under water equipment, stun grenades, belt cameras, etc.

P K packages their components in some unique ways including disguised as capacitors that can be wired directly onto a telephone circuit board and in a little bit of putty that's designed to stick on any place on a wall, in a nail that works as a spike

mike and transmitter, in watches, in pens, in small boxes, in telephone mouth pieces, and in one thing that is eloquently known as a grain of rice transmitter.

P K has begun a less than subtle shift in their marketing strategy; selling to various government agencies has made them a bit more cautious about selling to the general public and, in fact, P K US will not sell most of the things in their neat catalog to anyone without a badge. This decision left a definite hole in the civilian marketplace so P K diversified beginning a company known as:

Personal Protection Products, or P3, 405 Park Avenue, Suite 1203, New York, NY. P3 stocks low-end surveillance gear including sub-miniature cameras in cigarette lighters, pin hole lenses, through wall mikes, video surveillance systems built into attache cases, video body wires, cameras in master's paintings, personal communication receivers, miniature microphones, high capacity recorders, and a whole variety of telephone analyzers and countermeasures gear. They do not, however, sell the best goodies any more except through P K.

Positive Control Systems, 575 South Dawson Dr., Suite 207, Camarillo, CA 93010. Pen registers and dialled number recorders for law enforcement.

Probity Electronics, Inc., 574 Meacham Ave., Elmont, NY 11003. Crystal-controlled transmitters with matching receivers, body wires, parallel crystal phone taps, sound-activated recorders and a nice little calculator transmitter. Law enforcement only. At least for the transmitters.

Productive Products, P. O. Box 930024, Norcross, GA 30093. A Panasonic recorder which has been "re-engineered" to obtain maximum sound reproduction quality at ulta low tape speed giving 12 hours of recording time on a single 120 cassette (6 hours per side). Vox activation with adjustable triggering sensitivity.

Protector, P. O. Box 520294, Salt Lake City, UT, 84152. Another reprint of other people's catalog catalog. They feature research electronics equipment, some VMI cameras and lenses, various dropout recorders and Capri countermeasure stuff.

PULNIX America, Inc., 770 Lucerne Dr., Sunnyvale, CA 94086. Miniature and sub-miniature CCD cameras as well as a variety of lenses for macro and micro field viewing with auto irises and various focal lengths.

R

Research Electronics, Inc., 1570 Brown Ave., Cookeville, TN 38501. Primarily an OEM countermeasures gear producer, their equipment is both moderate in price and effective. The basic unit, at the time of this writing, is the CPM 700, a wide-band receiver for total spectrum coverage from 200 Hz to 3 GHz that can be configured in a variety of ways with such things as carrier current test transmitters, infrared probes, phone adapters and acoustic leakage probes. They also offer a tape recorder detector, some telephone security and masking devices, a nice little scrambler, and a decent through wall mike.

REI has been in business for some time and I can personally attest to the validity of their equipment.

Ross Engineering, Inc., 7906 Hope Valley Court, Adamstown, MD 21710. James Ross runs seminars, produces the surveillance expo, puts out a newsletter entitled *Surveillance,* and sells a portable spectrum analyzer configured for countermeasures work as well as some speciality receivers including Scanlock.

R&R Speed and Cycle Shop, 4804 Stamp Rd., Temple Hills, MD 20748. Mobile surveillance systems designed in vans and other covert vehicles.

S

S. A. M. Electronics, 2701 Belmont, Chicago, IL 60618. A self-contained earphone amplification system designed for "hearing conversations at 100 yards and a TV at 2 blocks, birds, dogs, yelling at 2 miles." I'm not sure what the birds and dogs have to yell about but I guess that's their affair.

Saul Mineroff Electronics, 946 Downing Rd., Valley Stream, New York 11590. Mr. Mineroff has spent a decade or so in cooperation with the DEA, the FBI, and various other best unnamed agencies, modifying and developing specialized tape recorders. He apparently stocks some other manufacturer's gear but his primary push at this time is something known as SME 700, which is a small cassette recorder that seems to do many of the things the Nagra JBR does at less cost and with more user friendly features. The SME 700 is a tiny recorder that records in stereo and incorporates a fast acting ALC, along with special filters and compressing circuits, to record the human audio range quite well. The tapes are then played back in a specialized playback unit which has a dynamic noise reduction circuit built in which limits background noises during playback.

The SME is designed to be worn as a body wire and uses stereo to obtain conviction level audio. The SME can be set up so once it's turned on it cannot be turned off by the agent and it does not contain an erase head, basically what-you-hear-is-what-you-get. Mr. Mineroff also sells a modified RN 36 recorder which will record 4 hours of conversation on one tape and a nice little miniaturized SME high gain booster microphone that acts as a preamp for any low impedance microphone allowing long cable runs and better sensitivity.

Mr. Mineroff prefers to deal with persons of the law enforcement persuasion.

Security and Defense Marketing Services Ltd., 14 Hollywood Rd., London SW10 9HT, England. Electronic countersurveillance gear.

Sensor Imaging Inc., 400 Travis St., Suite 1805, Shreveport, LA 71101. Remote sensor video packs designed to operate in remote or hostile environments without human intervention. These packs contain video cameras, sometimes infrared sensitive video cameras with boosters or passive thermal detectors, and some sort of triggering device. When activated the pack powers up from its "sleep" mode, grabs video of whatever is going on, and then transmits the video via radio or cellular phone system to its portable video display.

Remote sensor packs are often used to back up physical alarms in high security installations.

Security Systems, Inc., 3017 Hudson Place, New Orleans, LA 70131. Xeroxed catalog of other people's stuff, things from REI, a couple of Japanese companies, Capri, Lorraine Electronics, various stun guns, and tracking systems. One should always verify that the equipment is, in fact, in stock when ordering from any value-added retailer.

Shadow Systems Incorporated, P. O. Box 447, Tempe, AZ 85281. SSI sells an infinity transmitter known as the VF-1.

Sherwood Communications Associates Ltd., Box 535, Southampton, PA 18966. Sherwood is the Sears and Roebuck of surveillance. Probably my all-time favorite supplier for a variety of reasons:

1. They have damn near everything one could imagine in stock and can get anything that might not be.

2. I have yet to see a lower price on just about anything Sherwood sells.

3. Service is rapid, the personnel is extremely knowledgeable about all the equipment.

4. Sherwood carries a number of very hard to find items that are either made by their engineers or imported with fairly minor markup.

5. Sherwood will rent many of their units (full price held as a deposit) difference returned when the unit is returned in good shape. A real rarity in the surveillance field.

6. Sherwood offers the largest selection of used surveillance and countermeasures gear I've ever seen. Every couple of months they put out a list of used gear in stock at pretty reasonable prices. As one might suspect, they will also buy used surveillance or countersurveillance gear.

Sherwood stocks a complete line of video goodies, many of which they have brought into the country themselves or modified to be more effective, transmitters, extended play recorders, special cabling, extremely sensitive microphones I have yet to see in any other catalog and generally the most complete stock of surveillance gear I've seen in one place. One stop shopping...

SHERWOOD COMMUNICATIONS
The Sears and Roebuck of Surveillance

PINHOLE LENSES

Designed for use on concealed cameras, the Pinhole Lenses are useful in any Undercover surveillance work. Compact size and minimal front exposure ensure discreet observation.

No. 5020 Straight Pinhole Lens: 9.0mm/F3.4
No. 5021 R.A. Pinhole Lens: 9.0mm/F3.4
No. 6000 Straight Pinhole Lens: 5.5mm/F3.0
No. 6001 R.A. Pinhole Lens: 5.5mm/F3.0
No. 6002 Straight Pinhole Lens: 11mm/F2.3
No. 6003 R.A. Pinhole Lens: 11mm/F2.3
No. 6004 Camcorder/35mm Lens: 8mm/F2.0
No. 6005 Camcorder/35mm Lens: 11mm/F2.0
AUTO IRIS ALSO AVAILABLE

$260.00
$310.00
$325.00
$425.00
$320.00
$360.00
$320.00
$320.00
CALL

MINIATURE MIC AND LINE DRIVER SYSTEM

Features ultra minial electret element for e of concealment. Comp with 18 to 24" c cable and subminial locking connectors. be used alone for sl wire runs. Miniature line driver permits microphone runs in excess of! feet. Increases sensitivity on short mic runs. Linedriver improves sign: noise ratio. Power supply operates linedriver/microphone system from audio recorder. Operates on 9V battery. Complete with 50' cable.

No. 2404 Miniature Mic & Linedriver System
Additional Cable -

$450
$1.00

SURVEILLANCE MICROPHONES

Specialized high performance miniature microphones that are easily installed and concealed. Proven in years of service with government agencies.

No. 2409 Micro Mini Electret Mic For Use w/Body Wires
No. 2410 Micro Mini Electret Mic For Use W/Recorders
No. 2411 Tube Mic for Use With Body Wires
No. 2412 Tube Mic for Use With Tape Recorders

$ 99.00
$135.00
$ 99.00
$135.00

UNDETECTABLE MICRO-RECORDER

This two speed, palm size, microcassette recorder is constructed in a manner which causes it to avoid detection from recorder detectors. Unit has fast forward/rewind, cue and review, mic jack, remote control jack and ear jack. Includes a tape counter, pause switch and built-in microphone, silent stop and remote mic capability.

No. 2502 Undetectable Micro-Recorder
No. 5009 90 Minute Microcassette
No. 9003 AC Power Supply
No. 900112 VDC Vehicle Adapter

$119.
$ 8.
$ 12.
$ 12.

Shomer-Tec, POB 2187, Bellingham, WA 98227. Good selection of low end surveillance and countermeasures gear including a nice infinity transmitter plus tear gas, flare alarms for those of you that still miss Vietnam, weapons, survival gear and lock picking equipment.

Sierra Digital, 5675 Spyglass Lane, Citrus Heights, CA 95610. A touchtone display (DTMF detector) that allows for instantaneous display of digits as they are received and also for review of previously received digits which are stored in an onboard 32 character buffer. The input can be from a telephone line, scanner, or from a recorder.

SIG-OPS International, P. O. Box 4882, Poughkeepsie, NY 12602. Another other people's stuff catalog but a good one. SIG-OPS has assembled an eclectic collection of swords, umbrellas, tear gas, super-powerful search lights, night vision equipment, countermeasures gear, linemen's handsets, dropout recorders, preamplifiers and compressors, and in-ear earphone microphone systems, and long play recorders.

Sony Corporation of America, 15 Essex Rd., Paramus, NJ 07652, Security Systems Division. Camcorders designed specifically for surveillance such as the MAX-8, EVC-X7, which takes a variety of lenses (C-mount), offers good imaging and low light sensitivity together with a compact light weight design and remote control operation plus a superimposed date-time clock makes this an ideal surveillance unit.

Spectrum Communications Corp., 1055 W. Germantown Pike, Norristown, PA 19403. A couple of kits consisting of transmitters, body wires, one case receiver/recorder units, and long range repeaters. Spectrum has been in the two-way business for many years and is just starting to get into surveillance applications.

STAR-TRON, P. O. Box 11526, Pittsburgh, PA 15238. Probably the most popular law enforcement night vision equipment made (originally a division of Smith and Wesson), they offer a large line of varied scopes and occasionally have something unheard of in this business; sale prices.

Surveillance Technology Group, 102 Midland Ave., Port Chester, NY 10573; P. O. Box 3077, New York, NY 10163. STG is the law enforcement arm of one of the grandfathers in surveillance gear, CCS, (Communication Control Systems). For years CCS sold high-price countersurveillance gear that made them a sort of mail order sweep center along with a number of rather unique surveillance items. Some years ago they had a minor brush with the law over selling restricted goods to certain countries who were not allowed to buy said goods and the owner was allegedly given the choice to cooperate with the feds or face God know's what. One can well imagine his decision—so for a number of years anything purchased from CCS could also be considered to be purchased from the FBI.

STG has taken a much more law enforcement only stance on most of their equipment and they have quite a selection although it appears to be drawn from other sources rather than OEM. Night vision devices, little transmitters, phone taps, ashtray transmitters, through wall probes, microphones, the usual camera hidden-in-a-plant, and lens hidden-in-an-antenna, carrier current video transmitters, what appear to be TRON-Tek, filters, digital processors, Nagra recorders, investigator's "kits," etc.

STG even offers an executive jet surveillance system which enables covert operation and monitoring of all passengers, flight crew, ground staff, and/or intruders. Once the system is camouflaged and in place, all activity on board the airplane can be recorded while in flight or on the ground. For those of you who don't trust your company president, this looks like a real bargain.

However, it doesn't compare to the Sky Eye Airborne Video System that allows one to conduct video surveillance over inaccessible or mobile targets without camera installation. The Sky Eye Video System is also capable of tactical military reconnaissance as well as border patrols because it uses an ultra-miniature CCD camera with a zoom lens, mounted in a model airplane that will fly some 200 kilometers per trip, spying from 2 kilometers overhead with its rapid focus zoom lens system. Not something everyone would want to use, but one of those hard to find items that when you need it, you really need it.

SWS Security, 1300 Boyd Rd., Street, MD 21154. SWS specializes in electronic tracking devices (bumper beepers—see Steve's article in this book), radio communication equipment both clear and encrypted, night vision equipment, audio and optical surveillance equipment, video equipment including covert briefcases, covert auto applications, law enforcement audio equipment and countermeasures service.

SWS is comprised almost exclusively of former law enforcement and intelligence officers that are familiar with the equipment and needs, and they provide technical services for many agencies throughout the U.S.

T

Tacticx/Applied Protection Technologies, Inc., 100 West Old Marlton Pike, Marlton, NJ 08053. A miniature remote-controlled, battery-powered video event recorder which operates with any black and white or color camera and offers a recording time from 5 to 300 seconds per event. As they so succinctly put it, Tacticorder is a lawful video bug.

Tel-E-Tel, 1011 High Ridge Rd., Stamford, CT 06905. Specialized miniature transmitters that send real time full motion video over ordinary twisted pair wire including dedicated phone lines or alarm wires.

Toshiba America, Inc., 82 Totowa Rd., Wayne, NJ 07470. OEM sub-miniature CCD cameras and time lapse video recorders.

Transcrypt International, 1620 N. 20th St., Lincoln, NE 68503. Frequency hopping transmitter.

T.R.D.Inc., 177 Main St., Fort Lee, NJ 07024. A slick catalog that includes a briefcase recorder system, what looks like a modified Merantz surveillance recorder, dropout recorders, a Radio Shack-like pen register, a digital pager monitoring system that works on what appears to be an ICOM receiver, and a dedicated fax bug, which simply reroutes fax transmissions to a recorder or another fax machine, plus low light systems, linemen's handsets, radio direction finding equipment, vehicle tracking systems, etc.

Trend Telecommunications Limited, Knaves Beech Estate, Loudwater, High Wycombe, Buckinghamshire HP10 9QZ, England. Encrypted fax machines that meets Tempest standards.

Tactical RF Incorporated, 8 Hill St., Norfolk, MA 02056. Complete portable listening posts, intelligence kits, transmitters built into pagers, wallets, envelopes, belt buckles, or of course, the ubiquitous baseball cap, plus base and repeater stations and custom design.

Technology Service Enterprises, Inc., 3850 Holcomb Bridge Rd., Suite 235, Norcross, GA 30092. Secure telephones produced by AOE International using the DES Encryption algorithm as well as a facsimile encrypter and a couple of analog scramblers.

TRON-Tek, Inc., TRON-Tek specializes in law enforcement surreptitious and downright sneaky video installations that include their covert briefcase models, their transmitters with directional antennas, and their transmitters mounted in telephone company splice jacks, electric company cans, and by now, well, who knows?

TRW Electronic Products, Inc., 1050 Southwood Dr., San Luis Obispo, CA 93401. Fax encrypter that uses a public encryption key that is randomly generated before each transmission to promote security.

TSA/Technical Services Agency, Inc., 10902 Indian Head Highway, Suite 304, Ft. Washington, MD 20744. Run by a consummate pro in the countermeasures business, TSA manufactures and sells the Eagle Plus receiver (which is right there with the Scanlock, as far as I'm concerned), a nice countermeasures-oriented spectrum analyzer, carrier current receivers, their own acoustic rangefinder—the Rangelock—which in conjunction with any receiver or amplifier instantly calculates the range to any transmitter, a small spectrum monitor, line tracing systems including a UHF line tracing system that sends an inaudible tone down the wire, metal detectors, voltage kits, etc...

V

Vanguard Research, Inc., 2810 Old Lee Highway, Suite 200, Fairfax, VA 22031. Slow scan video that operates over normal telephone circuits.

VCS, Inc. 262 Carlton Dr., Carol Stream, IL 60188. High resolution CCD cameras for security and surveillance.

Ventronic, 94 Galli Dr., Novato, CA 94949. Ultra-miniature fiberoptic transmitters and receivers that fit directly on the back of cameras and monitors to transmit video for a distance of up to 5 miles without repeaters.

Ventronic sells complete installations, kits, and components and they are one of the more reasonably priced entries into this fairly new field.

Viking Electronics, Inc., 1531 Industrial St., Hudson, WI 54016. Automatic routing switches so fax machines and telephones can share the same line, DTMF controllers that operate equipment via touchtone requests, and phone line simulators which create dial tone, battery, and ringing without benefit of any telephone company. Ideal for fax and data interception, among other uses.

Viking International, 150 Executive Park Blvd., Suite 4600, San Francisco, CA 94134. Surveillance equipment supplier specializing in infrared light systems and filters including spotlights, flashlights, and rechargeable battery packs, plus an extremely high efficient proprietary "night flash," a high performance I. R. marker beacon that can be pulsed or continuous for covert lightning as well as boosting infrared photography. Viking is one of the pioneers in improving this kind of equipment and their beacons seem to have work better than any others on the market. Viking still offers some of the best extended play recorders for covert recording because they don't just slow the units down but include compensation circuitry.

Their mic compressor is a gem, powering any electret mic and offering increased range and clarity.

Also very nice video transmitter/receiver systems; low priced (in comparison) and quite powerful. Law enforcement or export only on the video...

Visual Methods Inc., 35 Charles St., Westwood, NJ 07675. VMI is one-stop shopping for video gear. A huge inventory of straight and right angle pinhole lenses, fixed iris lenses, miniature CCD cameras, disguise cameras, lenses in industrial ceiling sprinklers, fiberoptic setups, etc.

VMI is operated by a gentleman who has written many good papers on video and covert surveillance and probably ranks as one of the leading experts in this field. VMI makes some things, sells others, as well as packaging off the shelf items in a unique way.

An instance of the latter would be their XC42122, a black and white video camera that will operate in .00093 foot candles of light with an amazing 570 lines of resolution. This is a C-mount camera that accepts front end lenses from any other video camera including pinholes. Because it is so sensitive to low light, the unit ranks at about the same level as Second Generation night vision devices. This means one can, for about an outlay of

$1,600, have what is effectively a night vision device that will also work in the daytime and allow recording of the images.

VMI also stocks monitors, time lapse recorders, and unique transmission systems.

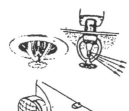

CT822 Sprinkler Head

Attaches to any camera. Available in brass or chrome finish. This 22mm pinhole lens sees an image 3' x 4' from 15 feet away. Screwdriver adjusts downward angle, and can be rotated in any direction.

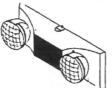

CT803 Emergency Light Fixture

A standard Emergency Light Fixture in a hallway or vestibule becomes a valuable tool for loss prevention. With a CCTV camera, pinhole lens and rechargeable battery pack, this fully operating Emergency Light monitors the activity you require. When used in conjunction with a time lapse recorder of VCR, past activity can be reviewed.

CT808 Exit Sign

Standard Exit sign with a CCTV camera and pinhole lens covertly installed inside allows observation of problem areas.

CT832 Clock Surveillance Kit

Stop office theft with this unique pinhole surveillance kit that uses an ordinary wall clock to conceal the CCTV camera. The kit consists of a working clock, 8mm auto iris lens , monitor and cable.

Pencil Sharpener Surveillance

Unobtrusive pencil sharpener stops pilferage in office areas. Place on desk, or other problem areas, and observe what's going on. Concealed inside is a miniature camera and lens which provides you with an output that can be video-recorded.

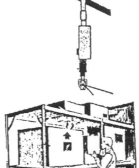

TV Sprinkler Hangs From I Beam

Entire sprinkler lens and CCD low level TV camera, encased in 5" x 2" box with video and power cables hidden in 1.2" pipe, is moved in to TARGET area, and with a magnet is attached to an I Beam. Cables are run along beam out of sight. Turn camera to target area and adjust mirror.

Racking Systems

XC16 camera inserted into frame and wedged at proper height, lens looking through adjacent holes in frame. Run cables out through the top of the rack beam.

Tool Chests and Rolling Cabinets

Locking compartment conceals VCR and video camera. Rolls into position anywhere. Can be AC or battery. No set up, just leave in target area and walk away.

W

Watec America Corp., P. O. Box 6686, Thousand Oaks, CA 91360. Watec is a Japanese manufacturer of sub-miniature video cameras which are incorporated in many other people's systems or sold at a considerable markup.

Wood & Douglas, Unit 12-13, Youngs Industrial Estate, Aldermaston, Reading, Berkshire, England RG7 4PQ. Security monitoring specialists who make a carrier current video transmitter and receiving system allowing one to send both video and audio over existing AC supply lines.

X

Xandi Electronics, Box 25647, Tempe, AZ 85285. Low-cost kits for broadcast band, room bugs, phone taps, dropout recorders, and bug detectors.

Good Hunting…
—lee

US

INTELLIGENCE INCORPORATED presents the most unusual catalog of intelligence assimilation aids, services and surveillance equipment in the world. Our collection is unique because we combine our own books and videos with the best examples from a few well chosen professionals. Most of our equipment is designed for us by our own engineers and cannot be found in other catalogs. We do what we do very well.

SOFT STUFF—Books, Videos and Reports that feature hard and fast, hands-on information unobtainable elsewhere. Written and directed by top pro's like Lee Lapin, Fay Faron and Paul Van Houten, Ph.D. Our videos are shot and edited on state of the art, broadcast quality equipment and reproduced on top of the line 3-M cassettes. Our books are well known for being jam packed with "inside" information. We are proud to say our materials are used by most major intelligence agencies, many police agencies and thousands of PI's. **HARD STUFF**—A brand new selection of solid electronic and mechanical equipment including state of the art video surveillance gear and the most amazing entry equipment around. Our products do what they are supposed to at a reasonable price. **SERVICES**—I² now provides you with the *best* in people locating, skip tracing, background and pre-employment checks along with DMV, criminal, and asset searches. We're better because; A. We use several of the best databank groups for *every* search, not just the most popular one like most companies. B. We hit special databases that others don't and... C. We're good, after all, we did write the book on Getting Anything On Anybody.

For a look at our latest catalog send $5.00 to:

Intelligence Incorporated
2228 S El Camino Real
San Mateo, CA 94403